D0425683

Illness, Gender, and Writing

Illness, Gender, and Writing ∞

∞ The Case of Katherine Mansfield

Mary Burgan

THE JOHNS HOPKINS UNIVERSITY PRESS

Baltimore and London

© 1994 The Johns Hopkins University Press
All rights reserved.   Published 1994
Printed in the United States of America on acid-free paper
03 02 01 00 99 98 97 96 95 94   5 4 3 2 1

The Johns Hopkins University Press
2715 North Charles Street
Baltimore, Maryland 21218-4319
The Johns Hopkins Press Ltd., London

Library of Congress Cataloging-in-Publication Data will be found at the
end of this book.
A catalog record for this book is available from the British Library.

ISBN 0-8018-4873-3

For all the Margarets:

Margaret Caroline Walsh, R.N. (1909–1982)

Margaret Caroline Heagarty, M.D.

Margaret Caroline Ash

ꙮ *Contents*

∽ *Illustrations*

∽ *Abbreviations*

EXCEPT for several citations of the uncensored version of "*Je ne parle pas français*," all citations of Mansfield's stories, including the *German Pension* stories, are from *The Short Stories of Katherine Mansfield* (New York: Knopf, 1967). Other abbreviations are as follows:

A   *The Aloe with Prelude*. Edited by Vincent O'Sullivan. Wellington, New Zealand: Port Nicholson P, 1983.

ATL   The Alexander Turnbull Library, Wellington, New Zealand.

Berg   Henry W. and Albert A. Berg Collection. Astor, Lenox, and Tilden Foundations. New York Public Library, New York, N.Y.

BTW   *Between Two Worlds: The Autobiography of John Middleton Murry*. New York: Julian Messner, 1936.

CL   *The Collected Letters of Katherine Mansfield*. Edited by Vincent O'Sullivan and Margaret Scott. 3 vols. Oxford: Oxford UP, 1984–93.

DE   *The Stories of Katherine Mansfield: Definitive Edition*. Edited by Antony Alpers. Auckland, New Zealand: Oxford UP, 1988.

JMM/KM   *The Letters of John Middleton Murry to Katherine Mansfield*. Edited by C. A. Hankin. New York: Franklin Watts, 1983.

LJMM   *Katherine Mansfield's Letters to John Middleton Murry, 1913–1922*. Edited by John Middleton Murry. London: Constable, 1951.

LKM   *The Letters of Katherine Mansfield*. Edited by John Middleton Murry. New York: Knopf, 1932.

LM   *Katherine Mansfield: The Memories of L.M.* By Leslie [sic] Moore. London: Virago, 1985.

Russell   Countess Russell Collection. Huntington Library, San Marino, Calif.

Texas   Harry Ransom Humanities Research Center, University of Texas at Austin, Austin, Tex.

TLR   "Katherine Mansfield: The Unpublished Manuscripts." *Turnbull Library Record.*

∞ Introduction

KATHERINE MANSFIELD is remembered for writing a number of brilliant short stories that helped to initiate the modernist period in British fiction, and for the fact that her life—lived at a feverish pace on the fringes of Bloomsbury during the First World War—ended after a prolonged battle with pulmonary disease when she was only thirty-four years old. Mansfield's short fiction, like her short life, has been thoroughly canvassed, but the relations between them have not been studied in the context of her illness.[1] While the life has been shown to be marred by recurrent emotional and physical afflictions of the most extreme kind, the stories have seemed to exist, depending upon the changing preoccupations of the critic, in relatively serene perfection as stylish expressions of the "new," as romantic triumphs of art over tragic circumstance, as regressive extensions of Mansfield's preoccupation with her childhood, or as wavering expressions of her early feminism.

Exploring Mansfield's illness as in many ways the ground of her writing, this study presents the writer as a woman whose life history is both a case history in medicine and a representative model in an effort to confront mortality through the achievement of narrative. Under such a view, Mansfield negotiated a series of illness crises in a paradigmatic way for the study of women's creativity as inflected by the trials of their bodies; in one way or another her art was implicated in a broad spectrum of "women's" illnesses—the crisis of oral nurture in infancy; a psychosexual alienation of the body in bisexuality; the gynecological crises of aborted pregnancy, venereal disease, and then sterility; and finally the bacteriological crisis of affliction by the most virulent plague of the early twentieth century—tuberculosis.

In gathering these specific health problems together under the rubric of "illness," I investigate not only the medical aspect of each biological or physiological incidence but also the "psychosocial experience and meaning of perceived disease." Thus I am following the lead of medical anthropologists such as Arthur Kleinman, who differentiates *disease* as physical malfunction from *illness,* which includes secondary personal and social responses to a primary malfunctioning (disease) in the individual's physiological or psychological status (or both). Illness involves processes of attention, perception, affective response, cognition, and valuation directed at the disease and its manifestations (i.e., symptoms, role impairment, etc.). But also included in the idea of illness are communication and interpersonal interaction, particularly within the context of the family and social network. Viewed from this perspective, illness is the shaping of disease into behavior and experience. (72)

Without neglecting the "primary malfunctioning" of her physical state itself, I believe that probing the network of illness in her life under such an expanded definition can sharpen the interpretive focus on Mansfield's fiction—exposing her urge to inscribe symptomatic sensory detail in her work, locating and historicizing the material base of her resolutely mimetic modernism, and pointing to the therapeutic aspects of her urge always to write in and of the body, to "examine" it, so to speak, in journals and letters and, once the "diagnosis" had become clear, to inscribe the interpretation in fiction.

In turn, I believe that a study of Mansfield's reconstructive response to illness can help to critique some of the theoretical suppositions about writing and the body which have flourished in the poststructuralist effort to bypass the positivism of early science and the sentimentality of simple phenomenology. Such suppositions have revolutionized and enriched our insights into the ways in which the self, gender, political discourse, and narrative presence are constructed by both socially and psychologically determining forces. And indeed, such thinking has influenced medical history as well as literary history. In medical history, however, no theory is more controversial than that of the "social construction of disease." To be sure, the analyses of medical discourses have shown that some ailments of mind and body have received medical consideration only after they have been named and classified by nosological systems. Thus the location of historical actualities in language has been a fruitful pursuit, but practicing physicians are resistant to such a conception of disease when the question of individual, physical fatality is involved. Indeed, at one recent convention of the American Association for the History of Medicine, a doctor threatened to bring in a diseased organ in all its deformity to the next meeting, to reinsert a modicum of medical materialism into the thinking of his colleagues. I sympathize with his impulse, for it seems to me that the materiality of the body, especially the female body, is the site of important truth not only about illness but also about the dynamics both of writing and of cure (not to mention practical politics).

It is at this intersection of the body and interpretation, then, that my study seeks to make some contribution to that growing interchange between medicine and literature which is now designated by such labels as "the medical humanities." As the hermeneutics of current literary theory becomes available for clinical diagnosis, some medical theorists, such as Edward L. Gogel and James S. Terry, are struck by the possibility that "clinical medicine and the formal study of interpretation have much in common." They welcome the flexibility for training medical students through involving them in literary interpretation's "analysis of contexts and subtexts, in the clash of incommensurables, in the search for hidden meanings" (avoiding "absolutes without deteriorating into pure relativism") as well as a shared preference for "attention to particular texts or patients above attention to generalizations or abstractions" (215). What I hope to retain of medical insight as I read the bodily "contexts and subtexts" of Mansfield's illness is not only the concreteness of Mansfield as a particular "text or patient" but a sense of her own interpretations of her illness.

In emphasizing Mansfield's bodily experience of illness, I above all seek to emphasize the purposiveness of her agency in response to invasion by disease, and I also strive to accent the unpredictable and highly individual detail in the narratives in which she represented her sensory alertness to pain. Katherine Mansfield's case indicates that the truth of the sources of illness lies somewhere along a continuum between physical malfunction or bacteriological invasion and the discursive imperatives that turn these into writing. Along both the epidemiological and the psychological axes, then, familial and social definitions conjoin with individual, willed reactions in illness; to emphasize one over the other is to substitute theoretical or polemical refinement for what William James has called the "sentiment of rationality" (63). It is my hope that the delineation of the extremities of the body in this study may point to a pragmatic engagement with clinical facticity as well as literary theory.

Though this study might be termed a "pathography," I do not subscribe to the notion that the succession of diseases that invaded Mansfield's body defined her totally. Rather, I assume in Mansfield's life the efficacy of her striving for self-definition beyond her incessant role-playing, her exasperation with her feminine body . . . her cough. Even though she was fully aware of determining contexts and the possibility of self-delusion in behavior, she was a woman who *acted*—decisively. Indeed, I find her active search for a selfhood that could withstand the dissolution of her body the particular attraction of her biography.[2] Under siege by the bacillus of tuberculosis, she would have found the notion of the "death of the author" an ominous threat more than an enabling conundrum: her writing was a conscious defense against fragmentation rather than accession to it. The fiction of the self has its uses when life is in jeopardy.

Thus in considering her writing, I suppose that the narratives that Mansfield devised constitute the most significant result, as well as the most revealing evidence, of her urge to articulate her own diagnosis and to enact the best therapy she could manage. I do not find her writing, however, the sublimated cure for the artist's wound as posited by Freud; she would have written without mortal disease, though I suggest that she would have written differently. Moreover, questioning notions of an *écriture féminine* that privileges the rapt, nonlinear, gnomic, submerged, and prelinguistic resistances to language, I value the formal care, rhetorical aggressiveness, comic play, and emotional risk taking in Mansfield's stories. Understanding and critiquing without mercy the power of patriarchal language, she did not surrender common language to patriarchy. She appropriated universals, metaphors, rhetoric, the wit of dialogue as projections for forthright moral judgments rather than as screens for subversion. Thus her writing was always gendered but never eccentric, always personal but never obscure. It reached towards a clear understanding with her readers, and her need for understanding was, as I say, intensified by the rapid approach of her death.

My study thus takes seriously Mansfield's often expressed effort to define, as a matter of survival, the core of a "self which is continuous and permanent; which, untouched by all we acquire and all we shed, pushes a green spear through the dead leaves and through the mould, thrusts a scaled bud through years of darkness until, one day, the light discovers it and shakes the flower free and—we are alive—we are flowering for our moment upon the earth" (*Journal* 205). This is a conception of the self which emphasizes its developmental dynamic—resisting the notion of settled scenarios and programmed reactions; it emphasizes as well the origin of the self in childhood, its frequently provisional development over time, and its function as a locus for a vital dialectic between the outer manifestations of cultural determination and the inner, "real" self. Mansfield's belief in such a self is precisely the kind of faith most called into question by postmodern revelations of the innate duplicity of such resolutions. Nevertheless, my interest is in the often observed power of the ill person to wrest a few more days, a few more years, from the fragmentations of fatal illness. I suggest therefore that the synapse between the functionally acting ego and the socially constructed subject may be bridged by notions of an applied, clinically based psychology in which medical crises are presumed to give rise to choices and responses that bear upon survival.[3]

The conviction of the sovereignty of the self may be a culturally constructed one, and the individual struggling for identity may be forced to work through a plethora of coercive roles, but finally in the actuality of illness, an ego that is curatively inclined must exert itself or else it will die before the body does.

Giving due notice to the ubiquitous workings of the cultural milieu in forming the self, then, I nevertheless assume that Mansfield's avid cultivation of continuity and coherence in her inner life embodied a drive to get well, to live, to flourish within an enabling identity.

~

In interpreting the intersection between Mansfield's enactments of "patienthood" in her life and in her fiction, I have drawn upon a variety of methodological resources—the contemporary studies of illness influenced by Susan Sontag and Michel Foucault; medical histories, including Edward Shorter's *History of Women's Bodies*; clinical reports such as those of Oliver Sacks; theories of early childhood development by object-relations theorists (especially D. W. Winnicott); the psychological and historical studies of homosexualities by such historians as Jeffrey Weeks; and the emphasis on the female body by feminist theorists Hélène Cixous, Julia Kristeva, and others. From the illness studies I have attempted to derive a phenomenological approach to Mansfield's sense of the body as the instrument of a perception mediated by the culturally determined metaphors of sickness, especially feminine sickness.[4] In sketching the outward contexts of illness, I do not want to slight the reality of physical pain, however, for I believe that the problem of any kind of illness theory is its tendency to falsify the experience of the body through schematization. Thus, for example, the distancing of individuated physical sensation through the location of pain within the constructions of language is what has made a study like Elaine Scarry's *The Body in Pain* ineligible for me. On the other hand, David Morris's more anecdotal survey of the designations of pain in *The Culture of Pain* seems unaccountably impressionistic: although Morris devotes a chapter to "women's pain," for example, he centers on hysteria and all but ignores menstrual complications or childbirth as the more characteristic instances of women's experience of the body. In my effort to track Mansfield's multiple illness experiences, therefore, I have approached her afflictions along a series of registers; at times I place her ailments in terms of their biological etiology and symptomology, and at other times I emphasize their physiological or their psychosocial determinants. But I want to remember pain in the category of *sensation* as well as *perception*,[5] and always I seek to let Mansfield's stories themselves both generate and test the explanatory power of my generalizations.

Given the imaginative strategies of her reaction to ill health, nonetheless, the totality of Mansfield's case cannot be compassed in an exclusive attention to physical disease; even as we attend to the issues of her physiological status, her psychological development must be assessed. The current theoretical emphasis on the relations formed in infancy—those nurturing, maternal interactions and symbolizations that establish the most primitive foundations for self-definition—seems most productive in understanding the troubled childhood that instigated Mansfield's continuing sense of herself as beset by illness. Accordingly, I have applied some of the Anglo-American formulations of ego psychology to my study of Mansfield's childhood. But in avoiding the suggestion that she was a mere victim of early confusion, or that she was somehow trapped at the oral stage (an accusation reflected in the standard negative view that Mansfield "never grew up"), I have linked object-relations theories with Erik Erikson's outline of latency and adolescence; here I want to pay attention to the complex initiatives of middle childhood, adolescence, and early maturity in identity formation.

Throughout, my preference lies with psychoanalytic theory that keeps contact with clinical practice. In such a therapeutic emphasis, I work against the easy assignment of Mansfield's story to the annals of psychopathology by insisting that *crises* of identity—no matter how bizarre—may be "normal" occurrences in the complexity of human development; thus I consider that flamboyant early symptoms may betoken future health as well as future sickness. In his refreshingly practical approach to the afflictions of the psyche, Winnicott suggests, "True neurosis is not necessarily an illness. . . . We should think of it as a tribute to the fact that life is difficult" (quoted in Greenberg and Mitchell, 208). Similarly Erikson emphasizes *process* in arriving at psychic equilibrium. His work is the foundation for contemporary American notions about the construction of identity through a complex of formative social interactions, developed and deployed with more or less effective motivation and design through the necessity that individuals must *do* as well as *be*.[6] Such an emphasis on development is useful in considering a writer whose achievements show the unevenness of a struggle broken off before its completion.

At the age of nineteen, in 1908, Katherine Mansfield came to England from New Zealand with the single purpose of escaping her middle-class family and dedicating herself to art. She changed her name from Kathleen Mansfield Beauchamp to Katherine Mansfield as a gesture of independence, and she embarked on a series of love affairs, a life lived on the margins of economic security, and forays from London to the bohemia of Paris and to various health spots on the Continent. But simple flight was no real solution, and the effort to achieve independence without wholly abandoning a past that was essential for imaginative creativity became a major imperative in Mansfield's writing. Moreover, from the beginning of her career (her first professional story appeared in England in 1910), Mansfield's flight from her family was challenged by physical breakdowns that intensified her need for domestic order. Although she endured a miscarriage, possibly one abortion, and the pulmonary disease that eventually killed her, she interpreted most of her illness as inherited from her mother. Thus her rheumatic pains, which were probably caused by undiagnosed gonorrhea, seemed a welcome, intimate link with her mother's body—indeed, almost the only link after her mother disinherited her in retaliation for the rashness of her marrying a casual acquaintance in order to legitimate her first pregnancy.

Her need for some kind of familial structure as an alternative to the conventional one she had left behind in New Zealand therefore became a curative motif throughout Mansfield's later illnesses; it may account for the intensity of her desire to settle at last with John Middleton Murry and to have a child. Depicting the female body as inscribed by social definitions that designated femininity as intrinsically diseased, moreover, Mansfield also provides us with portraits of women in ambivalent postures of submission to and rebellion against those familial "physicians"—doctors, fathers, husbands—who would cure through domination. In their place, she positioned images of more intimate, female "nurses"—grandmothers, mothers, friends, and strangers who participated in common class or gender subservience. Throughout her struggle with tuberculosis, she remained antagonistic to the masculine institutionalization of care as a feature in the humiliation of disease for women.

The return to the family to find health inevitably involves remembering some actual or idealized state of safety and care. Mansfield was a writer of memories that could be at times restorative, at times regressive. The line between remembrance and regression is very thin, but I believe that it has been oversimplified by those critics who have presented Mansfield's stories as the brittle products of a childishly nostalgic, sometimes hysterical sensibility. Heinz Hartmann has spoken of "regression in service of the ego" (368), and D. W. Winnicott has suggested that reliving the past can be a force in psychic cure: "Regression represents a return to the point at which the environment has failed the child."[7] In sorting out Mansfield's uses of memory, I suggest that she used regression in this curative way—reconstructing her originary environment to give her psyche the needed resources of community and hope.

~

Although my study draws extensively from Mansfield's biography and must therefore retrace some familiar ground, I have tried to avoid one more retelling of the famous life. I center, instead, upon particularly telling illness events, especially as they have been textualized by Mansfield's narrative versions of them both in her journal and in her most essential stories. My case history begins with the death of Mansfield's infant sister and the issues of maternal deprivation implicated in it; this first experience of death is the context in which I place Mansfield's insistent writing about the mortality of children in her earliest attempts at fiction and poetry. I read "The Doll's House" as haunted by Mansfield's dead sister.

In the second chapter, I move to body configuration, dimension, and weight as gauges of Mansfield's adolescent fear of sexuality in service of patriarchal power; here I suggest that images of orality in Mansfield's writing articulate a pattern of sexual repulsion that has roots in her mother's coldness and her father's sensuality. The threat of death which shadows anorexia and bulimia, I suggest, also figures in Mansfield's confrontation with the dead in "The Garden-Party," thematizing at once the gender issue of feeding women and the social issue of feeding the poor.

Mansfield's late adolescence in New Zealand, like her early life as a writer in London, was marked by heterosexual ambivalence, lesbian experimentation, and, eventually, a reactionary maternalism designed to resolve bisexual confusion. In Chapter 3 I assess the way Mansfield's susceptibility to the fear of her sexuality as diseased gave rise to a defensive strain of homophobia—perhaps the most repellant trend in her preliminary psychosexual adjustments, one that remained active in "Bliss," possibly her most anthologized story. Here I propose that Mansfield's participation in the discourse of post-Wildean aestheticism contributed to the vocabulary of disease in her representations of the transgressive sexuality to which she was drawn.

Chapter 4 analyzes Mansfield's first prolonged experiences of adult female sicknesses—those of pregnancy, miscarriage, abortion, and venereal disease. The designation of female sexuality as an affliction informs the stories of *In a German Pension,* Mansfield's first book. That cruel anatomy of early twentieth-century attitudes to "female troubles" shows how observant an epidemiologist Mansfield was, recording with almost scientific dispassion the varieties of psychosexual and maternal morbidity she encountered in prewar European culture. I also suggest that her sardonic reaction to Germanic mythologizing of maternity tends to demystify the anthropologically derived designation of "abjection" as intrinsic in women's bodily experiences, pointing to such designations as deriving from male rather than female subject positions.

Katherine Mansfield's gender confusions, and betrayals, were bracketed, if not alleviated, by the traumas associated with the Great War. In Chapter 5, I analyze the shattering of her personality by the death of her brother and her feverish attempt to reinvent herself in mourning for his death. Here I persist in reading her regression to her New Zealand past in "Prelude" and "At the Bay" as a therapeutic strategy. Engaging her own grief, I suggest, she was able not only to mourn her brother but also to confront the spectrum of women's punitive hysterias within her family. The remission she imagined involved a mother/brother plot in which the dead brother might instigate his mother's attachment to her children, thereby redeeming the memory of the mother both for himself and for his sister.

From the crisis of her brother's death, I turn in the next chapter to the environment of epidemic in the wartime existence Mansfield led in London—an existence of stress and deprivation which was surely instrumental in her susceptibility to tuberculosis in its most virulent form. Here I attempt to relate Mansfield's experiment in writing in the first person with the techniques of medical examination she experienced, emphasizing her experience of pulmonary disease as a private transaction that required listening in silence. Such silence can be the source of accommodation to or of bitter condemnation of a universe of disease and death. I see *"Je ne parle pas français"* as a disease story in its focus on the pathology of incessant self-examination as a substitute for living.

The invalidism of consumption threw Mansfield upon the nursing of her husband, John Middleton Murry, and her devoted female companion, Ida Baker (renamed by her as "Lesley Moore" and then "L.M."); her experience of disease thus involved a submission to care, even as it enabled her most autonomous period of writing. In Chapter 7, therefore, I look at Mansfield's stories of caregivers, exploring her recycling of past desire within the context of dependency—on masculine rescue, on the safe circle of childhood, on an alliance with sisterly servitude, and on a communal alternative. But always, I suggest, she preserved within the psychic habitat of the invalid a tonic relish for work and the promise of defeating her illness through her writing.

As she sloughed off the confusions of her past, Katherine Mansfield yearned for a reconciliation with her parents. She wanted a special wifehood with John Middleton Murry. And she longed to have a child. In many ways, then, her ideal of health was essentially conservative; indeed, it might be read to exemplify some notions that preoccupation with cure is an elitist stance—that it can signify a surrender to bourgeois comfort and control, turning away from both the democracy of suffering and the radical "truth" of the unconscious.[8] As I attempt to show in my final chapter, however, the liberating force of Mansfield's example is neither social revolution nor bourgeois complacency but a form of lyricism which retains a clinical edge of sensation—one that at times confronted, at times joined, her affirmation of the imperative to continue living within the imminence of her death.

In the last stages of her life, Katherine Mansfield approached an accommodation between her satirical instincts and her longing for mutual charity between men and women, parents and children, the powerful and the weak, the sick and the well. Finally, she posited the potential for a kind of necessary innocence in every individual—a kind of existential selflessness which could make the adult like a child again in spontaneity of feeling, without precluding competence, patience, or self-knowledge. She had explored this idea in her most memorable fiction, and in the very last days of her life, she carried the exploration further by going to live in an odd, transcendental "commune" on the outskirts of Paris. There she died in the season of Epiphany—making ready for a great communal celebration of "presence." We are apt to remember her now chiefly for the perfection of such stories as "Prelude," "The Garden-Party," and "The Daughters of the Late Colonel," but her authority springs as well from the fact that in freeing herself from the old modes of feeling in the ultimate isolation of disease, she asserted her solidarity with the sick. She compared herself with Keats and Chekhov because she knew she was to share their fate, but she became like them also in the simplicity of her ultimate refusal to limit the possibilities of her life either to private pleasure or to universal pain.

Illness, Gender, and Writing

CHAPTER 1

" 'Ah! Ah! Ah!' called the grandmother"

The Deaths of Children

ON JANUARY 10, 1891, a photographer was summoned to the Beauchamp residence at 11 Tinakori Road in Wellington, New Zealand, to record the image of Gwendoline Burnell Beauchamp, a four-month-old baby who had died of infant cholera the day before. Her older sister, Kathleen, was less than three years old at the time, but in a journal entry written some twenty-five years later, grieving for her brother's death in the Great War, she remembered the photographic session in detail, placing it at the conclusion of one of her memorial recollections of her childhood in New Zealand:

> Bridget dressed me next morning. When I went into the nursery I sniffed. A big vase of the white lilies was standing on the table. Grandmother sat in her chair to one side with Gwen in her lap, and a funny little man with his head in a black bag was standing behind a box of china eggs.
>
> "Now!" he said, and I saw my grandmother's face change as she bent over little Gwen.
>
> "Thank you," said the man, coming out of the bag. The picture was hung over the nursery fire. I thought it looked very nice. The doll's house was in it—verandah and balcony and all. Gran held me up to kiss my little sister. (*Journal* 103)

The memory is curiously distanced and faintly comic; its unemphatic selection of random impressions recaptures the consciousness of crisis by an immature witness who had no key on which to sort her perceptions. As a matter of fact, Mansfield prefaces the episode of Gwen's death with a remark about the embeddedness of such matters in the culture of her childhood: "Things happened so simply then, without preparation and without any shock" (101). The actual photograph she describes has been featured in a number of the biographies of Mansfield because it images both her beloved grandmother and the doll's house of her famous story, but Mansfield's narrative of its context is

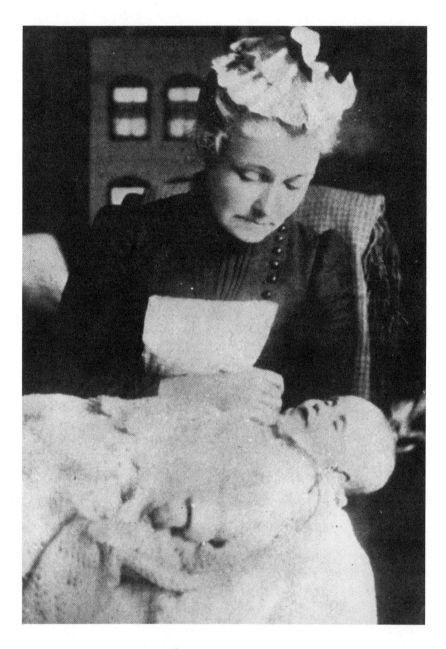

Margaret Mansfield Dyer, Katherine Mansfield's grandmother, with Baby Gwendoline and the doll's house. (ATL)

so indirect that none of the biographers seem to have noticed that the infant in it is dead.[1]

The broader framing memory of Gwen's death incorporates her birth as well. Mansfield begins the memory by presenting a scene of her mother's recovery from childbirth labor:

> They let me go into my mother's room (I remember standing on tiptoe and using both hands to turn the big white china door-handle) and there lay my mother in bed with her arms along the sheet, and there sat my grandmother before the fire with a baby in a flannel across her knees. My mother paid no attention to me at all. Perhaps she was asleep, for my grandmother nodded and said in a voice scarcely above a whisper, "Come and see your little sister." I tiptoed to her voice across the room, and she parted the flannel, and I saw a little round head with a tuft of goldy hair on it and a big face with eyes shut—white as snow. "Is it alive?" I asked. "Of course," said grandmother. "Look at her holding my finger." And—yes a hand, scarcely bigger than my doll's, in a frilled sleeve, was wound round her finger. "Do you like her?" said my grandmother. "Yes. Is she going to play with the doll's house?" (*Journal* 101)

It is significant that the reminiscence of Gwen's death has been instigated by a memory of a maternal disinterest, here only partially justified by the fatigue of the recent ordeal of childbirth. The grandmother tells the child to go and kiss her mother: "But mother did not want to kiss me. Very languid, leaning against the pillows, she was eating some sago" (101). The mother's weary rejection of Mansfield is not the only feature of anxiety in this seemingly innocuous reminiscence, however; there is also the invasion of a usurping sibling for whom rivalry is muffled, who is made less accessible to normal aggression, by her frailty.[2] Thus while birth giving is shadowed by the image of the mother's illness and apparent postpartum depression, birth is shadowed by the repellant morbidity of the infant with the face "white as snow." Katherine Mansfield, the observing child here, displaced by both illness events, has become a contemplative spectator.

Rebuked by her mother's preoccupation with eating an invalid's diet, the child turns to the grandmother, now taken up with the new baby: "All day, all night grandmother's arms were full. I had no lap to climb into, no pillow to rest against" (102). Submerged in this image of a paradise lost is the narrator's emphasis on the grandmother's breast—the "pillow" that signifies not only ease but a safe place to play:

All belonged to Gwen. But Gwen did not notice this; she never put up her hand to play with the silver brooch that was a half-moon with five little owls sitting on it; she never pulled grandmother's watch from her bodice and opened the back by herself to see grandfather's hair; she never buried her head close to smell the lavender water, or took up grandmother's spectacle case and wondered at its being really silver. She just lay still and let herself be rocked. (102)

Here the foster-maternal breast promises the envious child warmth, ease, the safety of an enclosed haven. Moreover, its accoutrements provide a range of images for explorative fantasy—the mysterious image of the moon and owl brooch, the timepiece with the dead grandfather's lock of hair as an icon of fidelity and continuity, and the familiar personal smell that denotes one specific human body and no other. Further, the child burrows into the breast, not for nutriment, but for the reassurance of the enclosing maternal body. In the context of rivalry for this enchanted body, the new baby's strangeness is defined more by her inability to interact with it than by her usurpation. Thus the young Mansfield's awe at her sister's quietude turns to fear of such passivity and is concluded by a resolution to protect the valued toys from Gwen's inability to look at them, to interact: "After that I felt frightened of Gwen, and I decided that even when she did play with the doll's house I would not let her go upstairs into the bedroom—only downstairs, and then only when I saw she could look" (102). In this recollection, the doll's house is a contested object of imagination—one that must be forbidden to the sick child for fear that her inability to see it might rob it of its magical power of consoling Mansfield for the psychic loss of her mother.

I have taken care to set up the narrative of Gwen Beauchamp's biography because many of the primary medical, psychological, and creative initiations of Katherine Mansfield's art are indirectly addressed in it. There is the threat of disease in birth and child bearing; there is the suggestion of psychological damage wrought by denial of the "primary" mother's breast and the interposition of the grandmother's breast as surrogate; and, finally, there is the embodiment in the narration of the child's negotiation of her fears and rejections through play. This retreat to the comfort of toys inaugurates later creative work—both the recollective narrative of Gwen's death itself and then a mature reworking of it in differing forms. The constructive work of regression, of reenactment of early rejection for the purpose of cure—of making pain into a new creation—is first evident in elegies for the deaths of children and allusions to the abandonment of children which mark almost all of Mansfield's earliest writings. These juvenile works can exhibit such a morbid, unsublimated narcissism that they might seem unworthy of extensive analysis, but I believe that they prefigure later, more interesting and more subtle reworkings of the trauma of Gwen's death in stories such as "The Doll's House." Here the anxiety about being the child who survived and the split of the self into the acute perceiver and the pathetic victim are transformed into a declaration of the survivor's mandate to liberate her imagination as a service to all neglected children.

∼

In his memoirs, Sir Harold Beauchamp, Katherine Mansfield's father, noted his infant daughter's death as a loss that was eventually recompensed by the birth of a son: "Our youngest daughter, Gwendoline, died at the age of three months of infantile cholera, a disease that is rarely fatal under modern treatment. You can imagine what happiness the arrival of the boy brought as the last of the family" (83). Infantile "cholera" was the late-nineteenth-century name for severe colic, a form of gastroenteritis, for which the pediatric record is sparse and indefinite.[3] Statistics suggest that one of the sources of such disease was the hand-feeding of infants, which deprived them of the immunities of breast milk. Among the benefits of breast-feeding, according to modern clinical studies of Third World infant mortality, is its preservation of the baby not only from such childhood diseases as measles but also from the kinds of bacterial invasion which cause fatal disruptions of fragile neonatal digestion.[4] If babies were hand-fed in the late nineteenth century, they not only lost their mothers' immunities, but they tended also to be subject to bacteriological invasion from poorly sanitized feeding utensils. The late-nineteenth-century techniques of feeding, practiced without awareness of the necessity to boil vessels or pasteurize milk, invited contamination. Moreover, there was much confusion about the appropriate substitute for mother's milk: cow's milk was not only inappropriate for infant digestion, but it might be tainted, and so a number of home remedies were contrived for infants who had to be "brought up by hand."[5] Household experts devised concoctions as diverse as bread soaked in beer, arrowroot paste or pudding, and beef "tea." Indeed, among the most critical advances of modern pediatrics has been the analysis of human milk, which eventually led to the fabrication of infant formulas; this advance, added to the general adoption of pasteurization, has led to the decline of infant deaths such as Gwen Beauchamp's.

Mansfield's childhood recollection cannot, of course, tell us whether or not Mrs. Beauchamp nursed her sickly daughter, and gastroenteritis in a baby does not automatically indicate that the mother has not provided breast-feeding. We must guess at Annie Beauchamp's techniques of mothering from a few biographical details and from hints in Mansfield's narratives. One clue that Annie

Beauchamp may actually have nursed her newborn daughter is her consumption of sago. Sago was a palm flour that formed the base for puddings that might be consumed in preparation for nursing; in cookbooks of the day, sago was a prescribed staple for nursing mothers as well as for invalids.[6] Although Mansfield's noting of the sago detail could imply preparation for nursing Gwen, Antony Alpers reports a neighbor's opinion that Mrs. Beauchamp "didn't handle babies" (*Life* 3).

Whatever the exact details, Annie Dyer Beauchamp did not attend very well to the feeding of her children. She is absent in Mansfield's account of Gwen's crisis of nurture, and she seems to have abandoned Kathleen soon after her birth. Mrs. Beauchamp had left Wellington on a trip when Mansfield was only twelve months old.[7] Isabella Beeton advises that the weaning period should "never be less than *nine*, nor exceed *fifteen*" months (1038), and so while Annie Beauchamp's trip might fall within the prescribed limits,[8] it usurps the time frame usually allotted for the essential working out of the child's separation from the mother's body. Furthermore, separation from the mother's presence is much more traumatic than weaning from her breast; modern psychology locates the essential activities of self-differentiation in this time.[9] Moreover, after several months' absence, Annie Beauchamp had returned to New Zealand preoccupied with her new pregnancy. Again, we can only surmise, but it is possible that her frequent pregnancies might have some relation to her not having the contraceptive benefits of nursing. She had one more daughter after Gwen, and finally, in 1894, she bore her last child—the boy mentioned by Sir Harold as the consolation that erased the memory of Gwen.

The rejection of care for children implies a resentment of bearing them and indifference to rearing them. And it is clear from the historical record as well as comments in Mansfield's autobiographical stories (see Chapter 5) that Annie Beauchamp resented the six pregnancies that she was forced to bring to term because of her husband's unyielding desire for a son. Her own happiness at the birth of the boy consisted, perhaps, more in relief than in maternal fulfillment. Once the son was finally delivered, Annie Beauchamp's pregnancies ceased—a fact that emphasized the attachment of the family's identity to the male heir and underlined the diminished status of the daughters as failed experiments in the effort to insure the succession of the patriarchy. Indeed, the failure to have brought forth a male child may account for Annie Beauchamp's lassitude at the birth of Gwen, for surely she was overwhelmed with the knowledge that her labors would not end with this birth—her fourth pregnancy in five years.

In many of Mansfield's fictions, the mother is presented as a semi-invalid, and in her journals and letters Mansfield frequently alluded to her mother's having had rheumatic fever as a girl. She assumed that the "weak heart" left by this illness—always a feature of her mother's aloofness—was an inevitable complication for pregnancy, and in "Prelude" she has the mother protest that her husband's desire for children will kill her (258). Thus Mansfield's mother seems to have experienced pregnancy as a diseased state, one that threatened her, more than other women, with death. In the episode of Gwen's birth, indeed, she assumes a funereal pose, "her arms along the sheet." Nevertheless, there is a quick undercutting of the fatality of her illness when the narrative shifts to find her calmly eating the sago. Is she hypochondriacal? Or is she a frail woman fated to the endless childbearing of late Victorian patriarchal culture?[10] Mansfield's portraits of mothers throughout her fiction tend to play on one or another of these diagnostic possibilities.

In the pregnancy rituals of her time and of her class, Annie Beauchamp would have spent the weeks immediately following the birth of a child in "confinement." Usually that period was aided, for families that could afford the expense, by a "monthly nurse"—the attendant who came a week before the expected birth and stayed for several weeks after to attend the mother and infant.[11] In Mansfield's recollection it is the grandmother who fills the role of the monthly nurse and of the general nursemaid later. Annie Beauchamp's own mother, Margaret Mansfield Dyer, lived with the Beauchamps during the early years of the family, acting as a general household manager and nurse for all. In the nineteenth century, the benefit of having a relative rather than a hired nurse for obstetrical events was the provision of a loving presence during the trials of labor and recuperation. Mansfield's reminiscences suggest, however, that the accessibility of the grandmother may also have had the negative effect of giving Annie Beauchamp a convenient excuse for never having to mother her children herself. As Antony Alpers remarks of the grandmother's ministrations, "When there was a baby in the house her daughter did not have to touch it" (*Life* 9). Thus her mother's role as intimate servant gave Annie Beauchamp the margin of leisure to maintain her lifelong illness role—that of the frail woman for whom pregnancy was a singular medical crisis.

Whatever the cause of her mother's illness and its mitigation of responsibility for her baby's disease, Mansfield's reconstruction of Gwen's death emphasizes its status as a crisis of misnurture: "Down in the kitchen one day old Mrs. McElvie came to the door and asked Bridget about the poor little mite, and Bridget said, 'kep' alive on bullock's blood hotted in a saucer over a candle'" (*Journal* 102). Annie Beauchamp is absent here; Mansfield recalls that other women engaged in the task of providing life-giving nutriment to her child. Their account of the nutritional measures devised to save Gwen's life mirrors domestic medical practice as the province of females at the end of the nineteenth century; Mansfield mentions a doctor's arrival, but only for the fact that his dog "rushed at [her] and snapped at [her] bare legs" (102). The concern for Gwen's therapy thus lies among the servants, who care for the child through the casual sympathy of women's gossip. The only maternal nurse is the grandmother; she is there at the moment of death.

Mansfield reconstructs the instant of Gwen's death obliquely, remembering her stiffen in the arms of the grandmother, upon which, for the only time in the recollection, there is a cry of sorrow for the death of the child: "I saw her tiny body stretch out and her hands flew up, and 'Ah! Ah! Ah!' called the grandmother." But there is no other comment, no mourning; the next paragraph turns to the appearance of the photographer on the following morning. Aside from hanging the picture in the nursery, there does not seem to have been much further effort to remember little Gwen among the family. As in Sir Harold's account, her life is quickly passed over in rejoicing at the later birth of Leslie Heron Beauchamp, Katherine Mansfield's beloved brother "Chummie."

Whether through preternatural powers of recollection from the age of two and a half or—more likely—an absorption of the family illness story, Katherine Mansfield retained a vivid image of her sister's death. Thus, although the birth and death of Gwen Beauchamp made minimal disturbance and were soon forgotten, the illness elements remained as major themes of her sister's childhood recollections.[12] The mother's illness may have provided the unwanted child with a rationalization for her own rejection as well as her baby sister's casual demise, but the rationalizations of illness could not satisfy the psyche starved for recognition by the mother. Who can absolve the observing child from guilt for the death of a baby sister who has taken her place? The grandmother was the rescuing surrogate, to be sure, but in her humility—her diminished status as servant—she could not give Mansfield the ultimate satisfaction of commanding the attention of her powerful birth mother. Nevertheless, as in the ancient photograph of herself with the dead Gwen, the grandmother's figure would be permanently etched as the presiding figure in the memorial iconography of Mansfield's narratives of childhood.

~

Katherine Mansfield's earliest writings are beset with images of the deaths of children. She was attracted to the romantic "Erl-King" theme—the story of the child stolen away by a threatening death figure while the parent stands by helpless, or in some cases mysteriously complicit. Although this theme was intensified by the sentimentality about lost innocence which infected the fin-de-siècle aesthetic writers—Oscar Wilde especially—whom Mansfield read in adolescence, I believe that its urgency derived from the complex of reactions instigated by her sister's death. The first of the "child-verses," written when she was fourteen, centers on death as a mother's embrace:

> Would I could die as thou
> Hast done this day
> In childish faith and love
> Be ta'en away
> Rest, my little one
> Flowers on your breast
> Safe in the cold earth's arms
> Ever at rest.
>   (Quoted in Hankin, 6)

Death, here figured as a sheltered enfolding in cold arms, beckons as a release from early disappointment. Although the "breast" belongs to the child and serves conventional elegiac imagery in this verse, its association with the cradling embrace of the grave figures Mansfield's obsessive positioning of child-hood death in the proximity of the rejecting maternal bosom.

Mansfield's tendency to imagine the deaths of children as reproaches against cold mothers invokes the breast as the object in a desire to be totally covered, indeed to be taken into the mother's body. The image of hiding in the mother reappears in "My Potplants," a prose piece written when Mansfield was six-teen. This death story summons one of a number of the shadowy maternal figures in her early writing; they appear only to disappoint: "I hid my face in her dress and sobbed wildly, madly. . . . She took me on her lap and brushed my thick heavy hair from my hot face and kissed me" (quoted in Hankin, 13). Such a positioning of the fated child at refuge in the breast returned whenever Mansfield's sense of illness and abandonment became intense, as it was in her early school years in London (1903–8) when she wrote a number of morbid prose poems. And the image continued to mark the experimental writings she produced during the first several years of her return to London (1909–12) when she was frequently ill as a result of love affairs, aborted pregnancies, or venereal infection—not to mention a lifestyle of skimped meals and little sleep. In a poem published in *Rhythm* in 1912 when she was initiating her vexed relationship with John Middleton Murry, she has the grass speak to a weeping child, "One day I shall open my bosom / And you shall slip in" (*Poems* 36). The word "pillow" frequently invokes the mother, especially when the sought-for breast is imagined as a locus for passive rest. Thus in "The Storm," one of the poems written after the death of her brother: "I put my arms round a tree / Pillowed my head against the rough bark / Protect me, I said. I am a lost child" (*Poems* 60). And in "Covering Wings," written in 1919 during a particularly severe pulmonary crisis, Mansfield addresses "Love" as a maternal, enfolding presence: "Love! Love! Your tenderness, / Your beautiful, watchful ways / Grasp me, fold me, cover me" (*Poems* 70). The maternal body is pleaded for incessantly in Katherine Mansfield's most fatalistic illness writings, but denial is always so incipient that the plea carries its own element of remonstrance.

When the breast represents the maternal function of enfolding and shielding, the remonstrance locates the lost child in an alien world. But the breast involves corporal nurture as well as hospitality. This oral aspect is submerged but frequently implicit. There is, for example, an image in the prose piece written when Mansfield was fifteen: "The poor little child, not knowing, stretched out his arms for her to take him up, and soothe him, and hold him to her breast."[13] The image of suckling as such is more evident in "The Grandmother," a poem written in 1909; remembering her grandmother as a source of nurture, Mansfield takes note of the oral reflex of her brother in her grandmother's arms, describing his mouth, which "moved as if he were kissing." Taken together with images of the breast opening up, such sucking imagery identifies the mother not only with protection but also with erotic satisfaction. As Hankin has noted, the sheltering figure in Mansfield's early writing may combine "the roles of protectress and soulmate, mother and lover" (13).

Several variations on the pathos of fated infants mark Mansfield's elaboration of breast images—the idealization of the child as specially endowed with an innocent trust in existence, the notion of child death as occurring in exposed isolation, the longing for the mother's embrace even if it implies dying, and the speaker's close personal identification with the dead or dying child. And in the insistence on satisfaction, there is also some sense of the disproportion of wanting so much that the demand is rightly rejected. Such an extremity of need/demand structures guilt as well as remonstrance in Mansfield's more eroticized invocations of the breast. Within this complex, the demanding child may understand that the mother's refusal is justified and accept the sentence to early death as a deserved punishment.

In her survey of Mansfield's juvenilia, C. A. Hankin suggests that her juvenile morbidity reflects an Oedipal conflict that involves wishing for the death of her parents and leads to ambivalent traffic between fantasy and dream worlds. Such a traditional Freudian paradigm gets at some of the gross manifestations of Mansfield's psychic "splitting" under the pressure of maternal rejection, but it has two limitations: first, it suggests that Mansfield's imagination was innately pathological, and second, it fails to register the bodily specificity in Mansfield's characteristic imagery of desire and loss. In such a paradigm the somatic ground of personality is either inaccessible or erased in the Oedipal grid.

In countering the simplifications of such an interpretation, I begin by insisting that Mansfield's fascination with infant death was the symptom of anxiety brought about by the *real* witnessing of the *real* death of her sister at close hand. Emphasizing this historical originary event, I want not only to defamiliarize the analysis of Mansfield's morbid fascination with childhood but also to move interpretation of it back into the clinical setting of the mother and child engaging in their earliest interactions. Thus I seek to read the splitting in Mansfield's imagination within a "relational" structure of ego development (through interaction with her mother and grandmother) rather than within the "drive" structure of inherent psychic urges that might categorize her, like Freud's Dora, as yet another example of female hysteria.[14] The combination of childish need and aggression manifested in Mansfield's breast imagery suggests Melanie Klein's observations of the infant's early sadistic attack on the mother's body, and eventually of "the desire to suck and scoop out, first directed to her breast, soon . . . to the insides of her body" (128). Klein links this sadism not only with worries about fulfillment but also with anxieties of loss which are allied with an early death wish; the ambivalences of infant ego development finally work themselves out in a sort of buildup of introjections of body parts and functions—moving from the oral/breast fixation, through flooding/urethral fantasies, into erotic imaginings of the Oedipal penis within the mother as well as the father.

Klein's approach, the foundation for later object-relations theorizing, sees the desire for the breast as a basic drive and so foregrounds the embodied nature of the child's fantasy life as well as its rich imagistic vocabulary. Nevertheless, I find its literalistic schematization of body parts, of sadistic drives, and of family power constellations too rigid to make a satisfactory fit with the environmental complexities in Mansfield's case. Klein's is a psychology of the psyche red in tooth and claw.

That there is a vexatious economy of positive and negative strategies, sadistic and masochistic moves, in Mansfield's depictions of childhood deprivation of the breast is not in doubt; the themes of infant mortality, maternal desertion, good and bad nurture, and rescue by a magical, eroticized mother constantly intervene in her writing. But the pattern these elements establish is not a static routine of infant deprivation and mourning, reenacted within the neurotic pathos of regression. What we see in Mansfield's more mature narratives of child death, as in her sketch of Gwen's dying, is a consciously achieved awareness that her own implication in the total context of her sister's death occurred within a layering of diverse environmental causes and reactions. In addition to the rejecting mother, the layers included the grandmother's servitude and surrogacy, Mansfield's own maneuvers for protection as a rival sibling, her precocious perceptual range, the power of her canny though rudimentary perceptions to identify injustice, and, finally, her recognition of the photographer's comic air as in some sense allied with her own secret recording of the event for future reference.

In assessing the possibilities of an inner life liberated from fixation on the mother's breast by such a creative understanding of the contexts of deprivation, I turn to D. W. Winnicott's elaboration of Kleinian formulations. My focus on the therapeutic dimensions of theory guides my theoretical choice here, for Winnicott was a pediatrician who elaborated Klein's founding version of object-relations analysis within his medical practice with large numbers of very young children; the demands of actual work with children inculcated a refreshing freedom from dogma.[15] Thus in his own critique of the Oedipus theory as the universal model for understanding children's psychological difficulties, Winnicott once observed, with characteristic plainness, "It is not just a 'resistance' on the part of parents and teachers that makes them impatient with the truths that are formulated in Oedipus Complex terms. These facts . . . tend to make people feel helpless. What can they do?" (*Human Nature* 35). The question of what can be "done" with the insights of child psychology in interpreting a literary life can be asked with the same appeal to a recognition that the self needs to "do something," to function in writing. The Oedipal "truths" tend to encapsulate the writer in enactments of archetypal conflicts, without accounting for the basic somatic foundations of her sense of material reality and of her imagination's primitive strategies to define and control it. In other words, without a theory of the subject's role in constructing her own self, *in the body* as well as in later complexes and in the coherent understandings provisionally posed through her rich fantasy life, a psychoanalytic reading must become a study in psychopathology.

Although Winnicott was a follower of Klein and referred to her gratefully in a number of his writings, he always made clear that he did not see the origin of the development of the infant self in terms of Kleinian drives but in terms of the mutuality in the mother-infant "environment" (*Maturational Process* 177). Thus the infant contrives the initiating awareness of its own basic existence in collaboration with the mother—the infant in being held (and the mother in holding) and the infant in needing the breast (and the mother in responding to that need)—resulting in the substantiating "theoretical first feed." The breast is not, then, simply a biological provision for getting milk into a baby, nor is it the introjected object of elemental psychic drives; it is a first marker of the incipient subjectivity's ability to function within the limits of reality—both by experiencing "omnipotence" in summoning the maternal fulfillment of an inside need and, eventually, by recognizing limits to its power to construct and control the outside by recognizing that the breast it needs is not its possession. In "good enough mothering," there is a creative mutuality between the mother's willingness to give herself to the infant's need and the infant's being able to move from the solipsism of a world it wholly creates to a world in which it lives.

The psyche's symbolic creativity in imagining the mother when she is absent prefigures all later forms of creative activity. Winnicott locates infantile creativity in the designation of "transitional" territories between the child and the mother, and the familiar appropriation of "transitional objects" such as blankets and toys, which can fill the space between desire and satisfaction. I quote at some length here because I refer to Winnicott's notions again in my discussion of Mansfield's childhood:

> After the theoretical first feed, the baby begins to have material with which to create. Gradually it can be said that the baby is ready to hallucinate the nipple at the time when the mother is ready with it. Memories are built up from innumerable sense-impressions associated with the activity of feeding and finding the object. In the course of time there comes a state in which the infant feels confident that the object of desire can be found and this means that the infant gradually tolerates the absence of the object. Thus starts the infant's concept of external reality, a place from which objects appear and in which they disappear. Through the magic of desire one can say that the baby has the illusion of magical creative power, and omnipotence is a fact through the sensitive adaptation of the mother. The basis for the infant's gradual recognition of a lack of magical control over external reality lies in the initial omnipotence that is made a fact by the mother's adaptive technique. (*Human Nature* 106)

Rather than freezing the development of the self in the rigidities of pre-Oedipal interpretation, such a schema foresees fruitful possibilities in children's negotiations with nurture through their ability to create "transitional objects." In so doing the child begins to create her own symbols for what has been lost, what can be hoped for from outside, and what must be made from inside.

Mansfield's strategy of survival—her adoption of her grandmother as a secondary mother—accents her maneuvering of the necessary transitional figure in her life into the realm of imaginative play as well as self-preserving nurture. Thus the grandmother is depicted as a source of spontaneous creative activity for the young child. Her lap, as we have seen, offers objects to investigate, interpret, handle. In the nursery setting for the textual memorial of Gwen's death, she permits free play with the doll's house. Because of such sponsorship, she is given the role of muse for Mansfield's later writing.

~

From a Winnicottian point of view, then, Mansfield's childhood might be seen to have commenced in a pathological crisis of orality—of inability to engage the mother in a satisfactory first feed. The sister who actually died of misfeeding was projected into this crisis, merged with the surviving sister in some of the child-death images I have listed, thus transforming the early Mansfield at once into the victim and the victimizer. Both in the photograph that hung over the nursery fire and in the creations of Katherine Mansfield's imagination, Gwen's icon sets up conflicting claims. It formulates the dialectic between the sentimentality of identification and the satire of sheer specularity. In reading this split in Mansfield's imagination as one that involves positioning her narrative self vis-à-vis the dead infant and the surviving one, we move from the conventional assigning of a split between "the world of dream and the world of reality" (Hankin 15) to a more therapeutic view; we see Mansfield's juvenile strategy of regression in times of illness as a creative confrontation with the source incident for her anxiety about dying an early death. As a mature writer revisiting this childhood trauma, however, Mansfield now has conscious choices to make about where she will stand; will she again take on the role of the dying child? will she position herself within the sheltering gaze of the grandmother's funereal posture? or will she "photograph" the event as a professional artist, called in to memorialize death?

Underlying these issues of self-presentation is the question of the source of psychic health that enabled Mansfield to overcome the failure of her mother's breast and thus an ongoing confusion about the nature of reality and of imagination. For the pathology of Katherine Mansfield's childhood would seem its most relevant feature for her mature writing if it were not for the enabling nurturance she drew from the memory of Margaret Mansfield Dyer, her maternal grandmother (the "Mrs. Fairfield" of "Burnell" stories of New Zealand). Her allusions to the grandmother in her journal indicate the richness of the grandmother's guardianship. She returned to Margaret Mansfield Dyer's image in periods of intense confusion and fatal illness, as in the winter of 1922 when she was in constant, demoralizing physical pain: "January 21 Grandma's birthday. Where is that photograph of my dear love leaning against her husband's shoulder, with her hair parted so meekly and her eyes raised? I love it. I long to have it. For one thing Mother gave it to me at a time when she loved me" (*Journal* 289). The transitional territory between the child's need and the mother's denial is here clearly taken up by the grandmother. Moreover, the grandmother's occupation of that space is not simply a provision of nourishment. It also provides the enfolding that gives structure and well-being to the body itself. Mansfield concludes her apostrophe to her grandmother's photograph with a striking bodily description, remembering "especially . . . her beauty in her bath—when she was about sixty. Wiping herself with the towel. I remember now how lovely she seemed to me. And her fine linen, her throat, her scent. I have never *really* described her yet. Patience! The time will come" (289).

Thus Mansfield's relation with her grandmother was a matter of intimate, sensual interaction with a maternal body. In a fragment from 1910—written when she was herself pregnant and alone in Bavaria—she wrote: "The only adorable thing I can imagine is for my Grandmother to put me to bed and bring me a bowl of hot bread and milk, and standing, her hands folded, the left thumb over the right, say in her adorable voice: 'There, darling, isn't that nice?' Oh, what a miracle of happiness that would be! To wake later to find her turning down the bedclothes to see if your feet were cold, and wrapping them up in a little pink singlet, softer than a cat's fur" (*Journal* 42). The grandmother is not only the protector but the lover of the child's physical body, then; her internalized image configures holding, warmth, feeding, sleep, in the proximity of the eroticized female body. It is within these memories that Mansfield can eventually recall her lost childhood not only as a time of the death of the child but also as a time of lyric joy and discovery.

It was not only psychosomatic reassurance that Mrs. Dyer gave, however; she also gave Mansfield conscious answers about the fatality of life. In the memory of the death of her son, Margaret Mansfield Dyer had an illness story of her own. In "At the Bay," Mansfield shows the grandmother remembering such a death; the granddaughter asks about death—whether it makes her sad, for example. The grandmother admits the fact of mortality and the sadness. And then, the child encounters a shocking awareness of the reality of death—her own and her grandmother's:

> "Does everybody have to die?" asked Kezia.
> "Everybody!"
> "*Me?*" Kezia sounded fearfully incredulous.
> "Some day, my darling."
> "But, grandma." Kezia waved her left leg and waggled the toes. They felt sandy. "What if I just won't?"
> The old woman sighed again and drew a long thread from the ball.
> "We're not asked, Kezia," she said sadly. "It happens to all of us sooner or later." (283)

The sharp recognition of mortality here filters through the relationship between the older woman and the child; the child is allowed, for a moment, to engage in fantasies of immortality, but she is also confronted with inalterable facts.

The terror of the facts is real, but it is also held at bay by bodily contact with the maternal presence, which in this episode dissipates fear in a bout of tickling. Kezia's pleading with her grandmother never to leave her by dying is forgotten in their play. Mrs. Dyer is thus the mother who can confront mortality, absorb its sadness, explain it, and then continue with her living through the affectionate and playful acceptance of the child's body.

The aura of virtue which surrounds the image of the grandmother in Mansfield's memories and stories is not limited to her ability to verify the child's physical existence, however. It also derives from a definition of the good mother as one who would not neglect her children even through the lassitude of illness. Her grandmother established for Mansfield an ethic of health ratified by work. Thus, although she sometimes wrote of her mother admiringly as a frail woman who had the courage to endure, Mansfield realized that Annie Beauchamp gave her no sense of a woman's capacity for serious exertion. Mansfield recalled this as another barrier to their understanding: "I often long to lean against Mother & know she understands things . . . that can't be told . . . that would fade at a breath . . . *delicate needs*—a feeling of fineness & gentleness—but what Mother hadn't is an *understanding* of WORK" (CL 3:212). The grandmother's capacity to make bodily contact, to let the child "lean against" her, was embedded in her spontaneous physical activism. She was the family servant, the one who took care of the flesh in feeding, in warding off illness, in contriving comfort, in explaining mortality. The care devoted to all these occupations gave her granddaughter a solacing sense of the possibility of a woman's capacity effectively to guard the child from death.

The grandmother-nurse was obviously Mansfield's childhood refuge from the threat of illness. But to some extent Mansfield lost this refuge in a strange lapse of her own attention. As she grew into adolescence, her dependence on her grandmother waned. She did remember and write about Mrs. Dyer during her high school years in London. Here is a little verse that frankly places the grandmother in the position of the rescuing sick nurse:

> I am sitting in the darkness
> And the whole house is still
> But I feel your presence
> Since I've been ill. . . .
>
> Granny darling, then I want you
> For I know you understand
> And I yearn for your presence
> And to feel you clasp my hand. . . .

> And I thought and thought about you
> Would you sorrow? Would you care?
> When you heard that I was blind
> And was left to linger here?
>   (Quoted in Hankin, 7; ellipses are Mansfield's)

Once she had returned to Wellington from the three years of schooling in London, where she had written this poem to Margaret Mansfield Dyer, however, Mansfield plunged into the new social life of her adolescence. In the busyness of her return, she neglected to visit her grandmother and thereby missed seeing the aging woman before she died suddenly on the last day of 1906.

~

The death of Mansfield's maternal mentor and nurse left her truly bereft. She turned again to her parents in her poems of childish illness, but without very great hope of comfort. In "The Sea Child," a poem written during convalescence from her first major adult illness in London, Mansfield made her last appeal to the primary mother as the rescuer of the dying child. The overwrought poem is interesting only for what it reveals about the prevalence of the romance of the death of children in her maturing imagination.

> Into the world you sent her, mother,
>   Fashioned her body of coral and foam,
> Combed a wave in her hair's warm smother,
>   And drove her away from home.
>
> In the dark of the night she crept to the town
>   And under a doorway she laid her down,
> The little blue child in the foam-fringed gown.
>
> And never a sister and never a brother,
>   To hear her call, to answer her cry.
> Her face shone out from her hair's warm smother
>   Like a moonkin up in the sky.
>
> She sold her corals; she sold her foam;
>   Her rainbow heart like a singing shell
> Broke in her body: she crept back home.
>
> Peace, go back to the world, my daughter,
>   Daughter, go back, to the darkling land;
> There is nothing here but sad sea water,
>   And a handful of shifting sand.   (*Poems* 32)

The structure of this variation on the theme of the fated child is clear. When Mansfield entered the dark world of the town to "sell" her treasures, it had not been a free act of liberation. Rather, she was forced away by her mother's coldness. Once her "rainbow heart," that special gift for life sponsored by the grandmother, has been broken in the dark city, her impulse is to steal home again to her sisters and brother. But the way is barred by the mother, who tells her, perhaps wisely, that she has forfeited her family. Like the Little Mermaid in Andersen's fairy tale, she has lost both her innocence and her home by de-siring more than a daughter ought to have. Though Mansfield developed, in one strand of her personality, the toughness to take advantage of her experi-ences, in another strand there was always the outcast, broken child, asking the mother for nurturing. This alternation between self-determined independence and immature sentimentality became one of the most problematical aspects of her writing, for even in some of her most mature fiction, the myth of the dying child breaks through.

And the myth breaks through in the very image of Gwen's corpse in the nursery photograph. Mansfield returned to that image to make reparation for her aggressive survival of Gwen in a number of stories in which the dead child does not actually appear but, rather, haunts the narrative margins with features from Gwen's funeral photograph. There is an evocation in Mansfield's satiri-zation of Monica Tyrell in "Revelations," for example. This spoiled, childish society woman deflects the reality of the death of her hairdresser's daughter by imagining herself buying funeral flowers for a figure like Gwen in the photo, "a tiny wax doll with a feather of gold hair, lying meek, its tiny hands and feet crossed." Monica's self-dramatization permits her to appropriate the pathos of infant death for herself: "From an unknown friend. . . . From one who understands. . . . For a Little Girl" (431). This story of the society woman's flight from the child's death seems to do penance not only for the death of Gwen but for the death of Margaret Mansfield Dyer as well. Mansfield rec-ognizes the insincerity of a sentimental melancholy that will not make the effort to do anything substantial for the ill and dying.

Hints of elements in the death of Gwen appear in other stories. There is an infant death in "The Child-Who-Was-Tired," for example. And "Sun and Moon" stages the destruction of the doll's house, now imaged as a confec-tionary dessert that the little boy covets for its imaginative magic but which his little sister eats in all too material a way. And in "Life of Ma Parker," the consumptive grandson, Lennie, is described as Gwen had been described— pale, with golden curls, and silent.

Nowhere is the imaginative transformation of Gwen's death so intriguing, however, as in "The Doll's House." Here at last the episode that Mansfield remembered from her earliest childhood is reproduced in symbolic restitution. But it is reproduced under the aegis of the surviving sister this time, without the mediating presence of her grandmother; even though the story centers upon the Burnell family, Mrs. Fairfield is never in evidence. The presiding figure is Kezia, Mansfield's autobiographical protagonist in many stories of her New Zealand childhood. The story begins with the arrival of the doll's house at the Burnells' and the reactions of the three sisters to it. It is Mansfield's Kezia who understands that the special magic of the new toy inheres not so much in its furniture, and certainly not in the stiff and outsized doll figures of mother, father, and two children, but in the little lamp that "seemed to smile at Kezia, to say, 'I live here.' The lamp was real" (571).

In the course of the story, all of the classmates of the Burnell children are allowed to see the house, two by two. The exceptions are the Kelveys, "Lil" and "Our Else," daughters of the local washerwoman. By the edict of Mrs. Burnell, these derelict children are not to be let into the yard. The mother's prohibition here not only reenacts the rejection of Annie Beauchamp but mimics the young Mansfield's determination to keep the doll's house from her dying baby sister. The story, however, permits Kezia to relent as Kathleen had not; after some time, and when the glamour of the toy has faded, Kezia disobeys the maternal prohibition and lets the little girls into the yard to share her vision of the house. Even without her grandmother, she now has the moral stature to be generous, to resist the rejections of mothers. Almost before they can fully take in the total effect, however, they are shooed out by Aunt Beryl, another personification of antimaternal woman in Mansfield's Burnell stories.

Of course, "The Doll's House" has a multiplicity of origins and references from Mansfield's childhood; there was, for example, a family like the Kelveys in the Wellington of the 1890s. It would be absurd to insist that the story is nothing but a reenactment of the death of Gwen Beauchamp. But none of the historical models for the rejected Kelveys quite explains the description of Our Else, the youngest—a silent and pale ghost throughout the story. The description of her costume emphasizes her infantile status; "she wore a long white dress, rather like a nightgown, and a pair of little boy's boots." Further, "she was a tiny wishbone of a child, with cropped hair and enormous solemn eyes— a little white owl" (573). The silence of this odd child, and the description of the whiteness of her face, associate her with the dead infant in the photograph that hung in the Beauchamp nursery for all those years. At last in "The Doll's House," a picture retaken, Katherine-as-Kezia can reanimate Gwen, making reparation for her rivalry with her dead sister by fighting the mature women of her family for the silent child's right of access to the treasured transitional object—the repository of identity. She can give the dead child voice at last. In sharing, she transfers to the ghostlike Else the capacity of the nurtured imagination to create and hold on to what is "real."

The real lamp embodies Mansfield's achieved capacity to separate the inner from the outer world, not by abandoning illusion, but by understanding its role in the construction of a reality that can nurture the self. Kezia's sharing places her in rebellion not only against her mother but also against the family that enforces the mother's prohibitions. They are all enemies of the symbol making that was to become Mansfield's tool in defining her own reality through a recognition of her sisterhood with the dying. Rejecting the self-satisfactions of the healthy, she was better able to take the part of weak and marginal figures like her dead sister. And so in alliance with Kezia, Our Else speaks the last words both for the child as victim and for the child as survivor: "I seen the little lamp."

CHAPTER 2

"They discuss only the food"

Body Images

In FORMAL photographs of the family of Sir Harold Beauchamp, one of Wellington's most successful self-made businessmen and later director of the Bank of New Zealand, the bourgeois family defines itself in self-possession before the camera; there are the commanding mother in exquisitely tailored dresses that bind her trim neck and wrists, the father bearded in Edwardian fashion and tending to corpulence, two neat and compliant older sisters wearing the standard costume of late Victorian adolescence, the youngest girl and boy in easy good behavior, and an elegant maiden aunt poised to move on into her own marriage. Kathleen, the middle child, however, frequently seems caught at an unsure perimeter of the group—wearing its uniform, perhaps, but seeming somehow deflected from the entourage. She does not conform to the family's discipline of gaze or of body control. In the pictures of her childhood, Katherine Mansfield is notable for being chubby, and the eyeglasses she wore at one stage give her the nearsighted person's shield of a reflective lens. In photos of her adolescence, she seems always to have a problem with hair or with blouses that won't stay tucked.

Mansfield glamorized such an outcast status as romantic rebellion in "Juliet," a novel begun when she was seventeen, during her last school year in London, and worked on during the following year when she was back in Wellington—fighting her parents to return to London in order to commence the kind of artistic life closed off by the domestic circle in New Zealand. In "Juliet," alienation from the mercantile family is shown to inscribe a split within the heroine herself, creating a "Mirror face" that reflects the only self with whom she can communicate:

> Since her very early days she had cultivated the habit of conversing very intimately with the Mirror face. Her childhood had been lonely, the dream-face her only confidante. She was second in a family of four. . . .

Annie Beauchamp (1864–1918). (ATL)

Opposite page, top: *The Beauchamp family, Wellington, ca. 1898.*
Back, left to right: *Vera, Jeanne, Kathleen [KM], Annie Dyer*
Beauchamp; front, left to right: *Chaddie, Mrs. Dyer, Leslie.*
(V. Mackintosh Bell Collection, ATL)

Opposite page, bottom: *Beauchamp family on board the* Niwaru *en route*
to England from New Zealand, 1903. Back, left to right: *Kathleen [KM],*
Harold W. Crow, B. J. Dyer, Vera; second row, left to right: *Chaddie,*
Annie, Captain Fishwick, Jeanne, Belle Dyer (Annie's sister); front: *Leslie.*
(A. L. Delahenty Collection, ATL)

The mother was a slight pale little woman. She had been delicate and ailing before her marriage and she never could forget it. . . . [The father was] a tall grey bearded man, with prominent blue eyes, large ungainly hands, and inclining to stoutness. . . . Juliet was the odd man out of the family—the ugly duckling. She had lived in a world of her own, created her own people. (*TLR* 3:7–8)

Even though she suggests a rare attractiveness in Juliet's whiteness of skin, the sensitive cut of her nose and lips, and the expression of her eyes, Mansfield also signals her heroine's difference from the family by implying some physical defect in her experience, some ugliness in this duckling. What was the flaw, then? Descriptions of Juliet embed size as a feature—"an unusual fullness over her brows," "the underlip too full for regular beauty," and hands that are "distinctive," but "large." She seems to have inherited nothing of the slight, delicate mother's form: in fact, the largeness of her hands allies her with her father's body type.

As the story progresses,[1] Juliet suffers alternating bodily changes. Alone in London and vulnerable to the crowds, she feels diminished: "She was thinking, thinking. How absurd everything was. How small she was" (17). At a later point, however, seduced, abandoned, and pregnant, she thinks of her body as grotesquely large: "How very very heavy she had grown. She could hardly hold up her head now . . . [Mansfield's ellipsis] It is quite extraordinary—like a dead body, she thought. All the six undertakers couldn't lift her now" (23). Thus within the idealized context of romantic rebellion that she herself was acting out at the time of writing "Juliet," Mansfield indirectly confronted the question of the body of the late adolescent and the way its configurations both split and mirrored her inner life. (Not coincidentally, the heaviness of the adolescent body is here linked with the image of early death, and Juliet does die eventually as a result of childbirth or abortion—the text is not clear about which.)

The reality of Mansfield's own alienation from her family—romanticized in her autobiographical heroine as both temperamental and programmatic—was neither so noble nor so self-assured in real life. It was, for one thing, founded upon the humiliation dealt by maternal disfavor that centered on her physique. A witness recalled Annie Beauchamp's chilly emphasis on Mansfield's weight as she distributed her greetings to the family after one of her travels: "Finally it was to Kathleen she spoke first, for everyone to hear. 'Well, Kathleen,' she said, 'I see that you are as fat as ever.' And in my first glimpse of Kathleen I saw her eyes flash, and her face flush with anger as she turned away with a toss of her ringlets."[2]

That body weight should have been a major issue between Katherine Mansfield and her mother refocused in latency and adolescence the oral issues of Mansfield's infancy. The demand of Annie Beauchamp that Mansfield control her weight was at variance with the daughter's positive self-identity gained through interaction with her grandmother—that intimate confirmation of bodily existence attained through being held and fed. In "Mary," a memoir of childhood published in *Harper's Monthly Magazine* in 1910,[3] Mansfield proudly attributed her childish plumpness to her grandmother: "I was a strong, fat little child who burst my buttons and shot out of my skirts to grandmother's entire satisfaction" (274). The dietary prohibitions of the mother denied the value of this "strong" identity by rejecting its manifestation in Mansfield's flesh. Furthermore, Annie Beauchamp's intolerance of her daughter's body seemed especially wounding because it contrasted sharply with her acceptance of the appetitive body of her husband. Accordingly, it was within this paradox of fleshiness forbidden for females while accepted for males that Mansfield's Oedipal crisis was transacted.

As we have seen, Mansfield's earliest imagination was marked by her sense of a fated split between the starved baby self of Gwen and the greedy surviving child self of Kathleen. A strategic result of the split was the double adult/child point of view taken in the recollection of Gwen's death and in the verses about child death. Thus, ironically, Mansfield's narrative stance was always to be divided between the perspective of the child as victim and that of the child as observer of a primal scene of early death. The mother's denial of Mansfield's body in latency superimposed upon this dichotomy another set of self-contradictions. Built upon the images of fat versus thin initiated in the psychic setting of mother/daughter antagonism, these contradictions designated body weight as a marker between the inner and the outer self. And so contending body images inform a string of associated oppositions in Mansfield's self-presentation—the self that belongs to the heavy father versus the self that belongs to the slight mother, the masculine self versus the feminine self, the spontaneous self versus the role-playing self, the loving self versus the rejecting self, and—finally and decisively—the healthy self versus the diseased self. Such a network of self-oppositions would be evoked in dialogue with a whole series of "mirror faces," recorded in Mansfield's journal and dramatized in many of her stories of confused young women.

~

One product of her adolescent preoccupation with body image was Mansfield's association of eating with ceremonies of acceptance. As I have already noted, her juvenile stories and verses emphasized the breast as an Edenic source of welfare in which suckling is hinted but never described openly. A more detailed vision of the paradise of food is played out in a strange narrative of Mansfield's early period—one of the many pieces written around 1910 in London, when her imagination was engaged by her sense of exile from her parents.

"How Pearl Button Was Kidnapped" tells of a toddler who wanders off from her family home—designated by her childish imagination as the "House of Boxes"—with two fat Maori women.[4] These friendly vagabonds are described primarily in terms of their physical amplitude and maternal affection for the child. The most intriguing aspect of the fantasy narrative, told from the child's point of view, is the imagery of being held and fed within the admiring sponsorship of the two native women who are enchanted by the difference of her body—her white teeth and blond curls. For example, when Pearl becomes too tired to walk, one of the women carries her, allowing the child to burrow into her body: "She was softer than a bed and she had a nice smell—a smell that made you bury your head and breathe and breathe it" (10). Such details of enfoldment within a fragrant bosom recall the infant fantasies that Mansfield associated with her nurturing grandmother.

The native women in "Pearl Button" do more than carry the child away, however; they also feed her generously. When the juice of a pear runs down her dress, they tell her not to worry about the mess. And when they leave their log house to travel on to the seaside, one of them again holds Pearl in her ample embrace:

> She nestled closed in the big lap. The woman was warm as a cat, and she moved up and down when she breathed, just like purring. Pearl played with a green ornament round her neck, and the woman took the little hand and kissed each of her fingers and then turned it over and kissed the dimples. Pearl had never been happy like this before. (11)

When they reach the shore, Pearl is strangely terrified by the sea—an image of the maternal in Mansfield's early writings, according to C. A. Hankin (263). I suggest that this story divides the maternal, however, setting up a contrast between the universal sea mother as a destructive force and surrogate human mothers as everyday protectors. On the one hand, there is the fearful sound of the sea mother's voice, all enveloping but threatening in destructive possibilities. On the other hand, there are the individual representatives of approving nurturance—servants and strangers who make no mythic claims in their representation of domestic tenderness. Applying Lacanian terminology, we may say that the sea represents the "phallic mother," the echo of the terrifying alienation of the other that in giving birth also contains the signifier of generative power.[5] Pearl's sea terrors are calmed by a regression to the register of the "imaginary" embodied in the wordless big women, and under their care she can play by the sea, finding the water warm and friendly.

In her presentation of the primitive Maoris, Mansfield emphasizes the erotic dimensions of the nurturing woman more openly than she can in the descriptions of Kezia's or her own interactions with the grandmother. The primitive innocence of the women may sanitize the narrative of any hint of incestuous love, but it also suggests the illicit appeal of the lesbian sensuality as a residuum of suspended Oedipal identifications (we will return to this theme in the next chapter). The heavy erotic texture of the child's interactions with the natives is especially significant because it so firmly associates sexuality with feminine largeness. And thus the issues of a freely fostered nurturance of the child self play into issues of sexual differentiation for Mansfield. She was unwilling to surrender physical amplitude exclusively to the male; she seems to have wanted to retain the possibility of body power for the female. But female weight is physical power without the avidity of masculine appetite: we never see the two Maori women eating in "How Pearl Button Was Kidnapped."

Mansfield's allegory makes clear that Pearl's escape into the arms of the fat women is also an escape from the conventional mandates of the forbidding mother and the aggressive father who, again using Lacan's formulation heuristically, embodies Law; indeed, the allegory enacts a fantasy of abandoning the environment of the bourgeois Oedipal family which segments itself into tightly defined spaces. Comparing her former home with the bliss of her new environment, Pearl asks the women, "Haven't you got any Houses of Boxes? . . . Don't you all live in a row? Don't the men go to offices? Aren't there any nasty things?" (12). She is both delighted and confused by her liberation from these constraints. Spontaneous play is now open to her, signified by transitional objects like the jade ornament around the woman's neck and the protected space of the seashore. When night falls, Pearl is fed once again under the approving eyes of the two foster mothers: "She ate meat and vegetables and fruit and the woman gave her milk out of a green cup. And it was quite silent except for the sea outside and the laughs of the two women watching her" (12). But eventually this rare interlude of play within the primitive arena of spontaneous sensuality is broken by the intrusion of society, and the story ends with Pearl looking up to see the arrival of "a crowd of little blue men to carry her back to the House of Boxes" (13). The world of men is one of capture, surveillance, and bodily discipline.

Although Katherine Mansfield's fixation with the heavy female body as the repository of the "good breast" seems to border on the neurotic in her earliest writings—and the allegorical spaces of "How Pearl Button Was Kidnapped" approach surreality—there is little sign that she herself suffered from any of the clinical eating disorders of adolescence. Her body weight exceeded the norm only in the eyes of her fastidious mother; from her photographs we can estimate that she was not obese, exceeding ordinary childhood variations. And although the young Mansfield worried about her weight from time to time, she seems to have avoided unnatural dieting, bulimia, or anorexia. Her comments on her weight indeed accented the comedy of her anxieties: in an allusion in one of her earliest letters, she writes to a cousin about walking in London: "I expect to come home quite thin, I am sure I quite deserve it. So far I can see no signs of 'Skeletonism,' I grieve to say" (*CL* 1:6). Moreover, throughout her life, her writing about food reveals the hearty gustatory sensibility derived from her grandmother's nurture; few writers of her generation could describe the pleasures of food more graphically. Take, for example, her description of the satisfactions of eating a cream puff: "Two minutes later Jose and Laura were licking their fingers with that absorbed inward look that only comes from whipped cream" ("Garden-Party" 541).

Although there is no sign of somatic eating disorder during Mansfield's adolescence, then, there is ample evidence that she suffered from the same kinds of confusion about body image which do motivate severe illness among adolescents. In a helpful survey of these confusions, Hilde Bruch has made an inventory of the meanings for food in the lives of adolescent girls:

> Food may symbolically stand for an insatiable desire for unobtainable love, or as an expression of rage and hatred; it may substitute for sexual gratification or indicate ascetic denial; it may represent the wish to be a man and possess a penis, or the wish to be pregnant, or fear of it. It may provide a sense of spurious power and thus lead to self-aggrandizement, or it may serve as a defense against adulthood and responsibility. Preoccupation with food may appear as helpless, dependent clinging to parents, or as a hostile rejection of them. (44)

Given such a plethora of possibilities, Bruch and other clinicians show, eating disorders in female adolescence are associated with internalized images of the body. Although Mansfield did not suffer the anorectic syndrome's physical manifestations, she clearly suffered from the kinds of body confusions that trigger the disease. For example, Mansfield's centering of "How Pearl Button Was Kidnapped" on the provision of forbidden food incorporates rage against her parents as well as longing for erotic gratification within the toddler body of the child. Further, the fear/desire of impregnation as a feature of body anxiety surfaces a number of times in Mansfield's adolescent writing; thus Juliet's feeling of heaviness encodes her fear of pregnancy before the narrative reveals its actuality.[6] Moreover, the figuration of Pearl and Juliet as small creatures confronting the dangers of an overwhelmingly large world emphasizes the elements of dependency in Mansfield's relativizing of size; the small, defenseless form is always shadowed by the heavy, controlling body of the father. But most important, Mansfield's conflicted introjection of body sizes into her child and female characters inflects their presentation with intransigent rebellion against the power of her parents.

Although the father's image is rarely so prominent as the mother's image in the self-reflections of her "small" characters, the false self in Mansfield's dialogues with the "mirror face" is frequently associated with the desire to appeal to the male, no matter how repugnant he might be in his omnivorous appropriation of all things to satisfy his appetite for approval. Mansfield's early satirical stories define men as eating animals and register the indignity of women's feeding them, even though her emphasis on body weight as the distinctive feature of the gendered body shifted focus with her later, more subtle stories about women as complicitous in such domination.[7] In these she came to understand that it was not any particular conformation of fat or thin which signified body image as distorted in women; it was, rather, the very proliferation of internalized images which set up a bewildering competition between refracted false selves and the ever elusive "real" self.

~

The imagination of the obese body as a patriarchal construction is best seen in Mansfield's delineations of Harold Beauchamp—in her journal and letters and then fictionalized in a series of fathers in her stories. In most of her early descriptions, she emphasizes his stoutness, his hairiness, and his bulging eyes. The hair signals sexuality, and the gaze indicates a voracity not only for food but for control of his daughter's behavior. Sexuality and power are, moreover, inscribed in the father's orality—the feature of the male which most repelled Mansfield. The intensity of her adolescent formulation of this repulsion erupted in Mansfield's remarkable description of her parents' behavior on board the ship that returned her and her two elder sisters to New Zealand in 1906 at the conclusion of their three years at school in Queen's College in London:

They are worse than I had even expected. They are prying and curious, they are watchful and they discuss only the food. They quarrel between themselves in a hopelessly vulgar fashion. My Father spoke of my returning as damned rot, said look here, he wouldn't have me fooling around in dark corners with fellows. His hands, covered with long sandy hair, are absolutely cruel hands. A physically revolted feeling seizes me. He wants

me to sit near. He watches me at meals, eats in the most abjectly, bla-
tantly vulgar manner that is describable. He is like a constant offence, but
I cannot escape from it, and it wraps me in its atmosphere. When I pass
him the dishes at the table, or a book or get him a cushion, he refrains
from thanking me. *She* is constantly suspicious, constantly overbearingly
tyrannous. I watch him walking all the deck, his full hideous speckled
trousers, his absurdly [illegible] cap. He is like a cat sometimes, I think—
except that his eyes are not like a cat's eyes, they are so full, so frightfully
offensive, when he is astonished or when he eats anything that pleases
him, I think they must start from his head. He watches the dishes go
round, anxious to see that he shall have a good share. I cannot be alone
or in the company of women for half a minute—he is there, eyes fearful,
attempting to appear unconcerned, pulling at his long drooping red-grey
moustache with his hairy hands. Ugh!   (*Journal* 6–7)

Clearly at this stage of her young life, Mansfield had moved from the situation of a vulnerable, confused child like Pearl Button to that of the sharp
diagnostician of body forms and their implications. The furtiveness of childhood sequestration in hapless chubbiness is exchanged for the aggressive self-
definition of a late adolescence in reaction against the body conformations of
her parents. The enmity centered on her father's fixation on feeding as a measure of control seems also a rejection of her mother's strictures against Mansfield's weight. The mother's service of this father's gluttony is here rendered as
a vicious form of feminine hypocrisy: "They discuss only the food."

According to classic Oedipal theory, the adolescent Mansfield should have
transferred desire for her mother to her father, or (in Nancy Chodorow's in-
fluential version) she should have turned *partially* to the father as relief from
her primary identification with the mother (*Reproduction* 123). Such accounts
of the Oedipal resolution of gender presuppose, however, a conventional triadic
mother/father/daughter field of psychic force; they feature the transfer of identifications in a romance of primary parent-child anxieties and affiliations. As
we have seen, Mansfield's Oedipal situation was more complicated—marked
by the tenuousness of any pre-Oedipal identification with her mother. Moreover, she possesses a precocious awareness of her mother's revulsion against
the father's sexuality which precluded her own competition for it; the seductiveness in the father upon which an Oedipal turn is supposed to be based was
therefore negatively charged. Mansfield thus identifies the mother and father
as combined in league against her. Annie Beauchamp is the phallic mother who
appropriates her husband's power with a vengeance; even as she rejects his
sexuality, she is the leading accomplice of the father's harsh law. It may be that

the cessation of parental eroticism after the birth of their son, the relocation of the source of their relationship from the sexual embrace to the partnership of familial governance, drained the Beauchamps' alliance of any of the affect that might have energized Mansfield's relations to them. As her shipboard diatribe implies, their conjugal alliance was especially confusing for the daughter because it provided no margin for instinctual erotic loyalty, no object for family romance, no relief from discipline. That romance, rather, resided in the relatively asexual *fourth* female figure in Mansfield's Oedipal situation—her grandmother. Thus her identification was with the female rather than the male, as suggested by her father's homophobic concern that she not be alone "in the company of women."

The psychic and familial situation during the efflorescence of Mansfield's Oedipal crisis in adolescence was thus fraught with implications of "illness," at least as it was defined by her conventional family. Indeed, there are hints in later intrafamilial letters and comments upon Mansfield's bohemian life in London that the entire family was alert to Kathleen's "erratic" behavior and united in varying ways to contain it.[8] Some biographers suggest that the polymorphous perversity of Mansfield's behavior during the two years between her return to Wellington and her decisive departure for London forced the family to surrender to her "acting out" and to let her go (Alpers, *Life* 60 ff.).

Despite insistent warfare against her patriarchal family, however, Katherine Mansfield maintained some ideal of its traditional values and uses; she made occasional gestures towards her father in early and later writings, even though these gestures were always tentative and frequently marked by despair of finding in the father the necessary liberation from identification with the mother. This ambivalence is captured in "The Little Girl," an early, though extraordinarily well controlled, story (probably written in 1910 but published in 1912). This story, which diagrams the toddler's Oedipal relationship with her father,[9] commences with the declaration of the child's perpetual fear of him:

> To the little girl he was a figure to be feared and avoided. Every morning before going to business he came into the nursery and gave her a perfunctory kiss to which she responded with "Good-bye, Father." And oh, the glad sense of relief when she heard the noise of the buggy growing fainter and fainter down the long road! (138)

Reading again through the Lacanian account of the Oedipus complex as involving an entry into language under the "law of the Father," the details of this story become especially significant, for they emphasize that speech and wordlessness are experienced by the little girl as under the father's command. The child is turned into a stuttering idiot when her mother asks her to serve her father in any way, and she is deafened and amazed on Sundays by his patriarchal vociferousness at church: "He said his prayers so loudly that she was certain God heard him above the clergyman" (139). In a pattern of characteristic images, this father is given, in addition to his gaze and his loud voice, overwhelming size that suggests a power to gobble up the child: "He was so big [that was what frightened the little girl]—his hands and his neck—especially his mouth when he yawned" (139).[10]

Responding to her grandmother's effort to help her make peace with this alien creature, the little girl sews him a pincushion. She discovers some papers on her mother's bed table and tears them up to stuff her peace offering. The papers turn out to be her father's "great speech for the Port Authority," and Kass's father and mother are both outraged at her usurpation of his words (140). She must be severely punished. Seeking comfort for his cruelly smacking her tender palms with a ruler, Kass later asks her grandmother, "Why did Jesus make Fathers for?" (141). Thereafter she hides her hands whenever her father approaches; "the child never forgot" (141). The father is not only law but language, and part of the child's recognition of the world of law is discovering that she is powerless to make herself understood and therefore to be treated kindly. Her audacious destruction of his speech—his language—sets her apart from him and her mother forever.

But eventually there is some relenting on the part of the child. She observes other children with more spontaneous fathers and is tempted by that ideal. When her mother falls ill and the daughter is left alone with her father, she makes a tentative rapprochement with him. She climbs into his bed to escape from a bad dream of a butcher with a terrible smile who wants to kill her. Nestling her against his breast, he invites her to "rub [her] feet against [his] legs and get them warm" (142). This physical contact with a hardness that was "nice," but harder than her grandmother, moderates her resistance to her father; she sees him as pitiful in his overwork and frustrations. At the end of the story, she moves closer and speaks to him fondly: " 'Oh,' said the little girl, 'my head's on your heart; I can hear it going. What a big heart you've got, Father dear' "(143). This reconciling comment echoes Little Red Riding Hood's exclamation to the cannibalizing wolf in the fairy tale; thus the father's seduction of the daughter here is so fraught with the threat of being devoured that it offers no secure entry into language, no indoctrination into the justice of law, and no clarity of decisive heterosexual identification. Thus, under all versions of the psychoanalytic formulation, the Oedipal transaction leaves the daughter in a confusing suspension of identifications.

The father's image in the shipboard outburst, as in "The Little Girl," is so embedded in his hateful bodily manifestation in hard, glowing health that it offers little compensation for the loss of the soft maternal form. Nevertheless, Mansfield turned to an idealized image of her father intermittently. She addressed him in a poem of 1911 at the time of deepest exile and rebellion. "To God the Father" reveals her longing for a maternal father, no matter how patriarchal he might seem:

> It is centuries since I believed in you,
> But to-day my need of you has come back.
> I want no rose-coloured future,
> No books of learning, no protestations and denials—
> I am sick of this ugly scramble,
> I am tired of being pulled about—
> O God, I want to sit on your knees
> On the all-too-big throne of Heaven,
> And fall asleep with my hands tangled in your grey
>   beard.   (*Poems* 37)

The wistful dependence of this verse constitutes a radical departure from the inner resolve with which Mansfield had experimented with various forms of sexuality at the risk of losing her family's protection (as we shall see, she appears to have flirted with men and women during the voyage to Wellington which so concerned her parents). For a major characteristic in the regressive urges of her later adolescence and early adulthood was an attitude of childish vulnerability in which she sought a strong, fatherly man for protection. As she rebounded from the kinds of risks which would leave her in both physical and psychic jeopardy, she was tempted to assume the posture of the prodigal daughter who had traded her approved feasting in the patriarchal home for a mess of pottage.

To some extent, Mansfield internalized the slim mother and the heavy father as the always accusing and judgmental voices that called her back to childhood helplessness. Permission to grow into her full embodied and sexual self was sanctioned only by the grandmother in Mansfield's working out of her Oedipal pattern. And her identification with the male through the father was gradually dispersed into the notion of a figure who would be less a repository of appetitive power than a brotherly conspirator in testing the limits of the law. In her stories as in her life, then, Katherine Mansfield's male friends and lovers were finally imagined and pressed into service as coconspiratorial children in the fight against the father.

A late sketch in Mansfield's journal suggests the pathology of her mother's complicity in confusing Mansfield's self-image by rejecting the father and thereby trivializing herself as a creature of fathers. The mother presented a blank rather than a mirror that might reflect back to the daughter a usable identity. Mansfield remembers the vivacious Annie Beauchamp confiding the regrets of her life in an intimate moment; she explains that she had always wanted to be an explorer, adventuring through the "Rivers of China": "Then she said 'If Father hadn't died I should have travelled and then ten to one I shouldn't have married.' And she looked at me dreamily—looked through me, rather" (*Journal* 234). Characteristically, here Mansfield sympathizes with the mother's sense of loss; the echo of refined slang in the phrase "ten to one" and the extravagant fantasy of the "Rivers of China" are both comic and endearing. But embedded in the sketch, it is clear—for the narrator goes back to notice accurately—the daughter has disappeared: "she looked . . . through me, rather." Thus, just as in her infancy Mansfield was left behind to make her mother's travels possible, so her adolescent presence is nullified by the mother's regrets about the limitations of having had children. Mansfield often sought to rationalize this kind of self-involvement by viewing her mother as the child and herself as the more knowledgeable parent, translating her mother's indifference into an attractively childish idiosyncrasy. Charming and beautiful women did not need to grasp the kind of stable feminine identity which could mirror the daughter's self back to her in a collaboration of identity formation. Annie Beauchamp was absolved of this parental mandate by her sense of the injustice of her own feminine fate. Thus, rather than recognizing her child, she could "look through" her.

D. W. Winnicott's essay on the mirror stage in identity formation designates the mother's face as the child's first reflection: "When the average girl studies her face in the mirror she is reassuring herself that the mother-image is there and that the mother can see her and that the mother is *en rapport* with her" (*Playing* 113). This insight may help to interpret the transaction recorded in Mansfield's memory: a mother who is unable to define her own life cannot assure her daughter of a self-image. The daughter's reaction to this lack may be the construction of a false self—created in compliance with the mother's depression or need. The daughter's inability to see her true self in the mother's mirror image and her tendency to try to make up for its blankness are often featured in the mirror episodes of Mansfield's fiction.

The challenge of sorting through the mirrored identities proffered to the adolescent girl by the mother within the confines of the bourgeois family is laid out most clearly in Mansfield's famous story "The Garden-Party." Here the autobiographical "Sheridan" family is defined as a locus of conspicuous consumption of food and of social power: indeed, the occasion of the story is its public celebration of itself with feasting. That story has had many interpreters, but none has been able to make a convincing explanation for the significance of the heroine's young brother, Laurie, who appears at the end of the story to help her make an inconclusive comment upon the meaning of her confrontation with "life."[11] Reading the plot, however, as engaging Oedipal confusions that seek parental allegiances in dealing with the confusions of body imagery, it is possible to view Laura Sheridan's brother as the last-resort sibling accomplice in her negotiation of a new code of feeling beyond the narrow ethos of her family.

The story opens with Laura Sheridan's morning survey of the forthcoming garden party. As the "artistic" one of the family, she is given the job of deciding where the marquee should be placed on the lawn. Her mother has delegated all of the supervisory roles to her daughters, announcing: "I'm determined to leave everything to you children this year. Forget I am your mother. Treat me as an honoured guest" (534). With the family power thus transferred, Laura self-consciously approaches the workmen she is supposed to direct—unsure of her own gender and class status, idealizing their working-class camaraderie, and seeking to join it. Naive as she is, the only way she can show her fellow feeling is through the small gesture of taking a bite out of the piece of her breakfast bread and butter in their company: "Just to prove how happy she was, just to show the tall fellow how at home she felt, and how she despised stupid conventions, Laura took a big bite of her bread-and-butter. . . . She felt just like a work-girl" (536). Here, as in "How Pearl Button Was Kidnapped," eating is imagined as an activity of solidarity. But it is also an activity circumscribed by familial prohibition; in taking the bite, Laura has transgressed something.

Abundance of food within a circumscribed, though public, familial setting is a class signifier in the economy of the garden party. The menu includes fifteen kinds of sandwiches as well as the paradisal cream puffs mentioned earlier. These are not so much tokens of the mother's prodigality of nurture as they are tokens of the father's success and the family's ability to engage cooks and maids and workmen and delivery boys in service to it. It is in the kitchen, however, that the baker's man delivers news that a laborer who lived down the lane from the Sheridans' house has just been killed in an accident.

As yet not totally absorbed in the family's enclosed identity, Laura moves immediately to cancel the party. Her older sister responds with a proclamation of class isolation: "Of course we can't do anything of the kind. Nobody expects us to. Don't be so extravagant" (541). Laura's next appeal is to her mother.

But Mrs. Sheridan is as self-protective as the sister: "People like that don't expect sacrifices from us. And it's not very sympathetic to spoil everybody's enjoyment as you're doing now" (543). In the process of rejecting her sensibility, both senior women in the family tempt Laura with an image of the family as so defined in its absolute identity that it is removed from judgment or blame by its distance from the working classes. Indeed, this distance is emphasized geographically by the steepness of the descent from the Sheridan mansion to the little cottages of the working people right below. And these "lower" people have been seen not only as totally separate from the privileged family but off-limits for the Sheridan children because of their low morals and their diseases—"the revolting language and . . . what they might catch" (542).

One strategy of the women in distracting Laura from her anxiety about the tragedy in the lane is to quarantine her as "extravagant" or "absurd." But her departure from the family pattern has, in a manner of speaking, immunized her from such interdictions already. She has ventured into the lane with her brother earlier on the principle that "still one must go everywhere; one must see everything" (542). Her artistic sensibility has been indulged in this infraction, as in the assignment of deciding about the marquee, but it is not so decisively valued that it can challenge the family's solidarity. Instead it marks Laura off as an eccentric who must be isolated or brought around.

Mrs. Sheridan's manner of bringing her daughter around involves changing the child's self-image by offering an alternative that embodies her own sense of the essential female self. This she does by ending the debate about canceling the garden party by giving Laura her own hat to wear. At first Laura can't "look at herself; she turn[s] aside" (543). But after she goes into her own room, she has an encounter with her own mirror which transforms her from the authentic Laura of her original instincts into the Laura fabricated by her mother: "There, quite by chance, the first thing she saw was this charming girl in the mirror, in her black hat trimmed with gold daisies, and a long black velvet ribbon. Never had she imagined she could look like that. Is mother right? she thought. And now she hoped her mother was right" (543). Laura attends the party in the trance of this new identity, deflected from any further impulse to question it. Even when she begins to confide in her brother, she is thwarted by his comment on her looks in the new hat. Laboring under the compliments of the guests, she does her best to minister to their wants by playing at being a woman—offering tea and ices and making sure that the members of the band get something to drink.

Laura's diminishing hold on her identity is maintained by care for sharing food with the guests, and so it seems appropriate to send her down the lane with a basket of leftover food when the question of the laborer's death arises after the party is over. Significantly, perhaps, it is the father who mentions the accident, bringing some news from the outside world into the enclosed family circle. And the mother, now somewhat abashed, at last takes action by gathering food for the widow and her children. Laura worries about the sensibilities of the poor family but is overwhelmed by her mother a second time and so delivers the basket of party food to the dead man's cottage. At the revelation of death itself, especially in the presence of the corpse of the young workman, Laura's fragile self is totally obliterated. She cannot think how to respond to the powerful negation and beauty of the man's dead body: "What did garden-parties and baskets and lace frocks matter to him: He was far from all those things. He was wonderful, beautiful" (548). Unable to find anything to say to this vision of selflessness, Laura sobs out one sentence, "Forgive my hat," before she flees.

Her comment is at once trenchant and hopelessly confused. The episode leaves Laura with an indeterminate sense of herself and of how she fits into the scheme of human bodies that die. She has no authoritative guidance from her family, and so she turns to her brother, who has come to meet her in the lane. She wants to ask a question: "'Isn't life,' she stammered, 'isn't life—'" (549). But Laura cannot complete the query, and Laurie is little help, merely echoing her question with a class accent: "'*Isn't* it, darling?' said Laurie" (549). Thus "The Garden-Party" enacts an Oedipal and familial betrayal by substituting for Laura's best, real self a socially constructed reflection of uncaring femininity. As in the fairy tale, the young girl has been seduced by the mirror image offered by a false mother. And there is no male rescuer to wake her up from her sleep of appearances.

Mansfield's allusion to the "mirror face" of "Juliet," her sorting out of paternal and maternal bodies in terms of their external form, and her regular staging of eidetic confrontations in her stories of adolescent girls engage her sense of identity formation as involving a vital dialectic between a hidden, inner "real" self and the outer manifestations of false personae. This conflict between her often satirical unveiling of surface "subjects" and her celebration of the hidden self—perhaps available in its transcendent beauty only in death—can be framed in terms of the issues of identity which preoccupy current critical discourse. For the comforting notion of the purposive ego in search of a familiar "self," for example, Lacanian theory hypothesizes a more distanced and confused "construction" based on mirror reflections that structure the preconscious "I" as an always unstable site for the obscure movements of desire. The collection of psychic motions so created—so acted upon—Lacan calls the "subject." The possibility of any inner revelatory agency has no place in a theory that accents the subject's determined "misrecognition" of inner drives.

Even in the early, maternal register of the imaginary, the instability of fragmentary images bars direct knowledge of the self.

The satirical strain in Katherine Mansfield's fiction illustrates her recognition of some of the features of subjectivity as modeled by Lacan: she is a connoisseur of constructed selves, especially of feminine selves that have been made up in the image of the social expectations instituted by patriarchy. As in "The Garden-Party," she frequently uses the encounter with mirrors to portray the ordeal of the self as it confronts a reflection that presents neither ontological reassurance nor psychological integration.

And as Mansfield frequently shows, the mirror image can emphasize the transparency of its own source—putting the empirical sensations of spatial stability and temporal sequence into terrifying disarray as the perceiver confronts the splitting of mirror images as an aspect of her inner split. Thus although Mansfield's insistence on self-discovery as the essential issue in her fiction is better understood in the light of the therapeutic (or adaptive) notions of the self such as Winnicott's, Lacan's formulations about the refracted and misrecognized formation of the subject in the "mirror stage" may illuminate Mansfield's satire.

Indeed, the bodily contrasts of thin versus fat in constituting identity contributed a kind of graveyard humor in Mansfield's imagination at times during her last years of illness when she fearfully watched her body dissipate in disease. Her diet had become a matter of excruciating concern, the intake of warm milk (which she seems to have despised) the main tonic prescribed to return her to health. Indeed, tuberculosis ravaged her breasts, the main feature of her femininity, and she wrote ruefully to a friend referring to a buxom governess, "I wish Mamselle could spare me a little tiny bit of her *front*. Mine has *gone*" (*CL* 2:284–85). She also maintained her caustic attitude about the absurdity of male health as reflected in body weight. She wrote to the same friend about John Middleton Murry's robust body during a bout of flu: "I shall have him photographed in his singlet soon, lying on a mat, you know, a-goo-gooing with REARED FROM BIRTH ON SUET PUDDINGS written underneath" (*CL* 2:284). Thus Mansfield's experience of the body colored her final battle with an emaciating disease. As the imagery of the gendered body of the thin mother and the plump father encroached upon her awareness of herself, however, she retained enough of the conviction of the essential fragmentariness of subjectivity to turn from the melodramatic and sentimental imagination of death to the macabre and tough-minded recognition of the somatic reality of her condition.

Mansfield finally addressed the issue of body weight as disease wryly in a surreal narrative of the deaths of two opposite children, sketched in a very late entry in her journal. The first child was a chubby figure who didn't want to think about things: "At last she became so adorably chubby, so ridiculously light-hearted, that she fell down the stairs, and they made her a heavenly funeral, and the most warming little grave you can imagine." The second was a thoughtful, "thin little girl" who "became so disgustingly thin, so preposterously wretched, that she fell up the stairs, and they threw her into the darkest, moistest little hole you can imagine" (quoted in Hankin, 3). The plots of death by surfeit and death by emaciation pay grotesque tribute to the irony of Mansfield's fated "wasting" illness; though rich in the characteristic sensory evocations of death as warmth and embrace for the chubby child, death is terrifyingly claustrophobic for the thin one. This reenactment of the body-image fractures of her childhood thus manifests Mansfield's final rejection of the ideal of rational body control which so often drives anorectics to kill themselves with dieting. Instead, she plays on an ironic confrontation of the existential horror of dying through starvation with the serenity of plenitude, even in death. There could not be a more decisive rejection of her mother's preferred body image, nor a more playful acceptance of her own.

CHAPTER 3

"Your lovely pear tree!"

The Evasions of the Closet

THE IMAGERY of the search for the breast marks all of Katherine Mansfield's descriptions of lovemaking with women. During the two-year period that she spent in New Zealand between her school years in London and her return there to commence her artistic career, she explored her developing sexual allegiances with notable candor.[1] Midway through her time at home, for example, she describes an experience of existential nausea which initiates a physical engagement with Edith Bendall, an older friend who is staying with her in the family's summer cottage: "The noises began to creep so close that I went back to the bedroom, and in the darkness leaned out of the window . . . each moment my horror of everything seemed to increase. In the yard the very fence became terrible." She awakens her companion, whose enactment of a mother's nursing soothes her terrors:

> Somehow silently she woke, and came over to me—took me again into the shelter of her arms. We lay down together, still silently, she every now and then pressing me to her, kissing me, my head on her breasts, her hands round my body, stroking me, lovingly—warming me [a word illegible] to give me more life again. . . . I drew close to her warm sweet body, happier than I had ever been, than I could ever have imagined being. (*Journal* 13–14)

Here on the brink of adulthood (she was eighteen at the time), Mansfield takes up that positioning of the child in search of the mother's embrace so frequently invoked in her child-death verse and so implicated in the oral dimensions of her body imaging. Indeed, her description of the bliss of such an embrace echoes the total happiness she would assign to Pearl Button in the story that she wrote in 1910; in the maternal encirclement of one of the Maori women, "Pearl had never been happy like this before" (11). I have already suggested that the desire for the maternal breast in childhood prefigures Mansfield's choice of the female body as the locus of inner security in her adolescence.[2] But such a self-protective choice could not survive the urgency of Mansfield's drive for worldly, cosmopolitan experience. And this drive involved for her a decisive sexual alliance with a man. Mansfield's early descriptions of lovemaking with men feature the notation of risk, of flagrant and dramatic game playing, and of animalistic encounters that suggest rape.[3]

Her school days at Queen's College in London had been marked by passionate attachments to female schoolmates and male teachers alike, and when she returned to Wellington, she expanded this bisexual orientation both as a series of experiments in identity for herself and as a weapon against her parents in her battle to get their permission to go back to London. But though she fell in love with at least two young women during her time in Wellington (with Edith Bendall and with "Maata," a beautiful Maori girl), Mansfield boasted of turning down five marriage proposals before she finally left home (Boddy, *Katherine Mansfield*, 15). She was also in love, at a distance, with a young cellist named Arnold Trowell who was pursuing his career in Europe; in a third variation of desire—one designed to repair rejection by her parents' form of conjugal love—Mansfield attached herself to the Trowells, imagining herself as the daughter-in-law of a friendly, lower-class nuclear family in which she would become the doting wife and, eventually, a better mother than her own. That Mansfield's drive to domesticity was less a matter of heterosexual eroticism than an obsessive rejection of her own mother may be seen by the fact that she immediately turned her affections from Arnold to his twin brother, Garnet, when Arnold rejected her. This domesticity led to pregnancy in 1909 (when Mansfield was twenty), but it was largely suspended through the period of sexual experimentation which followed Mansfield's exile to Bavaria by her mother, the miscarriage of her pregnancy there, and her return to London to enter its bohemian culture (from 1910 to 1912). In early 1912, Mansfield met John Middleton Murry and soon attached herself to him as to a brotherly husband; under this rubric, her drive to "play house" with a man modulated, as we shall see in Chapter 5, into the presiding style of most of her later sexual activity as love between children.

During her voyage to New Zealand from school in 1906, Mansfield had anatomized her response to male and female in terms that suggest the extremity of her wish to find in sexuality an escape from the provincial limitations of her parents. It was during this voyage that Mansfield confronted her fascination, not with "one man or woman," but with "the whole octave of the sex" (*Journal* 5). Her father worried about both varieties of flirtation. At one moment on shipboard, he warned that he wouldn't have her "fooling around in dark corners with fellows" (*Journal* 6), and in another mood of surveillance, he watched his daughter's relations with women: "I cannot be alone in the company of women for half a minute . . . he is there, eyes fearful, attempting to appear unconcerned" (*Journal* 7). Considering a flirtation with a man on board ship, Mansfield articulates her rebellious, masochistic fantasies: "When I am with him a preposterous desire seizes me, I want to be badly hurt by him. I should like to be strangled by his firm hands" (*Journal* 5–6). The challenge to conventional safety by a liaison with the outlaw male leads Mansfield to envision a worldly-wise future gained through her sexuality: "He has seen so much, it would be such a conquest. At present he is—I do not know, I think intensely curious and a little baffled. Am I to become eventually une jeune fille entretenue. It points to it. O God, that is better than [being] the daughter of my parents" (*Journal* 6). Back with these parents in Wellington after the eventful homeward voyage, then, Mansfield not only pursued the solace of the love of women, but she also wrote of passionate love with men as the more physically threatening choice along the octave of the sex.

Given the ambivalences of her childhood—the longing for acceptance by her mother, the sensual bonding with her maternal grandmother, the confusions of a body consciousness shaped by attraction to her mother's frailty and repugnance against her father's burliness—it is no wonder that Mansfield's strategies to achieve erotic satisfaction should be scripted in alternating definitions of sex: as love with women on the one hand, and love with men on the other. And it is no wonder that this alternation between hetero- and homosexuality reinforced Mansfield's sense of division in her inner life, intensifying the practice of self-dramatization which we have already seen in some of the mirror monologues she staged in her stories and journal entries.

In this chapter I want to suggest that the anxious dialectic of the erotic in Mansfield's late adolescence and early maturity generated a plethora of roles to play, costumes to assume, and evasions to perform as she defined herself sexually. For even as she plotted the drama of leaving her parents, she moved between playing the role of a self-proclaiming but sexually immature lesbian who lived a life of transcendent sensations in a child's body, and that of a knowing, corrupt prostitute who lived in the violently heterosexualized body of the adult. Once she arrived in London in 1908, she played out these roles to extremes that eventuated in flamboyant self-display, temporary addiction to the barbiturate Veronal (and a lifelong addiction to cigarettes), and, almost simultaneously, pregnancy and venereal disease. If her bisexuality was not in itself pathological, its acting out profoundly endangered her health.

We will look at the physical consequences of Mansfield's sexuality in later chapters; the question of the inner compulsions that led to an illness vocabulary for her erotic discourse is our topic here, for no matter how flamboyant her

Oscar Wilde, 1882. (Library of Congress)

Katherine Mansfield, 1910. (Ida Baker Collection, ATL)

*Maata Mahupuku
[Martha Grace] at
Miss Swainson's
School, 1901.*
*(George Moore
Collection, ATL)*

"Kathleen Mansfield,"
*1910 (G. Morris Collection,
ATL)*

Katherine Mansfield
[identified by L.M. as
Beatrice Hastings], 1911.
(ATL)

Katherine Mansfield, 1915.
(ATL)

assurance as a sexual adventurer, Katherine Mansfield's actual sexual relations were always afflicted ones. The psychic forces animating the variations in Mansfield's sexuality are many and complex; nevertheless, they shared a single constant—Mansfield's continuing guilt about them. Thus, although Mansfield's bisexuality should not be considered an "illness" of itself, it is clear that she pathologized its manifestations. She internalized conventional attitudes that caused her to view her love for women as diseased, and her always active inner standard of total emotional authenticity compelled her to assess her lust for men as corrupt. Her journal meditations on her bisexuality inevitably took on the rhetoric of an unrelenting juridical proceeding: "In my life—so much Love in imagination; in reality 18 barren years—never pure spontaneous affectionate impulse. Adonis [a name she gave to Arnold Trowell] was—dare I seek into the heart of me—nothing but a pose. And now she comes—and pillowed against her, clinging to her hands, her face against mine, I am a child, a woman, and more than half man" (*Journal* 13).

∼

In journal passages such as this one, Mansfield's inner dialogue takes on the structure of a trial in which a verdict must be rendered about her betrayal of "spontaneous affectionate impulse." In mapping the position she assigned lesbianism within the structure of her sexual desires, I want to suggest that in coming to terms with her sexuality, Mansfield not only gave utterance to her parents' exasperation with her "acting out" behavior, but she also internalized the voices of defense and prosecution which featured in the wider public debates about homosexuality at the turn of the century. These debates—at least as she knew them—were instigated with the trial of Oscar Wilde and were embedded in the aestheticist and feminist controversies that Mansfield encountered through her reading during her postcollege time in New Zealand. She then enacted them during the years when she frequented the purlieus of avant-garde journalism which surrounded publications such as the *New Age* in which her earliest London stories appeared.

In a suppressed letter that she wrote but did not send in 1909, Mansfield confessed her lesbian bent in the lurid terminology of madness and degradation:

Did you ever read the life of Oscar Wilde—not only read it but think of Wilde—picture his exact decadence? And wherein lay his extraordinary weakness and failure? In New Zealand Wilde acted so strongly and terribly upon me that I was constantly subject to exactly the same fits of madness as those which caused his ruin and his mental decay. When I am miserable now—these recur. Sometimes I forget all about it—then with awful recurrence it bursts upon me again and I am quite powerless to prevent it—This is my secret from the world and from you—Another shares it with me—and that other is [Kitty Mackensie][4] for she, too is afflicted with the same terror—We used to talk of it knowing that it wd eventually kill us, render us insane or paralytic—all to no purpose—. . . . I think my mind is morally unhinged and that is the reason—I know it is a degradation so unspeakable that— —one perceives the dignity in pistols. (CL 1:89–90)

The designation of homosexuality as a systemic disease that affects body and mind, its variability as an imagined fever, the prognosis of radical physical and mental breakdown leading to early death, the terror of the taint which lurks in waiting to erupt, always incipiently subversive of rational control—these disease designations are all familiar elements in the discourse that developed during the trial of Oscar Wilde. Take, for example, the pronunciamento of the *Evening News* on the day of Wilde's conviction: "We venture to hope that the conviction of Wilde for these abominable vices, *which were the natural outcome of his diseased intellectual condition,* will be a *salutary warning to the unhealthy boys* who posed as sharers of his culture" (quoted in Weeks, *Coming Out,* 20; emphasis added). Katherine Mansfield proclaimed herself just such a sharer of Wilde's culture, embracing his aesthetic even as she felt both attracted to and terrified by the appeal of his sexual outlawry. Thus she could not embrace the culture of homosexuality without suffering the judgments of a criminalized medical diagnosis that she had internalized from reading fin-de-siècle literature and controversy drenched in the myths of perversion.

In the first volume of *The History of Sexuality,* Michel Foucault has suggested that the modern discourse of sexuality was strongly incited by the forms of repression in the nineteenth century. The situation in French culture, with its variations in the erotics of class, the omnipresence of self-inventory through the discipline of confession (which plays so central a part in Foucault's analysis), and the centering of international sexual savoir-faire in Paris, may seem to be of limited relevance to British, especially colonial British, culture at the end of the Victorian period. But Katherine Mansfield's sense of her provincial status impelled her to a fascination with Continental experience; she started her visits to Paris as a schoolgirl, and she used French insistently in her talk and prose as a marker of her superior culture. Indeed, Katherine Mansfield's lifelong attachment to France was an ambivalent rejection of British sexual conventionality; as we shall later see, in her most homophobic story, "*Je ne parle pas français,*" Mansfield decisively placed the perversion of male homosexuality within a Parisian setting. Whatever its geographical variables, then, Foucault's attention to the medical criminalization of homosexuality is useful in reading Katherine Mansfield's assessment of her own impulses.

It is commonly accepted that the disease classification of homosexuality began to predominate at the end of the nineteenth century. Historians associate the use of a medical classification to mask and erase homosexuality with the rise of sexology under the aegis of such writers as Edward Carpenter (whom Mansfield read while she was in New Zealand).[5] Jeffrey Weeks has linked the foreboding diatribes against "self-abuse" by doctors such as William Acton with the health campaign against homosexuality which rose in the furor of the Wilde trial, and as recently as 1967, he notes, a provincial newspaper still spoke of homosexuality as "a disease more dangerous than diphtheria" (*Coming Out*, 23). Mansfield's anxiety about becoming "insane or paralytic" recalls classic Victorian admonitions about the mental and physical effects of masturbation and, by extension, homosexuality. The repression had worked its prohibitions upon her, giving her a sense of herself as abnormal and forcing her to hide her secret: the confessional letter on her affinities with Oscar Wilde was found among papers she had left at her first husband's flat, with a warning posted on either side, "Never to be read on your honour as my friend, while I am still alive. K. Mansfield" (*CL* 1:90).

In addition to the early death and mental decay thought to result from sexual aberration, there was also the threat of sterility, which featured the vision of an empty future without spouse or children. For male homosexuals, this vision was founded upon worries about the loss of sperm through nonprocreative expenditure. For females, the fear was less of physical incapacity than of a total rejection of motherhood—woman's definitive mission. Sir Ernest Wild thus fulminated against lesbianism in a 1921 House of Commons debate about a law to criminalize the practice: "It stops child-birth because it is a well-known fact that any woman who indulges in this vice will have nothing whatever to do with the other sex. It debauches young girls, and it produces neurasthenia and insanity" (Weeks, *Coming Out*, 106). Here the threat of a breakdown in physical and mental health is attached to the prediction of a lonely, barren future for women who experiment in forbidden eroticism. Thus Vita Sackville-West's decision finally to leave Violet Trefusis after their aborted elopement in 1919 was intensified by her husband's appeal to her on behalf of their children. And thus Mansfield's lesbian sexual experimentation was always shadowed by her ideal agenda of eventually justifying herself as a daughter by becoming a more loving mother than her own had ever been. She could not, however, implement this agenda of rebellion against the patriarchal family in the imagination of lesbian motherhood, though she did temporarily adopt a slum child to care for on her own when she was recovering from her miscarriage (see Chapter 4).

The primary threat of lesbianism, then, was its challenge to future generativity; the damage to women's reproductive instincts was to come less from unimaginable acts of sex between women than from the total "inversion" of the feminine in lesbian women, a violation of the prevalent classification of male as "active" and female as "passive." The very self-assertion of feminists was, ipso facto, the sign of a diseased reversal of gender roles. George Chauncey, Jr., has emphasized this feature of Victorian homophobia against lesbians: "In the Victorian system . . . a complete inversion or reversal of a woman's sexual character was refigured for her to act as a lesbian; she had literally to become manlike in her sexual desire" (125). As "inversion" became more and more recognized as the distinguishing characteristic of lesbianism, all outward signs of masculine desire—from the political aspirations of the "first generation" of feminists to the hair and dress styles of "second generation"—cast women within the circle of suspicion.[6]

The first suspect generation of "New Women" whose behavior unsexed, or wrongly sexed, them were the suffragists; their devotion to political liberation at the expense of home and family made them major targets for homophobic anxiety as well as knowing satire. If they were not depicted as doddering old women who had missed the joys of heterosexuality, they were seen as either frustrated virgins or mannish lesbian women.[7] Such depictions tended to concentrate on their bodily repulsiveness and the formless, unfeminine dress they were thought to wear; they were often seen as prigs who forgot the care of their very bodies as they mindlessly toiled to effect reform. Even sympathetic "second-generation" feminists could treat these late Victorians with condescension, as Virginia Woolf does in her portrait of the inhabitants of the suffrage office where Mary Datchet works in *Night and Day* and even in her sketch of the deprivations of body and spirit in the "Fernham College" of *A Room of One's Own*. Katherine Mansfield herself participated in such stereotyping of early feminist activists, describing a couple of women at a suffrage meeting she attended in 1908 as looking "like two very badly upholstered chairs," pouncing on her to beg for help in the cause (*CL* 1:60).

The suffragists and reformers of the late nineteenth and early twentieth century were subtly labeled as "unfeminine" spinsters rather than lesbians, whereas what Virginia Woolf called the "cropheads" of the Slade School, like other bohemian women in London in the second decade of the twentieth century, were the first group of women defined as deviant by their appearance as well as behavior. The notoriety of such women was marked by their aesthetic articulation in dress, their proclamation of promiscuity through androgynous style, and their violation of feminine convention through the urban vices of public smoking, drinking, and unchaperoned roamings through all hours of the day and night.[8] Above all, they dissociated themselves from first-generation feminist earnestness through flamboyant rebellion against the "feminine," defined as the subjection of personality. Vita Sackville-West's memory of her first ventures in male garb provides a gauge of the liberatory experiences for such women in her description of the exhilaration of cross-dressing, walking about London and Paris as "Julian," in the years during and after the Great War. Throughout her interactions with bohemian and politically radical members of London's intellectual underworld, however, Katherine Mansfield studiously avoided any such dramatic revocation of the feminine in her own appearance, choosing instead to dress for the kind of effect which emphasized at once her strangeness and her femininity. Dress was for her always a form of costume which served the intricacies of role-playing, for testing her sexual orientation was only one facet of her experimentation with identity.[9]

Indeed, Mansfield was a mimic in her appearance as well as her behavior, and the portrait photographs of her early years in London—from 1909, say, to 1915—show her impulse to take on the look of the various objects of her transgressive desire. In New Zealand, she seems to have affected the sedate hairdo of Edith Bendall. In London, she liked to make an impression by dressing in Maori fashion, imitating Maata, and she affected the exotic poses of the aesthetes. Finally, after she cut her hair in the fashion of the day, apparently around 1912 (*LM* 73), she looked so much like her mentor, Beatrice Hastings, that Ida Baker asserted that one supposed photograph of Mansfield actually shows Beatrice Hastings (*LM* 58). The point here is not so much Mansfield's appropriation of the appearance of the "cropheads" (though her keeping her hair in an identifying "fringe" gave her always the look of an avant-garde intellectual) but that she became so self-identified with male and female figures in her bisexual orientation that she managed to make herself *look* like them.[10]

New Zealand had provided a limited setting for such experimentation either with appearance or with gender, but once Mansfield arrived in England, she commenced a bisexual lifestyle within a much wider range. Thus her sexual life in her early years in London not only oscillated between lesbian love and promiscuous heterosexuality, but at the lesbian pole it also vacillated between the "innocent" tie with her devoted school friend Ida Baker and her relationships with marginal female figures with whom she had fleeting contact and few ties of loyalty or commitment. In these relationships, the affectionate comfort of her bond with a maternal lover such as Edith Bendall was displaced by illicit, Wildean excess. Moreover, such excess was impossible with Ida Baker because to respond to Ida's need would be to subvert Ida's infrangible innocence as well as to submit to the coercions of its blind feeling. The furthest Mansfield could go in implicating her old friend in her erotic network was to rename her, linking the androgynous first name of her brother (Leslie Heron Beauchamp) with Ida's mother's name (Moore) so as to create the persona of "L.M.," the designation of faithful androgynous retainer which Ida Baker inhabited for the rest of her life.

A suggestive glimpse of Mansfield's confused and unpredictable bisexual behavior is provided by the witness of George Bowden, the bewildered older man Katherine Mansfield married in 1909, knowing that she was pregnant by Garnet Trowell. In some desperation, Mansfield contrived to marry the stolid Bowden—reportedly appearing for the ceremony accompanied by L.M., dressed in black and refusing to spend more than one night with her new husband (*LM* 46). She returned to Trowell briefly after this. Her pregnancy by Trowell is generally considered to have happened in the interval after the marriage to Bowden. I believe, however, that she must have married Bowden because of the pregnancy; legitimizing it seems the only rationale for her clear intent to gain Bowden's name and nothing else from the marriage. She went back to Bowden for another short period before her mother arrived in London and packed her off to a German health spa. Significantly, L.M. was implicated by Annie Beauchamp as a suspect agent in Mansfield's profligacy, and she was sent away to Rhodesia. Whether the Beauchamp family found their daughter's potential pregnancy more scandalous than her bisexuality is impossible to know at this point; in either case Mansfield's play along the octave of the sex managed to engage her mother's attention and to assure her final and permanent disapproval.

It is not surprising that George Bowden would have been the bewildered victim during most of his time with Katherine Mansfield (though he refused to free himself from her through divorce until 1918). He seems to have been fascinated by her talent, especially her talent at self-dramatization; he later recalled his amazement at her chameleonlike changes of costume and mood. In particular, he recalled one of her most extravagant manifestations in a meeting with him at a party in 1909: she appeared in Maori getup that lent itself to an "eerie . . . psychic transformation" that made her look like "Oscar" himself (Alpers, *Life,* 87). The theme of homosexuality is indistinctly suggested in this memory, which Bowden dredged up for Antony Alpers in 1949, but in 1919, in explaining to his future father-in-law his failed marriage, Bowden openly invoked Mansfield's sexual "perversion" as the cause. His statement is remarkable for its demonstration of the way in which lesbianism was likely to be cited as a hidden affliction, erupting unexpectedly (especially in talented individuals) and productive of deception even in the close relation of marriage:

The lady I married, although of excellent and well-to-do people, and herself of some literary reputation, was sexually unbalanced and at times was irresponsible, although at other times perfectly normal. While her people in New Zealand were aware of this, her guardian in London was not, and as we married after a short acquaintance, it was only then conditions became known to me. . . . I took no steps toward divorce on the grounds of this perversion—a proceeding only possible in camera. But later on learning she had been guilty of misconduct, I instructed my lawyer to proceed on statutory grounds.[11]

Bowden was not the only witness to Mansfield's "perversion" during her early years in London, however. Her career as a defiant bisexual was openly played out and textually displayed in a relationship she cultivated while sharing lodgings with the writer William Orton and his lover in 1911. Here in an idealized ménage à trois, she acted out one of her most flamboyant experiments with love "along the whole octave of the sex." Mansfield recorded the arrangement by interlacing journal entries of her own with Orton's: Orton published these in 1937 as part of his autobiographical novel *The Last Romantic*.

Mansfield wrote her entries in the highly wrought language of her aesthete models, prefacing her account of her brotherly love for "Michael" (Orton) with an account of lawless lovemaking with "the Man" who comes to her in their shared rooms. In the manner of her other descriptions of her heterosexual lusts, this passionate interlude is couched in the imagery of animal sensuosity and calculated posturing: "I crouched against him like a wild cat. Quite impersonally I admired my silver stockings bound beneath the knee with spiked ribbons, my yellow suede shoes fringed with white fur. How vicious I looked! We made love to each other like two wild beasts" (*Journal* 45–46; *Last Romantic* 280–81). The plot moves from this interlude of lust to rapturous accounts of the narrator's love for the more gentle Michael and his lover, "Lais." Michael is the safer, more sincere lover of the two—one who can help her create a new familial constellation: "Yet if there is any truth left in me I know that only together shall we two create and be fulfilled one in the other. Michael and myself alone are truthful. . . . I want to begin another life; this one is worn to the tearing point" (46; 281–82).

Thus heterosexual passion vies with domestic passion before the tribunal of authenticity; in an effort to exculpate herself from role-playing here, the defendant pleads illness, a life "torn" apart. Further on in this fragmentary account, the narrator turns from Michael to Lais: "She is so beautiful that I see no other beauty, and content myself with the sweet Lais. Her slim body in the grey frock—her hands cradling her vivid hair—she lay on the yellow pillows. . . . We are the three eternities—Michael and Lais and I. For Michael is darkness and light and Lais is flame and snow and I am sea and sky" (47; 282–83). The affectation of emotions in this prose emphasizes the display of costume, the studied artificiality of playacting. But the bisexual plot is not one that Mansfield invented for effect only; the scenario she chooses patterns the actual forms her desire assayed during her early years in London—the thesis of love for a sexual male, the antithesis of love for a female, and the synthesis of domestic love for a boyish man with whom she could build a new, innocent future. And indeed, Mansfield's scripting of her eroticism had a historical witness who commented on its actual effects. Edna Smith, the historical "Lais," wrote sardonically but forgivingly ("I never bore her any grudge") of Mansfield's lust for her in a 1977 letter to her daughter: "At nineteen my love affair came to an end for various reasons, one being Katherine Mansfield who rather took a fancy to my lover and myself. She played with us both for a little and then went on her way" (quoted in *CL* 1:108).

~

Edna Smith's account of Mansfield's bisexuality accents its "playing" as a kind of manipulation. Mansfield's own account seeks to avert such judgment by interposing a description of herself as ill. "I am very lonely and ill today. Outside my window the buildings are wreathed in mist. There is a sharp rapping sound and the cry of voices from the timber yard—drowned men are building a raft under the sea" (46; 282). Thus in her bisexual idyll, as in her child-death poems, Mansfield frames her attraction to the sexual masculine predator, the sexually available woman, and the domestic, brotherly male with the language of a psychic loss so profound that it amounts to physical illness. Given the physical afflictions surveyed in the next chapter, we can say that her bodily sufferings may have been genuine, and indeed William Orton discerned "her first serious illness of the lungs" in this period (279). Nevertheless, Mansfield's invocation of illness at such times of sexual confusion has the effect of relieving her of control and therefore of moral responsibility for her inclinations. She is acted upon by them. Her inner life is split asunder by the assault of convention and illness, and so her erotic strivings constitute an instinctive effort to cure the disease of fragmentation, to put herself back together again.

Thus, if part of Mansfield's suffering as displayed in her relationship with William Orton and Edna Smith was physical, it was also psychological and moral. For Mansfield's dealing with her own bisexuality involved deep betrayal, not only of aspects of her own psyche, but also of her relationships with other women, especially the one continuing female friendship in her life, that with Ida Baker. Mansfield tended to interact with women in a kind of conspiracy against the men in their lives, consorting with men only as comrades when she was not sexually engaged with them. Thus she segregated her allegiances in ways that confused her closest relations and brought less intimate friends to accuse her of treachery. One element in this segregation was the fact that some women, Ida Baker among them, were relatively ignorant about lesbianism.

As Jeffrey Weeks has suggested, the topic of female homosexuality was generally ignored in late Victorian discussions of sexual "deviance." There were two reasons for this silence: women's normal sexual drives were not thought to be sufficiently strong to warrant undue juridical control, and there tended to be some ignorance as to how women might interact sexually with one another in any case. What could not be imagined could not be a threat, especially given the notion that women's sex drives were at best extremely mild. More important, as Carol Smith-Rosenberg, among others, has shown, women were allowed a much wider range of affectional affiliations than men were. Sexual suspicion was not cast upon women's embraces, passionate friendships, or long-term affiliations—especially within the family and girlhood circle. And, as Martha Vicinus has argued, the sublimation of the erotic in these affiliations could intensify them (47).

The lonely Ida Baker entered eagerly into this practice of idealized feminine bonding. She had known Katherine Mansfield from her earliest days in London and was enchanted by her magnetic appeal as well as her need for protection from her own risk taking; she derived from the schoolgirl culture of Queen's College the ideal of selfless devotion to her friend—what she called years later "the silver line of our closeness and love" (*LM* 20). But Mansfield's journal indicates that while L.M. longed for reciprocation of this closeness and love, Mansfield could barely tolerate her, either physically or emotionally, except in desperation when her escapades had left her sick and alone. "I *loathe* female, *virgin* love," she commented about L.M. in a letter to Ottoline Morrell (*CL* 2:294).

Given the wide acceptance of female "crushes," it is no surprise that Edith Bendall, the object of Mansfield's first recorded lesbian embrace, should have been unaware of the nature of the desire that she inspired. Claire Tomalin has reported that in old age, Bendall rejected any lesbian interpretation—viewing her affection as a normal effort to console a troubled younger girl during a time of agitation (36). And L.M., reporting on her later discovery that she was considered Mansfield's "lesbian friend," confesses herself not only bewildered by the accusation but having been in total ignorance of what that term might have meant (*LM* 54).

If Edith Bendall and Ida Baker counted the closeness, the embraces, the sisterly kisses, and the cuddling together in bed as within the normal range of female expressions of affection, however, Mansfield herself was not so secure in her ignorance. As a reader of Wilde, Edward Carpenter, and J. A. Symonds, she was clearly aware of homosexuality as an erotic possibility. As we shall see in looking at verbal signifiers of lesbian desire in her stories, she seems to have come into contact with the full spectrum of lesbian culture, so far as there was a developing one, in bohemian London around 1910. That she was not able to reveal this to L.M., suppressing the confessional letter to her—and even within that letter placing her own desire for women in the past tense, as a fever from which she had now recovered—points to the "purity" of L.M.'s side of the friendship. But L.M.'s purity was a heavy burden for Mansfield to bear, especially in the context of her using her friend and then deserting her whenever she attached herself to a more eligible male or female.

Beatrice Hastings was one of those more eligible females, the only one of Mansfield's friends who drew L.M.'s retrospective scorn for leading Mansfield astray. Hastings was the assistant editor of the *New Age* and mistress of its editor, A. R. Orage. Mansfield became a regular contributor to that journal after her return from exile in Bavaria, and through her association with Orage and Hastings she entered literary bohemia. From the passivity of submission to her mother's control in suppressing the Garnet Trowell pregnancy, George Bowden marriage, and L.M. relation, she seems to have thrown herself into the aggressive promiscuities, rivalries, and posings of London's current Grub Street with the energy of a child who had been cut off from all familial ties. Her friendship with Hastings was, for a time, intense. Although the Hastings friendship was a homosocial bond—I am not suggesting that it was overtly lesbian—it is significant in this account of Mansfield's bisexuality because it occupies a position along the whole octave of the sex which underscores the duplicity in Mansfield's need to bond with women.

As a leading controversialist for the *New Age,* Hastings seems to have tutored Mansfield in the realm of corrosive satire, and her revulsion at the idea of woman as chiefly a bearer of men's children matched Mansfield's reaction to the humiliation caused by her own recent pregnancy. Hastings' greatest stir in the pages of the *New Age* derived from a series of articles in which she attacked the whole concept of motherhood because she felt that the processes of sex and birth were intrinsically degrading. During the period of her discipleship to Hastings, Mansfield may have become pregnant again, and she possibly ended the pregnancy with an abortion (but see the next chapter for the medical impediments to this supposition). The more conventional L.M. recalled the episode with great disapproval (it had taken place while she was visiting in Rhodesia): "We never discussed the matter; obviously it had all been horrible. I am sure that Beatrice Hastings had been in some way responsible"

(*LM* 65). L.M.'s animus against Hastings condemns her feminist bias against motherhood, for L.M.'s ardent conventionality included visions of serving Mansfield as nurse to her children.

After a year or two, Hastings and Mansfield had a falling out: Mansfield had met Murry, set up a journal with him, and stopped publishing in the *New Age*. Nevertheless, when Mansfield was in Paris in 1915, she visited Hastings— now an increasingly alcoholic figure who resided in Montmartre as Modigliani's mistress. Though Mansfield felt the pull of the old tie, she sought to free herself with a shudder of physical disgust at the degradation of Hastings' femininity: "Strange and really beautiful though she is, still with the fairy air about her & her pretty little head still so fine—she is ruined. There is no doubt of it—I love her, but I take an intense, cold interest in noting the signs" (*CL* 1:159). In this ambivalent attachment to Hastings, Mansfield may have felt an undercurrent of erotic attraction, but the "intense, cold interest" also denotes Mansfield's tendency to recoil from any tie that became too demonstrative and thereby too subjecting. Though she could accept the possibility of transgressive tendencies in herself, she became anxious when the relationship approached the status of uncontrolled infatuation on her part or that of her lover. For Mansfield, lust was a power that made her uneasy even as she cultivated it; passionate love was a value that she coveted in herself but feared in its reciprocation. Innocence is seen as the ultimate form of authenticity in her writing about her own desire; however, the continuing paradox is that it can only be judged so through the knowingness of one who has experienced corruption.

Classical psychoanalytic theory posits a linkage of feminine homosexuality with the growing girl's need for "protection against too strong ties with members of her family, especially against her ties with her mother" (Deutsch 1:338). And such theorizing makes sense of Mansfield's lesbianism in her relationship with Beatrice Hastings; it was another psychic maneuver in Mansfield's effort to preserve and assert her selfhood against her mother's destructive rejections. Thus, whereas Annie Beauchamp had abandoned Mansfield during her first, crucial pregnancy, Hastings could mentor the younger woman through her second pregnancy; rather than sending her away in disgrace, Hastings could enlist her as a heroine in the program of declaring women's freedom from maternity through abortion. Thus Hastings stood for the new, liberated order of women's lives. Indeed, the power of her foster-mothership may have been especially potent because of Hastings' startling similarities to Mansfield. Not only did they look alike, but Hastings also wrote under an assumed name, was an exiled colonial, and had a "bad" father and a beloved younger brother.[12] In short, she was both a mother and a twin to Mansfield. Helene Deutsch describes the kind of tie Mansfield seems to have had with her, relating such a relationship to the pubescent girl's narcissistic reaction to familial pressures. "The differences and similarity, non identity and yet identity, the quasidouble experience of oneself, the simultaneous liberation from one part of one's ego and its preservation and security in the possession of the other, are among the attractions of the homosexual experience" (1:346).[13]

The relationship with L.M. was more complicated, though it too involved Mansfield's need for a feminine alter ego in whom she could find what was missing in her mother. But if Hastings represented the older, more knowledgeable female self for Mansfield, L.M. represented the naive, unworldly self over whom Mansfield must exert the superior power of her experience. Knowing as she was about the nature of her attractiveness to L.M., she used her and then responded coldly to the timid demands for reciprocal affection. She records in her journal a remorseful encounter with L.M. when she returned to their flat from an assignation with her current male lover. In a fit of reparation she kisses L.M., coldly noting her own distaste even as she administers the longed-for affection: "'Oh' she breathed, when I asked her if she was comfortable. 'This is Paradise, beloved!' Good God I must be at ordinary times a callous brute. It is the first time in all these years that I have leaned to her and kissed her like that. I don't know why I always shrink ever so faintly from her touch. I could not kiss her lips" (*Journal* 54). In the relationship with Hastings, Mansfield could safely assume the passive feminine role; in the relationship with L.M., she was called upon to exhibit the mastery of an active lover. In assuming such a stance with a woman, however, Mansfield risked losing her self-image of innocence. Thus, although she toyed with mastery over L.M., its physical manifestation was repugnant to her. And in a later phase of the relationship when L.M. intervened to nurse her friend through tuberculosis, Mansfield rebelled even more against L.M.'s incompetence than against her need for love. Her hysterical irritation with L.M. could not be resolved until she reached an understanding of the domineering aspects of her own personality.

But if Mansfield's bisexuality was rooted in the role-playing that she took on out of her adolescent psychological needs, it was also based in the ideology of her reading of Oscar Wilde. The ideology was shared by L.M., and she joined willingly in Mansfield's acting in rebellion against convention in service of a higher ideal of love. Sydney Janet Kaplan is the best commentator on the formal influence Mansfield absorbed from Oscar Wilde, but in framing the question of Mansfield's turn against Wilde's homosexual model as a feminist issue, I believe she slights the psychic dynamics involved. Like many adolescents, Mansfield needed some ideological commitment to focus her chaotic effort to construct her identity outside the circle of her mother's influence. The ideal of ceaseless devotion and exquisite craftsmanship answered her need for competence and an idealism that would take her beyond her mother's bored maternity and her father's frantic commercialism into a higher realm. Moreover, the originality claimed by Wilde's aestheticism answered her urge to assert a special distinction within her bourgeois family.

An adolescence immersed in the writings of Wilde and Pater and Symonds answered Katherine Mansfield's needs in many ways, then. These writers reinforced her extravagant role-playing, to be sure, and they justified her cultivated aloofness from ordinary people. But they also had a less negative effect; they offered the idea of seizing experience without regard for social responsibility—an idea that may have given Mansfield the weapon she needed in her imaginative defenses against the suffocation of her family. This early reading— which legitimized psychic pretense and sentimentality[14] that would take years to overcome—also gave Mansfield the sense that experience could be self-justifying, that it need not be locked into the emotional and moral confusions of the past, that it could exhibit an independent interest and beauty. Later in her fiction, Mansfield explored this conception of experience by continually focusing on the momentary and fleeting rapture with "Life" in the ordinary experience of the characters. Her attention to the contexts and imagery of such moments constitutes one of the major values of her art. Nevertheless, in the long task of freeing herself from the pathological elements of her adolescent fascination with the extremes of the sexual continuum and her guilt for her seductiveness, Katherine Mansfield became suspicious of aesthetic pretentiousness, and her satirical stories ruthlessly undercut female characters modeled upon this lability of her adolescent self.

Through all the complications of her heterosexual loves and illnesses, Mansfield at last came to rely on L.M. as nurse, companion, and provider (see Chapter 7). Thus she eventually turned away from experimental bisexuality into a determined heterosexuality that emphasized companionship rather than passion with women, and the ideal of marriage as a safe refuge rather than an exploration of sensuous experience with men. Her commitment to John Middleton Murry was accompanied by an overdetermined homophobia that involved not only revoking earlier loves but expressing a lifelong ambivalence about her bond with L.M. In her turn away from her lesbian past, Mansfield may have had less of the conventional worry about restoring respectability through "marriage" to a man than a hypochondriacal fear of having become physically and morally marked by lesbian infection. Having run through a variety of loves in her early London years, Mansfield seems to have experienced some version of homosexual panic which centered her fears not only on her unworthiness to experience sexual bliss but also on having forfeited the capacity to bear children.

In erotic discourse, the pearl may symbolize the clitoris or the yoni.[15] Whether or not Katherine Mansfield was aware of this association when she named the protolesbian characters in three of her stories "Pearl" is impossible to verify. We have already seen that she gives the name to the lost child who longs for the comfort of mother love in "How Pearl Button Was Kidnapped." In another narrative configuration, she names the confidante of her protagonist in her first novel "Pearl Saffron."[16] Varying this configuration in "Bliss," one of her most famous stories, Mansfield gives the name "Pearl Fulton" to the female seductress of the young wife who is its center of consciousness. That these names point to a cluster of feelings gathered around lesbian affiliations is indicated not only by their common linkage with the suggestive first name but also by the similarities in the surnames—"Saffron," "Button," and "Fulton." Sandra Gilbert and Susan Gubar have suggested a number of possibilities for the lesbian signification of "button," and the designation of clitoris or nipple seems suggestive of Mansfield's usage.[17] Whether this usage was derived from her reading in the sexologists or her absorption of the argot of London's demimonde among whom such locutions would have been current is unknowable; whatever the case, it is clear that her naming invokes more or less traditional images of the lesbian female as genitally defined but lustrous, coolly removed, somehow "other" in her sexuality.[18]

The "Pearl" character is thus summoned in the context of homoerotic desire but under a variety of authorizations. Through the innocence of the child Pearl and her primitive abductors, the comfort of this desire can be absorbed gratefully by both parties—even though it will be brought to an end by the intrusion of the men who come to rescue the child. But in the stories of grown-up women, the Pearl figure is not such an uncomplicated repository of mutually engaged maternal eroticism; there her libidinal possibility is shadowed by the betrayal involved in her posturing as a friend to the protagonist while she is actually seducing the protagonist's male lover. Given the Mansfield/Edna Smith/William Orton triangle as the autobiographical template for the "Catherine"/"Lais"/"Michael" trio in *The Last Romantic,* where Mansfield seems to have been the lesbian aggressor, we might expect that Mansfield would provide all the Pearl figures in her fiction with authorial sanctioning. But the different "Pearls" occupy varying positions within the paradigm of lesbian betrayal of heterosexual love in Mansfield's stories: in one case subject, in the other object of narrative desire.[19]

Pearl Button is clearly such a subject, and the legitimacy of her desire for the maternal/lesbian breast is the narrative thesis against which the arrival of the men works a destructive antithesis. But while in "Juliet," Pearl Saffron may be the admired object of Juliet's homoerotic desire in one fragment, in the next she is transformed into the bourgeois enemy: this Pearl's eventual marriage with David, Juliet's first lover, mocks Juliet's ideal of free love. And Pearl Fulton, the mysterious presence in "Bliss," is at once the object of and inspiration for Bertha Young's first intimation of the erotic; reenacting Pearl Button's childish aspiration for escape through bonding with the maternal breast, Bertha seeks to attach herself to Pearl Fulton's mature womanhood and through that attachment feels her first desire for her husband. Here, however, the male's intrusion into the lesbian interlude is not an intervention from outside but a product of the same feminine allure that has seduced his wife. Pearl Fulton's seductive investment in the whole octave of sexuality makes her indifferent to Bertha Young's childlike movement of love and possibly to Bertha's husband's lust as well; she seems coolly impervious to both of them. And then in an additional reversal, one that marks "Bliss" as one of Mansfield's most vexing experiments in point of view, the vulnerable protagonist is posited as so childishly gullible about the eroticism of female bisexuality that she warrants authorial irony. I see this narrative irony as a displacement of Mansfield's guilt about the betrayals involved in her own seductions of women as well as men.

Thus, even though she is identified with lesbian love, the Pearl character in Mansfield's stories may enforce a punishment on the "innocently" lesbian woman—the one who mistakes eros for agape. Emplotted variously by Mansfield's ironic narrator, "Pearl" can seem at first a companion, a sister, a reflection of the desiring female narrator's own secret, passional self. But once the competing male's sexuality is called into play, the intimacy of a "Pearl" is revealed to have been casual rather than authentic; and her most decisive movement is towards the male rather than towards her desiring sister/friend. And so the lesbian "Pearl" becomes a treacherous enigma, trading familiar, loving bonds with other women for heterosexual lust with rapacious males—or for the security of marriage with domestic men who can offer children and a conventional feminine destiny.

"Juliet" outlines an early version of this pattern which Mansfield transposed ten years later into the narrative and thematic betrayals of "Bliss." In an exchange between Juliet Night and Pearl Saffron which prefigures a passage between Bertha Young and Pearl Fulton in "Bliss," the status of the women's attraction for each other is displayed through their open dialogue about their sexuality, punctuated by their affectionate kissing of each other. For example, they compare notes about dealing with feelings of sexual restlessness:

"You feel sexual" [says Pearl Saffron]. "Horribly—and in need of a physical shock or violence. Perhaps a good smacking would be beneficial." (*TLR* 3:16)

Following upon such advanced remarks, Pearl enunciates the same-sex exclusiveness of the bond between the two girls:

"Nothing could separate us, Juliet. All the comforts of matrimony with none of its encumbrances, hein? . . . Think of a man always with you. A woman cannot be wholly natural with a man—there is always a feeling that she must take care that she doesn't let him go. (16–17)

Despite the comfort of living as an enlightened feminist comrade with Pearl Saffron in London, however, Juliet longs for artistic experience, and that longing tempts her beyond the protolesbian circle of the girlhood bond. She is seduced by an imperious foreign musician in an episode of lurid passion, and from this liaison she becomes pregnant and then dies. Pearl Saffron, meanwhile, marries Juliet's more conventional suitor, David, and they live happily ever after—with only a shadow of Juliet's tragic life lingering to haunt their memories. The narrative of "Juliet" summarizes their subsequent life together sardonically—as a bourgeois conclusion to and commentary on Juliet's wildness of erotic choice:

David and Pearl were married as soon as [they] reasonably could after Juliet's death, and a year and a half later, when a girl child was born, they both decided she should be christened after "poor Juliet." Pearl gave up smoking cigarettes and published a little volume which she called "Mother Thought" . . . somehow the title does not seem intensely original. Also, when they realised the possibility of another extension to their family they bought a nice little house near Cricklewood, and David achieved no small measure of success with his gardening. (17)

At first, Bertha Young of "Bliss" would seem to parallel the earlier Pearl Button, or even the Juliet Night through whom lesbian desire is assigned with Pearl Saffron in "Juliet."[20] At the beginning of her story, Bertha also is shown to be beset by sexual restlessness, though she is far less able to seek release from it than either of the earlier protagonists. The story begins as Bertha Young surveys the limitations of her bodily freedom. In the excitement of preparing for a dinner party with artistic guests, she indulges in a Wildean flood of self-pity laced with apostrophes to "Life." So goes the first sentence of the story:

Although Bertha Young was thirty she still had moments like this when she wanted to run instead of walk, to take dancing steps on and off the pavement, to bowl a hoop, to throw something up in the air and catch it again, or to stand still and laugh at—nothing—at nothing, simply. (337)

Bertha's mental images are idealizations of herself as one capable of grasping experience spontaneously and fully, the way a child does. Objective as they may seem, however, the words that report Bertha Young's consciousness also record her imaginative limitations through the subterfuge of narrative objectivity. The syntax of their mimetic rendering of her thoughts damns her by placing actions of childish abandon in a series of exclamations that build to an empty climax, "and laugh at—nothing—at nothing, simply." The fancy pause indicates that Bertha must repeat her thoughts to get them right, and the word "simply" gives undue exaggeration to the exact shade of her feeling while lending some slight hint of upper-class diction to the whole sentence. Such undermining effects pervade the narrative. Bertha is caught and judged by the echoes of her own sensual banality in the voice that seems to tell the story of her awakening so dispassionately.[21]

In all of Katherine Mansfield's stories of the childish rich, the narrator presents the flow of consciousness through their self-flattering immaturity, backtracking phrases, exaggerated modifiers, and mock exasperation at the failure of language to penetrate to the core of those mysterious moments of being which are the special talent of the aesthetically gifted. The habitual connection of innocence with "real" experience denotes a peculiar obsession for experience in Mansfield's young women of indeterminate gender: separated in various ways from full realization of their bodies, they continually seek special moments that are transcendent in their promise of a full encounter with "Life." Frequently this search comes in the context of flight from resistant realities. With characters for whom the reader is to have some sympathy, the apostrophe to Life can show acceptance of the joyous complexity of living, or it can mark a wise summing up of meaning gathered patiently through many trials. In a story like "Bliss," however, it is a gauge to a lack of experience; the rapture that accompanies it is narcissistic. And the vagueness of the moment reveals a fear of any more coherent encounter with sex. Mansfield's critique of such moments reveals her ultimate rejection of Wilde's aestheticism as well as her turning away from the flaunted homosexuality that his case implied for her.[22]

The connection between the moment and sexuality is evident in the imagery of Bertha Young's epiphany:

What can you do if . . . you are overcome, suddenly, by a feeling of bliss—absolute bliss!—as though you'd suddenly swallowed a bright piece of that late afternoon sun and it burned in your bosom, sending out a little shower of sparks into every particle, into every finger and toe? (337)

This opening image of sunlight may suggest that her reversion to childishness is a search for release from the frigidity of her marriage into the kind of natural warmth and bodily freedom that Pearl Button had found in the Maori women who kidnapped her. A new erotic potential is apparent in the "little shower of sparks," but it is clear that this impulse has been thwarted by Bertha's gender imprisonment. Her thoughts move from the joy of sunlight to her sense of constraint: "Oh, is there no way you can express it without being 'drunk and disorderly'? How idiotic civilization is! Why be given a body if you have to keep it shut up in a case like a rare, rare fiddle?" (337–38). In this set of images, Bertha must reject society—"civilization"—and her comparison of her body to a "rare, rare fiddle" presents an important conjunction of the sexual with the social. Bertha evidently thinks of herself as an object of art; to be childish is to allow one's "rare" gifts to be liberated. Daydream images of such freedom are, however, tied to imagery of special protection, and so they indicate Bertha's infantine passivity even while they indicate the wishfulness of her desire to recapture the naturalness of childhood. In some ways Mansfield seems to attach Bertha's incipient lesbianism to the prohibitions of class as well as gender.

The first action that Bertha performs in the story signals her inadequacy on both levels, for she has forgotten the key to her house. Not only does the loss of the key carry the connotation of sexual lack, it also reveals that Bertha can always summon a surrogate servant to help her out:

"No, that about the fiddle is not quite what I mean," she thought, running up the steps and feeling in her bag for the key—she'd forgotten it, as usual—and rattling the letter-box. "It's not what I mean, because— Thank you, Mary"—she went into the hall. "Is nurse back?" (338)

The relationship between Bertha, the nurse, and Bertha's child is important enough to merit a full episode in "Bliss." Bertha's fecklessness has already been forecast by her forgetting the key, but we are to see in the episode of the nurse that Bertha is kept even further from reality by the intervention of servants. The nurse does not want Bertha to take care of her own daughter; indeed, when Bertha sees the nurse with the little girl, she feels like a child herself: "She stood watching them, her hands by her side, like the poor little girl in front of the rich little girl with the doll" (338). Quite clearly, if the childishness of Bertha Young has to do with an artificially cultivated innocence, it also has to do with positive victimization. The nurse in "Bliss" is able to rule Bertha's natural instincts in a way that gives her irresponsibility an element of pathos. In the presence of a real child, Bertha actually seems the more vulnerable of the two.

The nurse is the first of a number of threatening parental figures in "Bliss." Bertha's husband is another. He is a boor, but his ruthless adulthood is one of the things that attract Bertha; it can reinforce her feeling that she is essentially a child. At one point in the story, when she is complimented by her husband on her soufflé (which has, of course, been prepared by a servant), Bertha "almost could have wept with child-like pleasure" (345). But Harry Young has little time for children; he is interested only in females who have mature erotic potential. He speaks of his own child to a friend: "My dear Mrs. Knight, don't ask me about my baby. I never see her. I shan't feel the slightest interest in her until she has a lover" (347). This cynicism is partly a pose, but it is a real enough gauge of Harry's perverse masculinity to give the reader some sympathy for Bertha. Indeed, Bertha's vulnerability to the tyrannies of servants and husbands threatens to raise her plight beyond the solutions of satire.

Bertha's moments of bliss are trivial, but they are contrasted sympathetically with the predatory posings of her husband and the crowd of sophisticates who come to her dinner party. The dinner party sequence has moments of broad caricature. The guests are given grotesquely childish nicknames—Face and Pug, for example—and their conversation never reaches beyond the lisping banalities of a smart-set comedy. They seem to inhabit the same kind of borderland of gender which Mansfield portrays in her other major fictional allusion to lesbian seduction, the section of "At the Bay" in which the young Beryl (Pearl?) Fairfield is courted by a brazenly bisexual older woman for her own husband. With her cigarette smoking, her disdain of conventional society, and her constant posing, Mrs. Harry Kember could well be a dinner guest at Bertha Young's party. Her identification as a possession of "Harry Kember" might also associate her with "Harry Young" of "Bliss," the only other male character in Mansfield's stories who is given the masculine name that associates him with the hirsute, sexual male.[23] But Mrs. Harry Kember is a cold creature, impervious to the warmth of the sun:

> When she was not playing bridge—she played bridge every day of her life—she spent her time lying in the full glare of the sun. She could stand any amount of it; she never had enough. All the same, it did not seem to warm her. Parched, withered, cold, she lay stretched on the stones like a piece of tossed-up driftwood. (275)

It is possible that Mansfield's portraiture of this notorious woman might have come from the same source that inspired D. H. Lawrence's "Shame" chapter in *The Rainbow*.[24] Mrs. Harry Kember has the same appreciation of Beryl's slim body, and Beryl feels the same attraction/repulsion that Ursula Brangwen feels about Winifred Inger in Lawrence's novel. But in Mansfield's story, the lesbian woman turns into the predatory male in an image of surreal transformation which marks her seduction as corrupt.

> [S]uddenly she turned turtle, disappeared, and swam away quickly, quickly, like a rat. Then she flicked round and began swimming back. She was going to say something else. Beryl felt that she was being poisoned by this cold woman, but she longed to hear. But oh, how strange, how horrible! As Mrs. Harry Kember came up close she looked, in her black waterproof bathing-cap, with her sleepy face lifted above the water, just her chin touching, like a horrible caricature of her husband. (277)

The interpolation of forbidden heterosexuality with a diseased homosexuality could hardly be more clearly articulated than in this hallucinatory passage. Mrs. Harry Kember is portrayed as a characteristic temptress—a source of lesbian infection—in the adolescent Beryl's maturation. Mansfield's earlier description of the love of an older woman such as Edith Bendall as a remedy for existential fear has here been exchanged for a depiction of such love as "poison."

In "Bliss" Pearl Fulton is equally alien to Bertha Young, though she is not so threatening as Mrs. Harry Kember. She is cool and sure of herself; she talks very little, and what she says has no overtone of the cleverness of the other guests. There are suggestions that she is physically as well as mentally more mature than Bertha. At one point in the narrative of the party, when Bertha is imagining that she and Pearl are communicating with each other on a level deeper than that of the other silly guests, she thinks, "I believe this does happen very, very rarely between women. Never between men" (346). As the sense of a special intimacy continues through Bertha's dinner, it builds to a fulfillment of the sexual imagery with which the story began. First there is the women's mutual contemplation of the pear tree in Bertha's garden, described in terms suggestive of phallic force:[25] "Although it was so still it seemed, like the flame of a candle, to stretch up, to point, to quiver in the bright air, to grow taller and taller as they gazed—almost to touch the rim of the round, silver moon" (347). And shortly thereafter there is Bertha's intimation of desire for her husband: "But now—ardently! ardently! The word ached in her ardent body! Was this what that feeling of bliss had been leading up to?" (348). In this acceptance of her heterosexuality, in this surprising experience of real desire, Bertha undergoes the first motions of release from childish frigidity into a bodily freedom more positive and satisfying. But it is a crowning irony that she can be impelled towards maturity only through the agency of a full-bodied woman, who, she is to discover, really is her husband's lover. By contrast, when Beryl in "At the Bay" is approached by the voracious Mr. Harry Kember, she recoils from his sexuality and runs away.

The swift denouement of "Bliss" shatters Bertha's newfound sexual joy. She catches a glimpse of her husband with Pearl Fulton at the end of the party and suddenly realizes that they are lovers: "Harry's nostrils quivered; his lips curled back in a hideous grin while he whispered: 'To-morrow,' and with her eyelids Miss Fulton said: 'Yes'" (349). The detail in this fleeting exchange recalls the animal physicality and the languor of sexual appetite which Mansfield emphasized in episodes of heterosexual lust in her earlier bisexual narratives. In its insistence on the sensual constituents of heterosexuality, the revelation reinforces Bertha's sense of a bewildering animal impersonality in the grown-up world. The impersonality is repeated with devastating force when Pearl Fulton turns from the secret encounter with Harry to recall the spiritual moment she has shared with Bertha in bidding her good-bye: "'Your lovely pear tree!' she murmured." Bertha is too confused to be able to respond. She can only think, lamely, to herself, "Oh, what is going to happen now?" (350).

If "Bliss" were to end at this remark, Bertha Young would be merely pathetic, and the story would have been a troubling exercise in Mansfield's irony. There is one last provocation, however. Bertha turns to the pear tree for an answer to her bewilderment about human sexuality, and there is no answer: "But the pear tree was as lovely as ever and as full of flower and as still." This last statement in "Bliss" leaves Bertha adrift in her ignorance of the real facts of sexuality with all pretense of narrative empathy abandoned.

Throughout the story the only source of value has been the possibility of authenticity in an obviously artificial world. Without her feeble pursuit of beauty, Bertha Young would be as empty of moral interest as the broadly caricatured guests at her dinner party. Even though it is childish, Bertha's flutter of inspiration at the beginning of the story and her hope for some kind of deeper relationship with Pearl Fulton have wrapped a fragile web of incipient charity around her thwarted sexuality. The story could have been an act of tender nostalgia for the fulfillment of love between women, but its final sentence collapses such a possibility by inviting the reader to see how trivial Bertha's lesbian emotion has been after all. The final twist may have seemed a clever stroke of modernist sang-froid, but the deeper impression is that Bertha's weakness has been more seriously betrayed by the narrator's vindictive unmasking of her unacknowledged lesbianism than by Harry Young's infidelity. The operative infidelity here is, after all, the infidelity of the knowing Pearl Fulton and the narrator who shares her knowledge.

⁓

Uncomfortable with promiscuous heterosexuality, increasingly repulsed by the naive lesbian sentimentality of L.M., and driven to make reparation to her parents when she found herself isolated and ill, Mansfield finally seems to have invested all her sexuality in the conventional notion of attachment to one man with the dream of bearing his children. Even during her bisexual experimentation in New Zealand, when she had romanticized the distant object of her heterosexual love—the cellist Trowell brother she had named "Caesar" to avoid his conventional name[26]—Mansfield reverted to the vocabulary of conjugal sex: "To me you are man, lover, artist, *husband,* friend—giving me all—and I surrendering you all—everything (*Journal* 17, emphasis added). This vision of a male/female relationship eagerly embraced by the self-sacrificing woman eventually became the one note in Mansfield's octave of sex. Perhaps her later dreadful experiences of aborted pregnancy and venereal disease seemed fit retributions for transgressive desire. In any case, the definition of her lesbianism as disease undoubtedly led Mansfield to reject same-sex love with a homophobic vengeance, while embracing heterosexuality finally as a form of child love between brother and sister.

In the next chapter, we must explore in more detail the disease sources of Mansfield's impulse to protect her heterosexual identity by rejecting her earlier lesbianism. Having had two years of promiscuity along the whole octave of the sex after the ending of her first pregnancy through miscarriage, Mansfield paid the price of increasing ill health that sexually active women suffered before the advent of modern antibiotics and prophylactics. Her attachment to John Middleton Murry was based upon their mutual sense of being adrift in a corrupt world. And her quixotic initiation of their affair was accompanied by an overdetermined homophobia that required her to revoke earlier loves even as she domesticated the ambivalence of her friendship with L.M. by turning her into an accomplice—almost a chaperon—in the Murry relationship. In her turn away from her lesbian past, then, Mansfield seems to have centered her fears on her unworthiness to have sexual pleasure and on her desire to amend the past by creating a newer, purer love. Such atonement played a role not only in her betrayal of friends and lovers but also in the corrosive irony of a story such as "Bliss," in which spontaneous attraction to another woman is suggested as the agent of destruction for authentic erotic faith; significantly, Bertha Young's susceptibility to Pearl Fulton's appeal is in direct contrast with her inability to mother her child. Thus an association of the lesbian temptation with the inability to mature into a capacity for maternity—Bertha is too "Young," indeed—marks the source of the transposition of Mansfield's desire to connect with the maternal breast into an overwhelming urgency to become maternal herself.

CHAPTER 4

"Fatal—so fatal!"

Pregnancy, Miscarriage, Abortion, and Gonorrhea

KATHERINE MANSFIELD was one of the first modern women writers to make the physical pain of childbirth a predominant theme in her fiction.[1]

In the stories she wrote for the *New Age* and then collected in *In a German Pension* (1911), she drew from her experience in Bavaria in 1909, where she had been sent by her mother to recover from her marriage to George Bowden and her "unfortunate" relationship with L.M. Several of Mansfield's biographers, including L.M., contend that Annie Beauchamp was unaware of her daughter's pregnancy when she sent her abroad, but I agree with Claire Tomalin that such a supposition is hardly credible.[2] The potentiality of pregnancy is a shadow in which any sexually active young woman—especially one living alone—would have moved in the first decade of the twentieth century (or *any* decade of the twentieth century, for that matter), and mothers are the first to suspect. And so Mansfield went into exile "for her health," booked into a foreign environment by her mother, aware that she was bearing Garnet Trowell's child.

There are few letters from Bavaria; Mansfield seems to have recorded most of her responses to her stay there in the stories she wrote after she returned to London. But in a letter written to Garnet while she was traveling in Belgium after she had become aware of her pregnancy (but before her mother's intervention), she speaks of herself as polluted, ill, isolated, spiritually moribund, but also in potential comradeship with the external world and exultant in the expectation of delivering a boy child (Mansfield never imagined herself as a mother of girls):

'Tis a sweet day, Brother, but I see it not. My *body* [her emphasis] is so self conscious—Je pense of all the frightful things possible—"all this filthiness"—Sick at heart till I am physically sick—with no home—no place in which I can hang up my hat—& say here I belong—for there is

no such place in the wide world for me. But attendez—you must not eat,
& you had better not sleep! No good *looking* "fit" and *feeling* dead.
In the train to Anvers. I love Belgium for I love green & mauve. I wonder
when I shall sit & read aloud to my little son. (*CL* 1:91)

Here pregnancy has given Mansfield a new consciousness of her adult body,
despite the fact that she again entertains her familiar childhood fears of isolation. Totally invested, for the moment, in her ideal plotting of a heterosexual
bond that would entail the establishment of an idyllic family with a brotherly
"husband" and a son of her own, she is aware of herself as carrying a creative
potentiality. Her use of the word "filthiness," however, invokes a sense of the
childbirth as pollution, and her being metaphorically "sick at heart" may be
entwined with physical illness. Mansfield tends to be so melodramatic about
her feelings that it is difficult to tell, in early journal entries and letters, when
she is referring to physical pain and when to mental distress. In any case, the
possibilities for physical discomfort as the basis of this account are the fatigue
and morning sickness of early pregnancy, and it is important to consider those
symptoms as factors in Mansfield's interpretations of aspects of her pregnancy
as pollution.

The reason for emphasizing the materiality of Mansfield's descriptions of
pregnancy, childbirth, abortion, and venereal disease in her earliest published
work is the obverse of the need to emphasize the rhetoric of the discourse of
disease in her writing about homosexuality. In either case, the discourse stands
in some opposition to the actuality of her experience. But the discourse of
homosexuality as contagion helps to mask her instinctive desire and finally
engulfs it in an alternative ideal of heterosexual happiness. The common discourse of pregnancy and of female sexuality as pollution, on the other hand,
derives from a defensive patriarchal value system that she herself discerned as
destructive; the physical pain that she knew firsthand served as a critique of
the rhetoric of suffering and exalted maternity, even as she invoked it in describing her condition to the father of her child.

Thus the tiredness that she mentions in her letters to Garnet could be a result
of her pregnancy as well as of ill-advised travel to the Continent at such a
physically demanding time. Moreover, in another letter to Garnet from the early
days in Bavaria, Mansfield mentions the temptation of Veronal. That drug, a
weak form of barbiturate, was prescribed for intestinal disruptions—possibly
for morning sickness.[3] Thus pregnancy seems the first major somatic malaise
that Katherine Mansfield ever encountered, and its early physical symptoms of
lethargy and vomiting may have served as vehicles for her desperation as an
outcast. There are physiological bases for the fatigue of pregnancy, but the

Katherine Mansfield at Rottingdean, 1910, recuperating from surgery for "peritonitis." *(Ida Baker Collection, ATL)*

bases for morning sickness are intertwined with psychic reactions. Helene Deutsch has analyzed these extensively as a part of the normal ambivalence of pregnancy: "In vomiting, the conflicting positive wish to keep the child asserts itself in the relieved, triumphant feeling that predominates after the food has been expelled: 'And yet he remained inside.' One patient always looked with panic fear for fragments of the fetus in the vomit, and always laughingly realized the absurdity of her behavior afterward" (2:137).[4]

The connection between oral fixations and childbirth anxiety is common in the folklore and experience of pregnancy. Eating is an act of servitude to the physical order of life. The expectant mother is urged to watch her diet carefully for the sake of her child; in some ways both the father and the fetus seem to feed upon the mother's physical and psychic vitality. Deutsch has indicated that both the nausea of pregnancy and its craving for exotic foods indicate a "strongly ambivalent relation to the father of the child, and to the child"

(2:138). Mansfield's experience of pregnancy seems to have involved a trans-position of her revulsion against her own father's voracious, indiscriminate eating to a delicacy about the table manners of Garnet Trowell (and her later lovers). She could not bear to see the way Garnet ate his egg, and throughout her life, she was much distressed by any lack of delicacy in consuming food.[5]

Helene Deutsch's Freudianism, more formulaic than Freud's, emphasizes the triumph of masochism in the feminine psyche, and in her encyclopedic sur-vey of motherhood, that triumph is imaged both as Darwinian in its service to the species and as patriarchal in its service to the mother as recompense for the absent phallus. In either case, the mother's nonphallic body is the repository for something that is not herself. In her account of woman's accommodation to maternity, therefore, Deutsch surmises that the expectant mother's most significant anxiety involves a "fear of losing her personality in favor of the child." But despite this fear, Deutsch suggests, most women finally arrive at notions of solidarity and transcendent generativity which help them face their biological destinies.

The promise of a son in Mansfield's letter, as elsewhere in all her writing about obstetrical illness, seems to dissipate her hopelessness in the manner sug-gested by Deutsch, though, as I indicate in the next chapter, she could not favorably dispose of the past until she confronted the death of her brother, whom she began to think of as a brother/lover and foster son. Nevertheless, her first pregnancy—fraught as it was with prohibitions—could be leavened through anticipation of the child as implicated in a wider communion with nature: accordingly, the addendum from a happier stage in her Belgian trip restores Mansfield to a sense of participation in ongoing life through a fantasy of nurturing her son after he is born.

Mansfield's physical and emotional report to the father of her child not only portrays psychic anxiety but also gives extraordinary expression to the viola-tions of generativity through imagined pollution, to the blurring of inside/out-side body definitions, and to the penetration of social boundaries by psychic despair. In *Powers of Horror*, Julia Kristeva, following the anthropologist Mary Douglas, has analyzed these disorders as mythic as well as psychological as-pects of "abjection." In many ways Mansfield's expression would seem to fit into the paradigm elaborated there, for Mansfield marks herself as the maternal "abject" in her account of the fears of pregnancy: not yet individuated from her own mother because of a disastrous Oedipal attachment, Mansfield exults in an illegitimate pregnancy that both flouts the laws of the father (Annie Beau-champ used that law to legally disinherit her daughter immediately after she returned to New Zealand) and displays the irremediable otherness of the female body in gestation. Interestingly, the legislation of eating as an aspect of being "fit" intrudes in this passage, prohibiting orality for the pregnant woman; the body must be kept undernourished so that it may appear as dead as it feels. In pregnancy, then, oral nurture has once again become a signification for Mansfield's fatality rather than a support for her bodily triumph. The alienation from the maternal body seems profound.

To add to her sense of abjection—defined by Kristeva and Douglas as a boundary violation, a scapegoat phenomenon—Mansfield had to embark on her experience of pregnancy in a foreign land. The Germany chosen by her mother is not the French-speaking Belgium chosen by herself earlier, and she found the culture in Bad Wörishofen, a health spa, alien and suffocatingly bourgeois. It may well be that Annie Beauchamp had left her daughter with an unspoken understanding of the need to deal with her pregnancy by herself; Claire Tomalin has revealed that one of the Beauchamp English cousins had become pregnant at the age of fifteen and had her child "taken care of" (that is, born and adopted out) in Switzerland. Becoming pregnant (and by an ineligible man),[6] Mansfield violated the most sacred norms of her family and culture, and the force of retribution was emphasized by Annie Beauchamp's abandoning her to face the question of her future with the child alone. It is during this phase—in an episode of coping with a cold caught in Bavaria—that she recalls her grandmother as a source of intimate comfort (*CL* 1:92). Whether the option of aborting this pregnancy ever arose is difficult to ascertain, but it seems unlikely that Mansfield contemplated such a move, so excited was she at the promise of the child to fulfill her notion of forming a compensatory family through her conjugal brother love with Garnet Trowell. Abortion would have been easier to obtain in London than Bavaria, for one thing; German law required the registration of all misbirths. Further, Mansfield seems to have staged her erratic marriage to George Bowden to provide legitimacy for a child she meant to keep.

Nevertheless, in Mansfield's trip to Belgium and then her acceptance of exile in Germany, there is some sense of her need to enact childbirth out of the sight of her normal community. Expectant as she may have been of a future in which she might tell her child that he was born in Bavaria (*CL* 1:92), Mansfield also considered herself carrying a burden that she must wash away in ritual ablution. The spa that the mother arranged for her advertised itself as inculcating the "*Wasserkur*"; such a system of external and internal bathing seems to have been appropriate for such a desired cleansing of her physical and spiritual profanation. Founded by a Roman Catholic priest, the regime at Bad Wörishofen involved perpetual inspection of the inside and the outside of the body to discover impurities. Surely Annie Beauchamp, and Mansfield herself to some extent, wished that the violation, the sin, the mistake—the child—might be absolved or dissolved.[7]

Mansfield's pregnancy did miscarry in Bavaria, probably in late June (at three to possibly six months),[8] and social scandal was thereby avoided. Given the immediacy of Mansfield's later writing about the pain of childbirth, however, it is important to consider that her pregnancy was at such a stage of maturity that she would have suffered some version of labor pain in the process. In the usual biographical accounts, there is a suggestion that the loss of the fetus was spontaneous, caused by Mansfield's lifting a heavy trunk. But "natural" abortions are rarely instantaneous; the contractions that expel the fetus may last for hours, and the resulting physical as well as psychological debilitation may be profound. Mansfield needed at least six weeks to recuperate, and in her grief, she asked Lesley Moore to send her a slum child from London to care for.

During the remainder of her summer in Bavaria Mansfield atoned for her loss by taking care of the child, returning him to London in the fall. And then she seems to have begun to move about. She was in Bavaria from March 1909 to the end of the year, joining whatever artistic groups she found in the area, learning about Slavic writers—especially Chekhov—and taking up with a Polish artist, Floryan Sobienski. There is little evidence about Mansfield's daily life in Bavaria after her miscarriage, but it is clear that in a sexual rebound she allied herself with a new lover whose character was suspect. If it is true that she contracted gonorrhea from Sobienski,[9] her body shifted from one manifestation of its fated materiality to another.

The convulsive emptying of the womb in a flux of blood would, in this case, have been followed soon by manifestation of contagion at the very site of impregnation, now through a gradual and insidious discharge. Without engaging in unnecessary fascination with the necrotic here, I do wish to point to the kind of materiality which Edward Shorter insists upon in his study of the history of women's bodies. Shorter points out that until the medical advances of the mid-twentieth century, women's experiences of the body tended to involve an almost perpetual (and thus perhaps unconscious) affliction by diseased discharges (*Women's Bodies* 256).

Even though she works in a range of abstractions far afield from Shorter's medical materialism, Julia Kristeva's analyses of the conjunction of anthropological and psychological motives in the definitions of bodily abjection, especially as they relate to the flawed elaboration of the subject out of the maternal "other," are also useful in considering Mansfield's pregnancy and gynecological disease. In keeping with Shorter's insistence upon the body, however, I want to suggest that Mansfield's reaction, though inscribed in language of degradation and complaint when she is writing letters to her lovers, represents only a partial account of her reaction to the body's pollution. In some ways her writing may even reach the existential ecstasis that Kristeva invokes in her accounts of maternal scription of the body. Such ecstasis is for Kristeva—as it was for Mansfield—a manifestation of the late, Continental romantic agony:

> If "something maternal" happens to bear upon the uncertainty that I call abjection, it illuminates the literary scription of the essential struggle that a writer (man or woman) has to engage in with what he calls demonic only to call attention to it as the inseparable obverse of his very being, of the other (sex) that torments him. Does one write under any other condition than being possessed by abjection, in an indefinite catharsis?   (208)

Such a formulation tends to maternalize writing (by men or women, Kristeva insists) even as it ties discourse to the revulsion against the maternal function in the Oedipal triad, and it may apply to one facet of Mansfield's creative urge. In her conversion of her Bavarian experience into the fiction of *In a German Pension,* Mansfield embeds her narratives in the concrete, physical pain of the maternal body, but the result is less expiation than a clear-sighted revolt against an idealization of the female body which turns "demonic," which essentializes its obstetrical horror. Katherine Mansfield seems hardly "possessed by abjection." And so I want to suggest in her writing, rather, a second version of "something maternal"—a corporeal familiarity that exorcised the body of its "filthiness," demystified its secret life of flux and elimination, and satirized the romanticizing of its pains and material manifestations as a peculiarly patriarchal form of symbolization.

It is true that Mansfield seems to have recognized tragedy in the condition of woman's physicality as subject a of forced fecundity, as a bereft site of loss, and as a locus of materiality that needed to be sloughed off periodically, but in opposition to such melodrama, she also retained an essential sense of ease in her own body—rebounding from preciously expressed repulsions with vigorous assertions of the comic incongruities of bodily life. She was more forthcoming about the exasperations of her body to her women friends who, she assumed, took such matters in stride. As we have seen, she joked about her adolescent embonpoint, and we will later see how witty she could be about the worst bodily indignities of consumption. In another example (from an unpublished letter to L.M. in 1922), she describes a "terrific adventure" with a depilatory, commenting that she would have to "paint [her] whole face navy blue to match [her] upper lip." And then she adds, "What a curious, secret life one does lead to be sure!" (Berg).

In spite of her gynecological disasters, then, I suggest that Mansfield retained the gift of an essentially positive Oedipal resolution for her female identity through her grandmother's provision of the "good breast" and thereby the good body. Criticism of Mansfield's fiction frequently forgets the fact that she was a comic writer (just as Kristeva's discussion, like much psychoanalytic analysis, accents the ironic while it neglects the mysteriously dissipating possibility of self-deprecating comedy, even within neurosis). Although Mansfield's comedy can be brittle and laced with anger, especially in her early stories, it nevertheless projects a tonic capacity for satire in the stories in which she recorded the experience of childbirth and disease in Bavaria. She wrote these stories for the *New Age* when she returned to England, and collected them under the title *In a German Pension* in 1911.

~

There has been some analysis of Mansfield's childbirth stories of *In a German Pension,* but much of it has failed to perceive the way in which their imagery evokes anger against the woman's destiny to suffer the yoke of physical pain and engages an impulse to find a justification for acceptance of such pain which might transcend blind submission to sexual convention and patriarchal ideology.[10]

Mansfield wrote most of the *German Pension* stories out of memories of Bavaria. Thus in her first stories brute pain may be emphasized through the bitterness of personal revelation. Mansfield responds intensely to the injustice of this physical curse on women in the *German Pension* stories. Through her merciless satire on that modern patriarch, the Germanic father who ignores the pain of his wife because it is her religious and social destiny to suffer for him, Mansfield rejects the patriarchal God who would curse women with childbirth and load them down with the symbolization of abjection.

Mansfield's *German Pension* stories were first published in the *New Age* during the time when she was under the influence of Beatrice Hastings' anti-maternal polemics. The heavy touch of journalistic irony can thus be felt in all of the stories. Many of them are, for example, in the first person, a narrative convention that Mansfield rarely used in her mature fiction.[11] Furthermore, the narrator glories in a feminist savoir-faire. She is an advanced young British woman who scorns the solicitude of the matrons she meets at the German health spa that is the setting for most of her stories. Though in at least one sketch there is a hint that she herself is pregnant, she is always sardonic about the fecundity of the females she observes—noting their internalization of patriarchal maternalism with its emphasis on the prophylactic and symbolic uses of the water cure for a kind of purification which masks the grossest bodily materialism with a lumbering romantic rhetoric. And she is a devastating critic of the fathers and would-be fathers she encounters.

At first glance, it might seem that the main target of Mansfield's satire in these stories is German eating, but throughout the collection, eating fetishism is immediately associated with compulsive rituals of elimination. Thus Mansfield's adolescent association of gluttony with patriarchy returns with a vengeance when she locates its justifications at the site of anality in the *German Pension* stories; time and again her narrator contemplates Germans at meat and contrasts their gluttony (which she associates with their penchant for large families) with their clumsy efforts at self-purification. She is quick to recoil from their obsession with the body's functions—from diet to the finest details of sweating, belching, and defecating. In a significant number of Mansfield's "eating" sketches, therefore, there is submerged a reference not only to impregnation but also to evacuation—of food or of child, and in either case of a by-product whose bodily elimination repairs overindulgence. For example, the first story of the collection, "Germans at Meat," centers on accounts of eatings and washings among the boarders at the pension:

> "If I drink a great deal of Munchen beer I sweat so," said Herr Hoffmann. "When I am here, in the fields or before my baths, I sweat, but I enjoy it; but in the town it is not at all the same thing."
>
> Prompted by the thought, he wiped his neck and face with his dinner napkin and carefully cleaned his ears.   (39)

Childbearing can be heard as an accompanying motif in this kind of talk; at one point in the dinner conversation, the narrator turns down an offer of sauerkraut, though proclaiming herself a vegetarian. In excited response, the widow at the table discourses on the relationships between motherhood, eating, and the social order:

> "Who ever heard of having children upon vegetables? It is not possible. But you never have large families in England now; I suppose you are too busy with your suffragetting. Now I have had nine children, and they are all alive, thank God. Fine, healthy babies—though after the first one was born I had to—."   (38)

The narrator breaks in to forestall any further physical revelations, only to be forced to hear of another mother who gave birth to four babies at one time, a feat that inspired her husband to give a supper party and have the babies placed upon the table. In other sketches when food and the water cure are discussed, the allusion to childbirth is again overheard: for example, one sketch listens in on a clutch of women talking about a daughter "who was in that very interesting, frail condition. . . . 'But it is bound to be quite satisfactory. . . . The dear married a banker—the desire of her life'" ("The Baron" 42). The commodification of childbirth in this remark reveals Mansfield's understanding of the social and economic imperatives in women's maternity. Middle-class women pay for their physical security by bearing their husbands' children without complaint.

But there are many complaints by men in the *German Pension* stories. Several of the stories center on the odd, demanding males who come there for the cure. The title character of "The Baron," for example, lives in such guarded isolation that the narrator finally tries to penetrate his secrecy, only to find that he spends every minute of his day eating according to some bizarre regimen. In another story, one of the young men has an impulse to kiss a young woman but pauses in his ardor to explain, "'But you know I am suffering from severe nasal catarrh, and I dare not risk giving it to you. Sixteen times last night did I count myself sneezing. And three different handkerchiefs'" ("The Sister of the Baroness" 49). Thus, although the women talk about health incessantly, disdaining English reticence about such matters—"'You do not seem to enjoy discussing the functions of the body. . . . How can we hope to understand anybody, knowing nothing of their stomachs?'" ("Frau Fischer" 52)—it is the men who seem engulfed in a continuing discourse of abjection.

Beyond a series of relatively unplotted sketches that anatomize the Germanic patriarchal preoccupation with physical impurity, *In a German Pension* contains more highly formed stories that make the satirical complexities and ramifications of Mansfield's feelings about childbearing even more explicit. In a piece derived from Chekhov entitled "The Child-Who-Was-Tired," for example, Mansfield dramatizes the domestic violence that can result from the unendurable weariness of caring for small children. This story is so closely dependent upon the Chekhov original that it has been the focus for a continuing argument about Mansfield's possible plagiarism;[12] what is most interesting about it to me, however, is its thematic aptness, given Mansfield's reaction to her own pregnancy. The story depicts the weariness of the illegitimate child servant of a brutal peasant family, who becomes so overwhelmed by caring for an infant that she finally smothers it in order to get some rest. The fact that Mansfield would have fastened upon this particular Chekhov story indicates her interest in the justice issues of childbirth—who has the pain? who bears the burden? The answer is the child itself, in this case a real child, but in other stories the young mother is herself a childlike victim. Mansfield's experience of childbirth in Germany seems to have accentuated her child-rescue fantasies; having earlier dreamed of herself as a child needing rescue, she now demands justice for those who are tired because of too much birthing. Her request for the London slum child to care for may reflect such a reformist stance in her fiction; moreover, the image of the brutalized child in her reworking of the Chekhov story may have been intensified by her status as a child cast out by her own mother and who is herself the mother of a rejected child as well.

But Mansfield is usually interested as much in the psychological as in the physical violence of overburdened motherhood, and this is evident in three of the most important stories from the *German Pension* collection. "Frau Brechenmacher Attends a Wedding" dramatizes the consciousness of a young matron as she remembers her wedding night. "A Birthday" follows the meditations of a father on the day of his son's birth. And "At Lehmann's" registers a young virgin's awakening to reality as she hears the sound of an older woman crying out in labor. As Mansfield surveys childbirth from this variety of angles, we see her complicating her feminist account of sex and its ramifications with mordant wit that energizes her impulse to accent the degradation of childbirth. It is seen as a painful process, but Mansfield's focus is not so much the suffering of the maternal other as the father's projecting his guilt for causing such suffering onto images of the otherness of his wife.

"Frau Brechenmacher" examines the thoughts of the wife of the village post-master as she watches another woman embark on the round of childbearing which has already drained her of all energy. The coarse, peasant hilarity about sex and fertility at the wedding party—the bride already has an illegitimate daughter—oppresses the young wife:

> She stared round at the laughing faces, and suddenly they all seemed strange to her. She wanted to go home and never come out again. She imagined that all these people were laughing at her, more people than there were in the room even—all laughing at her because they were so much stronger than she was. (61)

The young matron is wordless under the pressure of a culture that takes for granted a woman's blind servitude to fertility. When they return from the party, her husband obviously intends to finish off the celebration with sex, and he tries to engage his tired wife in a bit of conjugal banter. But when he reminds her of their own wedding night, his words reveal the mindless brutality that has transformed her into a passive drudge: " 'Remember the night that we came home? You were an innocent one, you were. . . . Such a clout on the ear as you gave me. . . . But I soon taught you' " (62). Frau Brechenmacher turns aside this memory with guarded good nature, but as she prepares for bed, her re-sentiment rises: "'Always the same,' she said—'all over the world the same; but, God in heaven—how *stupid*.'" Her rebellion is short lived. At the prospect of her husband's affection she is transformed into a hurt child. "Then even the memory of the wedding faded quite. She lay down on the bed and put her arm across her face like a child who expected to be hurt as Herr Brechenmacher lurched in" (62).

"Frau Brechenmacher" has little of the narrative finesse that Katherine Mansfield would later bring to studies of domestic tension. But the image of womanhood as a form of helplessness becomes a complex source of satire in her later stories; although she is angry at the abuse suffered by helpless German women, she eventually becomes less sympathetic with more sophisticated women's acceptance of maternal abjection as their own destiny. She considered such acceptance a mode of neurotic collusion with patriarchal and societal power (see Chapter 5). Less transformed in Mansfield's later stories of maternity is the image of the shamelessly self-satisfied husband. Such a patriarch is the subject of "A Birthday" in the *German Pension* collection, a subtle study of the consciousness of the young burgher, Andreas Binzer, on the day of his wife's delivery of his third child. The cries of his wife in labor punctuate Binzer's meditations on the inconvenience that her pain is causing him. He feels that the world of women is against him, taunting him by making so much noise about childbirth. He is pathetically open to self-doubt as a father, which easily merges into self-pity.

The story follows Binzer's strategies for escaping any blame for having caused his wife's suffering. His need for reassurance increases as his wife's cries intensify and fill the corridors of his house. Looking at her picture, as her delivery reaches its climax, he notes her strange frailty: "Delicate she looked even then; her masses of hair gave her that look. She seemed to droop under the heavy braids of it, and yet she was smiling. Andreas caught his breath sharply. She was his wife—that girl. Bosh! it had only been taken four years ago" (90). When another cry interrupts his reverie, Binzer manages to accuse his wife of treachery: "In the half light of the drawing-room the smile seemed to deepen Anna's portrait, and to become secret, even cruel" (90). The alienation of her suffering turns his wife into a stranger—the threatening, exotic icon of unknown experience in the body. The smile—a continuing image for impersonal sexuality in Mansfield's stories[13]—here judges the husband on a scale of human pain which he can never understand.

While Andreas Binzer is attempting to dissociate his wife and her alien suffering from himself, the cries cease. At first Andreas thinks that his wife must have died. When the doctor comes to tell him that she has borne a son, Andreas staggers in a faint and has to be caught. Such a bodily gesture of anxiety salves his sexual guilt by validating his own frailty as a participant in shared maternity. "A glow spread all over Andreas. He was exultant. 'Well, by God! nobody can accuse *me* of not knowing what suffering is,' he said" (91).

This last sentence in "A Birthday" helps to explain the characterization of fathers in many of Mansfield's later stories. In them, Mansfield shrewdly notes the rationalizations fathers make to pretend that their own lives carry pain commensurate with that of childbirth. Earlier, when the doctor has talked of Binzer's wife's courage, Binzer thinks, " 'Now *he's* accusing me. . . . That's the second time this morning—first mother and now this man taking advantage of my sensitiveness' " (88–89). To such men, domestic life is a minefield of female insults and implied accusations. There is some secret conspiracy among women which men must distance through solidarity and patriarchal law. A whole structure of ritual prohibitions and purifications for women is thus implicated in the male ablutions that frame the stories of *In a German Pension*. Under Mansfield's satirical ethnography, these rituals are as exotic as the sexual pollution rites that Mary Douglas describes among threatened males among the Nuer of the Sudan, the Nambudiri Brahmins of Malabar, or the Lele of the Congo (140–58).

Mansfield implies in her early stories that women actually do share a tribal secret in their more intimate, lived experience of the origins of life in pain and blood. And this secret derives not only from the physical trauma of giving birth but from the daily burdens of nurturing life. In "At Lehmann's," however, there is some indication that the "secret" in generation and sex is so profound that neither male *nor* female can understand or control it. In this story of childbirth told from a virgin's perspective, Mansfield turns aside from the resentments of the female and the egoism of the male to represent the impersonality of the sexual drive itself.

Early in the story, Sabina, a young servant girl, thinks about the existential implications of her mistress's pregnancy:

Frau Lehmann's bad time was approaching. Anna and her friends referred to it as her "journey to Rome," and Sabina longed to ask questions, yet, being ashamed of her ignorance, was silent, trying to puzzle it out for herself. She knew practically nothing except that the Frau had a baby inside her, which had to come out—very painful indeed. One could not have one without a husband—that she also realised. But what had the man got to do with it? So she wondered as she sat mending tea towels in the evening, head bent over her work, light shining on her brown curls. Birth—what was it? wondered Sabina. Death—such a simple thing. She had a little picture of her dead grandmother dressed in a black silk frock, tired hands clasping the crucifix that dragged between her flattened breasts, mouth curiously tight, yet almost secretly smiling. But the grandmother had been born once—that was the important fact. (73–74)

The problem of childbirth is here generalized beyond the reactions of social and ethical anger at the girl's ignorance of what awaits her at the hands of the male. The secret smile of Sabina's grandmother, a woman who has gone before her in the life cycle, indicates that the threat of birth involves more than physical pain; it involves death as well. Thus, though there are some familiar satirical thrusts at details of German domestic life, "At Lehmann's" represents a significant variation on the thematics of childbirth.

A nameless "Young Man" appears at Lehmann's Inn and attempts to seduce Sabina. Unsuccessful at first, he does make her aware of her body in a new way. He returns again on the day of Frau Lehmann's delivery. While the mother is in labor upstairs, he renews his seduction by attempting to kiss Sabina and then to fondle her breasts. But her confused encounter with the sexuality that leads to conception is interrupted by a "frightful tearing shriek" (78) from the woman overhead. Hearing this, the girl repels herself from the Young Man. She has found the answer to her questions about the "important fact" of birth in the contrast between the sweetness of sex and the revelation of childbirth pain. When this contrast is verified by the sound of a new baby crying, Sabina can stay in the room with the Young Man no longer. Her frantic flight from him ends the story.

"At Lehmann's" suggests that no matter how painful, how shocking, how polluting, how impossible to accept, childbirth is part of the virgin's destiny. And though Mansfield is most interested to note the injustice of this distribution of the hardships of maternity in her first stories, she also prepares to acquiesce in the implication that the inevitable must be made to fit somehow into the patterns of women's lives. But the gestating female body is not to be accommodated so easily in the patriarchal paradigms of purification. There is a conscious intention in Mansfield's stories to resist the distancing of the physical experience of women by the male habit of converting maternal pain into the metaphors of Germanic matriarchalism.[14]

~

Katherine Mansfield's encounter with masculine fears of sexual pollution did not end with her return to England from Germany, for it was in that return that she "found herself with a hideous new sexual problem, hardly less difficult to cope with than the previous year's" (Tomalin 75). Claire Tomalin has done the medical detective work necessary to trace all the diagnostic implications of

Mansfield's lingering physical malaise. She notes, for example, that Mansfield reported to a friend the symptomatic discharge of gonorrhea (though, as Shorter has indicated, discharges from varieties of vaginitis seem to have been constant for most women of the time). We cannot know what other intimate signs Mansfield may have experienced. The disease can be relatively mild, but its more virulent form can cause fever, extreme vaginal irritation from the discharge, and abdominal pain; the genital presentation is much more recognizable in the male than in the female. In the usual progress of the disease, this genital phase subsides, even while the infection passes "from the uterus to the tubes and beyond," in the words of a contemporary textbook (Taylor 163). This final, systemic phase of the disease is silent and not necessarily associated with the vaginal infection (which is difficult to diagnose as gonorrhea without microscopic inspection). It might cause a general infection leading to "painful and ultimately crippling arthritis in the joints; pericarditis (i.e. inflammation of the sac around the heart) and pleurisy (inflammation of the membranes surrounding the lungs)" (Tomalin 76). Such generalized physical symptoms began to appear in Mansfield's journal and letters after her return to London to begin her literary career there in 1910.[15] She underwent an operation for "peritonitis" in the spring in London, and the fragments of description of this medical trauma encapsulate major features of "medical purification" as practiced in the late nineteenth and early twentieth centuries.[16]

First, as Tomalin has pointed out, the doctor that Mansfield consulted, perhaps unwisely, removed her left fallopian tube and ovary. Secondly, the doctor kept the origin of her illness from her; she was only informed of it in the process of undergoing a thorough examination for tuberculosis by her most trusted physician, Dr. Sorapure, in 1918. And, most significantly, she had counted her "rheumatiz" and her heart flutterings as the most important, tangible links with her invalid mother (Mantz and Murray 310). Finally, the first doctor, who had operated rather than treating her disease systemically, seems to have used the nature of her illness to display "an unprofessional interest in her body" (*LM* 54). Recovery from the operation was made all the more difficult by the behavior of this doctor, and Mansfield suffered alone at a "second-rate" nursing home until Lesley Moore came to rescue her.

Thus immediately after the Bavarian exile for pregnancy, Mansfield discovered that even in England, women's genital illnesses would be presided over and exacerbated by an unreliable masculine power elite armed with coercive technologies. Her immediate recourse was to reopen the relationship with her closest female friend whose nursing could be trusted (another friend aptly named "Miss Good" helped to dress the wound). Moreover, she recuperated within the hope of eventually becoming pregnant successfully. Meanwhile, she was reassured of the normality, if not the health, of her female body by thinking often of her ailments as inherited from her mother and as genetic sources of solidarity with her. Although Mansfield sometimes speaks of women's frailty as a gauge of the kind of refinement she idealized in her mother, however, she also saw that refinement could be a form of denial of the body. The reticence of her doctors on the subject of her gonorrhea kept Mansfield in the dark about her fertility for years; although her surgeon's behavior conveyed his notion that she was a fallen woman, he never confronted her with the facts. His reticence may have seemed the sort of paternal kindness guided by the professional ethos of the time; nevertheless, this ethos tended to infantilize women by depriving them of true knowledge of their illnesses. And its shielding women from the facts of venereal disease also shielded the male sources of infection from blame.

Despite some remnants of Victorian "modesty" embedded in her memories of her mother's delicacy, however, Mansfield was amused and disgusted by the horror of men about the facts of the body, even as they talked about higher things. For example, in 1918 (before the revelation by Dr. Sorapure) she wrote to John Middleton Murry about flirting with a shady French doctor in Marseilles in order to get him to write her a chit to let her come home during wartime: "I am sure he is here because he has killed some poor girl with a dirty button-hook—He is a maniac on *venereal* diseases & *passion*—Ah! the filthy little brute!" (*CL* 2:129). Here, as in the *German Pension* stories, it is the conjunction of prurience with high-flying talk which inspires Mansfield's disgust; as for the body itself, she can use its eroticism as a necessary tool, so long as she doesn't have to let the disgusting doctor touch her. She remarks to Murry that she has not "felt so cynical for years."

Mansfield seems not to have reacted in self-loathing to the information that she had been infected with gonorrhea. Antony Alpers believes that the bitterness of her closing journal entry for 1918 reflects her sense of loss—a metaphysical loss in which she feels like a fly who thought herself glittering in the sun but has now fallen into a jug of milk—observed by God and "the smallest Cherubim and Seraphim of all, who delight in misfortune" (*Journal* 153; Alpers, *Life*, 289). Such language seems abject indeed, but it comes not so much from revulsion against the body—by this time Mansfield had faced full-blown tuberculosis with all of its own physical degradations—as from her sense of humiliating betrayal. All the signs she had looked for in her body—of continuing ability to have children, of connection with her mother, of maintaining her womanhood without the scars of the experimental sexuality of her late adolescence—were delusions. I believe that although she placed her condition within a trope of the kind of creaturely apocalypse which connected her with the lowest of insects, her shock was more the shock of existential betrayal than of self-pollution. And indeed, in most of her illness reactions, her questioning is more about God's providence than about the "filthiness" of her body, or of her sex.

I linger on this point because I want to suggest a contrast with John Middleton Murry's account of his response to the news that he had contracted gonorrhea from a prostitute before he met Mansfield (in 1911). Here is the way he talks about his casual meeting with a prostitute and the resulting infection:

> I straightway fell into an abysm of depression, from which I never re-covered. I was sorry for the girl, who got no pleasure out of me. . . . It was a sordid, miserable business; and I knew long before the end of it, that if my hope of liberation lay that way, I might as well resign myself to my chains. I simply was not made for such experiences.
>
> For some days after we were quit of it [the affair], I grew steadily more and more depressed. In about a week I felt downright ill. And then, to my horror, I discovered that I was. I went straight to a doctor, who was stern, but reassuring: hoped it had taught me a lesson. . . . I felt that I had touched a nadir: as indeed I had. Uncleanness had entered into my very vitals, and was festering there. The process of degradation which had be-gun when I fled from Margueritte [his first lover] was now completed. From my soul it had spread to my body. (*BTW* 183)

This kind of mentality, which sees the entire species as polluted in its physical manifestations but which invokes father/son bonding in male knowledge that the pollution can be learned "by a lesson" in keeping away from foul women, is characteristic of the male discourse of abjection. Murry is so detached from his own body that he cannot stand its venereal illness, and that seems to have been his response to Mansfield's body as well. He speaks of her always as much more "pure" than she ever saw herself as being. He suggests that their sex together was exalted and tragic because of her imagined self-pollution. In short, I am suggesting, Murry's self-pollution in his own initiatory sexuality illustrates the kind of masculine subject position which Kristeva's anthropological concept of the abject seems to take. Like all tribal males, he transforms his own bodily revulsion into a coercive representation of his beloved as an ethereal innocent whose first fall has made it mandatory that she be protected from further profanation. Murry's response to venereal disease was the *Weltschmerz* of romantic agony; Mansfield's was the literalism of the satirist. She articulated this difference between them in a letter to Ottoline Morrell in 1918 in which she spoke of the effect of the weather on her cough:

I feel that winter, cruel forbidding winter is content to leave nothing un-frozen—not one heart or one bud of a soul to escape! If only one did not feel that it is all so wrong—so wrong. It would be much happier if one could feel—like Murry—mankind is born to suffer—But I do feel that is so wrong—so wrong. It is like saying: mankind is born to walk about in galoshes under an umbrella. (*CL* 2:281)

Mansfield's critique of Murry's tendency to overdo the tragic extends her skepticism about male suffering from the *German Pension* stories into her relationship with Murry where, again, her comic sense of the absurdity of physical complaining forestalls metaphysical abjectifying.

~

The explicit attention to details of disease and prophylaxis played little part in Mansfield's stories after *In a German Pension*. Rather, in her later stories women's illnesses are subsumed under the general conditions of hysteria, pregnancy, and abortion. And, as I suggest in analyzing Mansfield's reactions to tuberculosis, the diagnostic perspective may have become a pervasive mode in her narratives of masculine pathologizing such as "*Je ne parle pas français*" (1918). In a few fictions between 1911 and 1918, she portrays suffering women, but with little sense of their afflictions as intrinsically gynecological. "This Flower," a short sketch written in 1919, returns to the narration of specifically sexual/obstetrical illness as a kind of fate which woman must face, positively isolated by the male's taboos and his denial of the physical actuality of the female body in pregnancy or venereal infection.[17] The story depicts the professional visit to a young woman by a seedy Bloomsbury doctor provided for her by her lover.

As the story opens, she is depicted in the full bloom of an epiphanic moment—"It was single, glowing, perfect: it was like—a pearl, too flawless to match with another" (406).[18] Such overwrought language would seem sheer transcendental blather if it were not apparent that the imagery has come as the result of defensive self-hypnosis during a pelvic examination. In this context, however, the words mask the discomfort of the procedure and the threat of pregnancy with the woman's ecstatic submission to life:

It was as though, even if she had not been conscious (and she certainly had not been conscious all the time) that she was fighting against the stream of life—the stream of life indeed!—she had suddenly ceased to struggle. Oh, more than that! She had yielded, yielded absolutely, down to every minutest pulse and nerve, and she had fallen into the bright bosom of the stream and it had borne her. (406)

Despite her orgasmic ecstasy, however, it appears that she has been given bad news by the doctor, who returns to the room drying his just-washed hands as she is dressing. Although his diagnosis is never made explicit, it seems that he has told her that she has some condition, probably pregnancy, related to her sexuality.[19] She asks him to conceal the truth of his findings from her lover, and—as the story closes—she submits to the lover's unknowing gaiety of relief: "'If you knew how frightened I've been,' he murmured. 'I thought we were in for it this time. I really did. And it would have been so—fatal—so fatal!'" (408).

The story reworks a number of the characteristic features of Mansfield's ironic/poetic gynecological narratives—the vulnerable female protagonist, her lyrical moment outside the body, the lover whose sentimental relation to the woman's pain is so contrived that it almost seems sincere. Without much ado, the woman recognizes the threat to their enclosed "innocence" from the harsh outside world of shady medical men, bodily profanation, and the threat of death. The key revelation in this story, therefore, is the woman's need to conspire with the medical expert to maintain her own anesthesia and to keep the harsh truth of her body from the male; the doctor has agreed to tell the lover that her only affliction is a "weak heart." The three-page story also exhibits Mansfield's characteristic exercise of narrative understatement so as to culminate in a last-line revelation of a failure of insight on the part of the male. The narrative calculation significantly conceals everything about the protagonist but her bodily condition, and even that must be hidden from her lover. We never know the woman's name, and the name given her lover—"Roy King"— is both an alias and a marker of satire against the regally insensitive male whose reaction to the woman's sexual predicament is to absorb it into his own romantic sense of cosmic fatality and then to want nothing more to do with it.

This story of illness thus veils the prognosis as well as the diagnosis implied at its outset. If the young woman has just found out that she is pregnant, she may be forming an alliance with the doctor to conduct the pregnancy in private. Or she may be expecting that he will perform an abortion; indeed, he may have already performed the abortion during the examination procedure that she has anesthetized with her epiphany. The biographical record of any experiential basis for the abortion hypothesis is unclear.[20] L.M. has stated that Mansfield had an abortion during the spring of 1911, even though she at first intended to carry the baby to term. But the clinical indications for such an episode are negative; given the infection and subsequent removal of one of her ovaries during the gonorrheal episode, it would have been very difficult, but not at all impossible, for Mansfield to conceive in 1911. The instability of her menstrual cycle, however, led Mansfield to think she was pregnant a number of times after her operation for "peritonitis." In any case, the description of the examination and interaction with the shady doctor in "This Flower" strikingly registers the thick detail of a firsthand experience. Thus, while the story records the humiliation of a vaginal examination, its center is the young woman's maneuvers to deal with the realities of her body's burdens. The girl is trapped in her illness with the doctor, who has told her privately, " 'Don't you worry, my dear. . . . I'll see you through' " (407).[21]

"This Flower" is an illness story, therefore, which emphasizes the manifestations of disease in the female patient's experience—the sensations of heightened existence betrayed by the danger of the prohibited results of sexuality, the deflection of humiliating invasion of the body by the medical professional through concentration on the interior moment, the repellant dependence upon untrustworthy male physicians, and the necessity to hide the "fatal" truth from the only source of economic safety—the denying lover. In her life, as in this story in which she portrays an actual clinical event, Mansfield stresses that "female troubles" require both internal sublimation and external concealment. And the cutting indictment of the doctor and the lover also suggests that it is the young woman who must find strength in her fragility: she cannot hide in symbolic imaginations of transcendent disaster. The threatened losses of economic support and health require her to scheme rather than to engage in self-pity.

The sources of cure suggested in "This Flower" image the "rest cure" regimen of rest and feeding which Mansfield's caretakers ordered for her when she became ill from tuberculosis—" 'She shall go away. She shall go away to the sea at once,' said he, and then, terribly anxious, 'What about her food?' "(407). Such a cure has a mixed reputation in feminist histories of medicine; although it could be seen as a provision of badly needed respite for the always slightly unhealthy late Victorian woman, it also involved an infantilizing of the woman.[22] In this story it not only registers the presumption of male supervision of the female body, but it also registers the woman's sense of her venereal condition as a secret that she could share only with the furtive professional who conspired with her to hide the truth from a lover who assumed that her suffering—like her body itself—belonged essentially to him: "He simply burst into her room, and she was in his arms, crushed up small while he kissed her with warm quick kisses, murmuring between them, 'My darling, my beauty, my delight. You're mine, you're safe' " (408). Thus for Mansfield, women's troubles were matters for a conspiracy of silence between the woman and the doctor in the light of the man's tendency either to ignore them or to abstract them into melancholy self-lacerations. Ordinary men could not confront the truth of women's troubles, and even the doctor/allies are likely to take an erotic interest—"He gave her a strange, quick, leering look, and taking off the stethoscope with shaking fingers he folded it into his bag that looked somehow like a broken old canvas shoe" (407).

Women, then, are essentially alone in the crisis of gynecological illness. Perhaps their only source of consolation, if not of cure, is their "moment," but theirs is not a moment of ritual elaboration. It is a moment of self-protective anesthesia stolen during the process of getting the bad news that will eventually have to be dealt with. Finally then, in her own illness, and the writing that released her from it, Katherine Mansfield's reaction to abjection at once embodied and critiqued the lyricism that Kristeva proclaims in her evocation of "maternal quietude" in "Stabat Mater":

> This maternal quietude, more stubborn even than philosophical doubt, with its fundamental incredulity, eats away at the omnipotence of the symbolic. . . . But it can also serve the speaking subject as a refuge when his [sic] symbolic carapace shatters to reveal that jagged crest where biology transpierces speech: I am thinking of moments of illness, of sexual— intellectual—physical passion, death . . . [her ellipsis]. (117–18)

In this realm, Mansfield well knew, it's the man who mythicizes and the woman who pays.

CHAPTER 5

"Lift my head, Katy, I can't breathe"

Hysteria, Mourning, and Rebirthing the Brother

"HYSTERICS suffer mainly from reminiscences," according to the initial formulation of the founders of modern psychoanalytic therapy (Breuer and Freud 7). In their emphasis on the memory of childhood experience as the originary illness for much of modern psychiatric practice, Breuer and Freud helped to transport hysteria from the site of the uterus—the classical organ of its origin—to the psyche.[1] Surveying hysteria in terms of the grotesque manifestations of the patients which he first witnessed in his work with Charcot and Breuer—the "conversion" dysfunctions of blindness, pseudocyesis (false childbirth enactment), or somatized paralyses and anesthesia, and the milder forms such as invalidism, obsessive daydreaming, animal phobias, and instability of affect—Freud built his interpretation on the supposition that cure lay in going back ever more deeply into the early configurations of family romance which instigated the syndrome. In the process of developing a fuller theoretical framework for such symptomology, moreover, his emphasis on the origins of the affliction as involving the seduction of the daughter, the anxiety of sexual initiation, and a hypochondriacal insistence on the incipient dissolution of the body continued the predisposition to gender hysteria female.

The question of cure for hysteria has always involved the mystery of the patient's agency in her illness. The characteristic hypochondria—the endless and enervated inventory of somatic complaints that derive from familial dysfunction rather than systemic disease—has inevitably suggested malingering; thus classic cures for hysteria have tended to carry about them the threat of discipline by the doctor. Silas Weir Mitchell's "rest cure" could even invoke the danger of the doctor's rape of the patient,[2] and Freud's implementation of Breuer's "talking cure," in the case of Dora especially, has seemed more and more a long-drawn-out episode of bullying than a cooperation with the troubled young woman to reach an understanding of her problems.[3] Further, the cultural supposition that woman's pain tends to be in her head can mask organic disease—mislabeling and neglecting genuine sources of physiological malfunction by attributing them all to hysteria. Thus Katherine Mansfield's symptomology of early anxiety about death, adolescent body image rebellion, flamboyant sexual display, emotional lability, vague and indeterminate aches and ailments, and even early surgery could play into a diagnosis of hysterical personality disorder. As a matter of fact, some early critical estimates of her traits as a personality and writer seem to have been based on such a diagnosis.[4] Significantly, such criticism did not have access to the fact that the sick role she assumed was in part founded in the physiological damage wrought by her early gonococcal infection (and, later, tuberculosis). Even so, she might seem a prime suspect for classification as a "hysterical personality," overresponding to physiological malaise, if she were evaluated according to one standard inventory:

> The hysterical personality is a term applicable to persons who are vain and egocentric, who display labile and excitable but shallow affectivity, whose dramatic, attention-seeking, and histrionic behavior may go to the extremes of lying and even pseudologia and phantastica, who are very conscious of sex, sexually provocative yet frigid, and who are dependently demanding in interpersonal situations.[5]

It is not my aim to decide whether or not Katherine Mansfield's case fits neatly within the nosology of hysteria, however. Rather, I want to show how the crisis of mourning brought about by her brother's death in World War I led to a form of reminiscence which might have seemed hysterical in its intensity but which actually enabled her to rework the past out of fragments of memory, dreams, and an eventual understanding of the origins of her destabilizing anxieties.

Freud elaborated melancholia, or pathological mourning, as a form of hysteria. In this form, the loss of the object is taken into the ego itself, so that the bereaved ego installs the narcissistically invested lost object as part of itself, displacing its anger against the disloyalty of the lost object, now embedded in the self, by engaging in dramatic complaint, scrupulous self-denigration, and eventual self-destruction. If Mansfield's bereavement had followed this pattern, as at first it threatened to do, "Prelude" and "At the Bay"—announced tributes to the memory of her brother—might be counted as extensions of her own hysterical trends. But John Bowlby's study of attachment and loss—enlarging the Freudian analysis of mourning by paying attention to clinical cases, primate research, and empirical observations of separation from the (usually maternal) attachment figure in children (and then of the death of loved figures in maturity)—suggests a less pathological pattern for Mansfield. Extrapolating from Bowlby's work, it seems clear that Mansfield's reaction to her brother's death was intensified by separation anxieties of childhood, for she had attached the network of relationships she left behind in Wellington to her brother's affection for her. And so the outcast and unmourned-for Katie must feature again in the narrative design of her memories of New Zealand evoked by Chummie's death. Although she proclaims in her journal that her writing in memory of him will be a reminiscence of the bright "undiscovered country" of the child-hood they shared, her re-creation is less a series of elegiac vignettes than a highly structured refabrication that imagines an eventual reunion between the lost brother and sister and the rejecting woman whose carelessness has wounded them profoundly.

The question here, then, is how Mansfield used one of her most borderline hysterical episodes, her sudden flight from England to the south of France fol-lowing the death of her brother, to engage in the kind of reparative reminis-cences which are the goal of psychoanalytic treatment. In this chapter I argue that she made such an engagement in rewriting "The Aloe," a relatively straightforward, chronological memory evoked by earlier sessions with her brother, into "Prelude," her first masterpiece of reparative recollection, and "At the Bay," its sequel.[6]

Here Mansfield in fact rejected the temptation to regress to dependency and infantilization that the idealized relationship with her brother had fostered in many of her adult attachments, especially the one with John Middleton Murry. Such relationships frequently enacted her own fantasies of dying alone and still unacknowledged by her mother. But Chummie's death objectified such sepa-ration anxieties, impelling Mansfield to confront the origins of such rejections as well as the pathos of their victims. Thus Mansfield's mourning found an outlet in resistance to hysteria, even as it opened an imaginative access to an understanding of hysteria in women as a possible form of self-absorption which can victimize innocent bystanding children, involving them in a generational cycle of the kind of recriminating self-splitting which Freud remarked in "Mourning and Melancholia." And so, although Mansfield's most ambitious remembrance of things past in "Prelude" and "At the Bay" finally plots a rec-onciliation between the mother and her child, it is also astringently diagnostic as it surveys the spectrum of hysterias that the women in the autobiographical Burnell family summon to justify their detachments.[7]

In connecting hysteria with Katherine Mansfield's writing, I am not, then, fully adopting some recent formulations that appropriate hysteria as a char-acteristically feminine discourse that must fight its way to utterance—frac-tured, dense, and nonlinear—through the restraints of patriarchal language.[8] Although it is clear that in her great New Zealand stories Mansfield was intent on creating a layered narrative that could represent the fragmentariness of rem-iniscence, I cannot make a case for her writing as inspired dictation taken from

Kathleen Beauchamp [KM], center, with her sister, Jeanne, and brother, Leslie, ca. 1908. (ATL)

Leslie Heron Beauchamp
ca. 1915 (ATL)

the imaginary realm of maternal, pre-Oedipal silence. In point of fact, she employs her associative, fractured form to range from episodes of generous femininity to those of feminine self-absorption. The mastery of this new kind of narrative in implementing her fixed intention to communicate judgments resists definition of her writing as hysterical.[9] On the contrary, Mansfield's writing is a willed resistance to the chaos of hallucinatory dementia. Its moral gestures militate against romanticizing the paralysis of physical hypochondria and the depersonalization of emotional anesthesia. Within her reconstruction of the Burnell family romance, such illness strategies are represented as having dire effects upon the well-being of children: hysteria is less a psychic signification of justifiable feminine recalcitrance than an instrument of evasion of responsibility which must be unveiled before reconciliation is possible.[10]

This is not to say that Mansfield's therapeutic project in her great New Zealand stories was single minded, prosecuted with a fixed purpose of recovery. It was enmeshed in her relationship with John Middleton Murry, with whom she had engaged in a rehearsal of the compensatory brother-love eroticism that sent her grieving for her brother towards borderline hallucination. Before approaching the texts of two of her finest stories, therefore, it is useful to review Mansfield's enactment of the pattern of her early attachment to John Middleton Murry. It was in this marriage rather than in her writing that she initiated a hysterical reparation—acting out a fantastic scenario of brotherly love. Her chosen brotherly lover could only fitfully preserve her inner child from guilt about the lesbian experimentation and the heterosexual eroticism that had finalized her mother's disownment during the crisis of Mansfield's first pregnancy. Murry's part in this scenario seems to have involved his own participation in hysterical regression, but that is not the story to tell fully here.

~

Katherine Mansfield began living with John Middleton Murry in 1912, and although she was not able to marry him until 1918 when her divorce from George Bowden was granted, she considered herself his wife from the start. L.M. remained in the background as a ministering angel, reappearing decisively when Mansfield became too sick to care for herself. But once she had committed to him, Mansfield took Murry as the center of her sexual and familial interests. She left him twice, both times after abortive attempts to begin some kind of community living arrangement with Frieda and D. H. Lawrence. First she fled from the claustrophobic patriarchalism of the newly forming group in 1915 for a brief romantic assignation with Francis Carco, a French writer whom she had met through Murry during an earlier time they had spent in Paris. The two reunited when she returned to London, and they shared a truly creative period together there and then again in late 1915 and early 1916 in the south of France after Mansfield fled there to work through the death of her brother. They were lured back to England to try a revival of the living experiment with the Lawrences in an isolated village in Cornwall, and Mansfield abandoned this stormy experiment in the summer of 1916, after only a short stay.[11]

After this last Lawrence episode, Mansfield established a private studio in London where she could pursue her writing in solitude, and she may have contemplated a final separation from Murry then. Her writing was now on track, and she had made friends among various of the literary figures of the time, having met Virginia Woolf early in 1917 and later spending time at Garsington with Lady Ottoline Morrell. She seemed confidently on her own, an up-and-coming writer whose next book would be eagerly awaited.[12] The sudden onslaught of tuberculosis in December 1917 revived her dependence upon Murry, however. During the extended separations necessitated by these illness episodes, both before and after tuberculosis, Mansfield's attitude about her relationship with Murry often teetered in balance between loving dependence and melancholic despair. As her health grew more precarious, she clung to a conviction that in essential ways the marriage was permanent—that in Murry she had found someone to whom she must give consistent allegiance because he would be her companion in work, the father of her children, and the guarantor of her survival.

I have already suggested that a third term in Mansfield's bisexuality was the imagination of a brother-love relationship—a version of heterosexuality which could retain the innocence of Mansfield's childhood while holding out the promise of reparation for rejection by her unloving mother, thus permitting her to become a better mother herself. In an ideal relation with a brother lover, she could be both childlike and maternal; the bond with Murry engaged this kind of psychic dialectic. During times of their separation, for example, Mansfield always wrote to Murry in the diminutive. One of her very first letters to him speaks of his being in London while she plays the game of keeping house in a cottage they have rented (CL 1:2). And then in a letter during her 1916 exile to work through her brother's death, she speaks more intimately of their physical play together: "I feel we are about 15 today—just children: you and I don't live like grown up people, you know. Look at the way we soap each other's backs and hop about in the tops of our pyjamas and scrabble into bed, winking our toes" (CL 1:255). In the 1918 exile caused by tuberculosis, she addresses him as "My little precious. My love, my child playfellow" (CL 2:9). In the midst of such effusions, however, she still maintained a fear that if the fantasy were disrupted, the relationship might end, and so she could become, in the very next letter, blackly pessimistic.

Thus Katherine Mansfield allied herself with Murry's own class-defensive sense of being set apart from the grown-up world. Murry's recently published letters to Mansfield show that he reciprocated in cultivating the aura of childhood in their relationship. For example, he wrote early on: "I thought you were more lovely and lovable than ever this last weekend. O Tig, you were so sweet, and so like a little child that I feel like crying when I write it. I adore you, darling" (May 1913, JMM/KM 22). One of the most significant features in this childhood bonding was the playful nicknames that the two gave each other. Because in their early publishing venture they were named the two "Tigers" by a friend, they took to calling each other "Tig." Mansfield's name eventually shifted into "Wig," which became Murry's main term of endearment for her. Before long, however, she drifted from "Tig" to calling Murry "Bogey" or "Boge," and it is by those nicknames that readers of her letters are most likely to recognize him. The significance of Mansfield's shift lies in the fact that "Bogey" was also her private nickname for her brother (though he was called "Chummie" by his family). Mansfield's ultimate domestic fantasy was to establish a home with Murry and name it "The Heron," in memory of her brother, whose full name was Leslie Heron Beauchamp (Alpers, Life, 263).

In many ways, then, Mansfield's marriage to John Middleton Murry was her construction of a dream of childhood that might open up a creative domesticity for both of them. Her constant attention to their living quarters, furniture, and housekeeping arrangements, even in the throes of galloping consumption, indicates the intensity of her longing for the stability of a home with a real name to it. The positive goal of her regression needs to be emphasized here, for Mansfield's construction required a difficult negotiation with Murry's more resistant childishness to maintain its reparative equilibrium. Thus Mansfield's leaving him for the erotic interlude with Francis Carco in 1915 was at least partly a result of her impatience with Murry's intellectual childishness as well as, possibly, his lack of ardor as a sexual partner.

In his autobiography, Murry downplayed the sexual side, reporting that he and Mansfield were brought together for the first time as a result of the conjoining of his metaphysical terror at thinking about infinity (inspired by a book he had been reading on Egyptian cosmology) with their shared sense of emptiness—made more poignant by observing a prostitute in a cafe. The peculiar blend of occult speculation, acute sensitivity to the "corruption" around them, and general morbidness—especially as these speculations forced them into a solidarity in their search for some private human comfort—marked the rest of their lives together. Whether or not this pattern of dependency was more crucial to Mansfield or to Murry is by now almost impossible to decide. Murry presided over Mansfield's reputation for so long after her death that his version of her initiation of their attachment seems to have taken hold.[13] Thus he describes her spirituality as deriving from too much, too soon by way of sexual experience: "Her wings had been more badly bruised than mine, because she had more bravely flown against the bars . . ." (*BTW* 207). And thus he insisted on the myth of her being too good for the world, which easily elided into idealizing her tuberculosis as a "romantic" disease that afflicted only the purest and the best.[14]

In many ways, the conspiratorial exclusiveness of the bond between Mansfield and Murry seems the most pathological thing about them. Real and imagined threats from the outside world reinforced Mansfield's and Murry's cultivation of an image of themselves as two fond children playing together in a cottage from which the rest of the world could be excluded. Such a confused set of ideals was expressed in one of the more regressive of the stories that Mansfield wrote during her early relationship with Murry. "Something Childish but Very Natural" is the pathetic tale of two young people who meet on a London train and begin a platonic friendship. Eventually Henry begins to press for greater intimacy, but Edna explains to him:

"Somehow I feel if once we did that—you know—held each other's hands and kissed it would be all changed—and I feel we wouldn't be free like we are—we'd be doing something secret. We wouldn't be children any more . . . silly, isn't it?" (174–75)

The boy agrees, for the time being. Indeed from the start, Edna's purity has given him a sense of their specialness—their superiority to all the other boys and girls in London. He explains that the source of their unusual ecstasy is their childishness.

"My God," he cried, "what fools people are! All the little pollies that you know and that I know! Just look at you and me. Here we are—that's all there is to be said. I know about you and you know about me—we've just found each other—quite simply—just by being natural. That's all life is—something childish and very natural. Isn't it?" (171)

Despite her hesitance, however, Henry arranges a weekend rendezvous with Edna. He waits for her, dreaming of their joy, failing to realize that she cannot bring herself to submit to the rising pitch of sexual desire which their being together arouses in him. The story ends with the onset of darkness as Henry reads the telegram she has sent to tell him that she cannot come: "The garden became full of shadows—they span a web of darkness over the cottage and the trees and Henry and the telegram. But Henry did not move" (183).

Mansfield wrote this little allegory of a lost Eden in 1914, but she never included it in the collections of her work published during her lifetime.[15] Murry himself published it after her death, using it as the title story for a posthumous collection (1924). He seems to have felt that his own relationship with Mansfield followed the pattern set up in "Something Childish," though perhaps with the roles reversed—Mansfield the suitor and he the reluctant virgin. As a matter of fact, Murry recalls having used some of the phraseology about "sex spoiling everything" when he describes their courtship in his autobiography (BTW 208). Murry's account of his own innocence is somewhat suspect—he had already had his own bout with gonorrhea. In any case, it seems clear that Mansfield's and Murry's capacity for erotic intimacy was blocked. Murry's official biographer indicates that there was very little sensuality in their lovemaking: "There were no caresses, no preliminaries; their love-making (such as it was) was a climax without crescendo" (Lea 31). From an erotic angle, then, Mansfield's story of defeated child love may have contained a sting; perhaps Edna's decision to jilt Henry had more to do with his priggishness than his pallid eroticism. Although I don't want to engage in another round of Murry bashing here, I do want to suggest that his childishness was a characteristic that Katherine Mansfield sought to dislodge, even while she clung to the ideal of naive simplicity for the both of them. Certainly, she never wanted Murry to publish her immature, sentimental stories.

While Mansfield recognized the dangers of playing at sex, however, she did not fully recognize that the fragile idyll of love as "something childish" could set up a screen narrative designed to shield the bereft child from recognition of a primal scene that would imply that her own mother and father participated in the kind of eroticism which could ally them against their children. The allegory of the destroyed ice cream house in "Sun and Moon" hints some such scenario, for the destruction of the confection by adults which so upsets the little boy in the story is accompanied by his bewildered awareness of the sexual desire that has aroused his mother and father after their dinner party. When the children are brought out to witness the fragmentary remainder of the party after the guests have left, the boy senses that the parents are tipsily distracted and that when the father "pretend[s] to bite [the mother's] white shoulder," she is not at all cross (383). He finds the change in his parents, like the debacle of the used dinner table, terrifying.

Mansfield dreamed this primal scene story, almost entire, during one of the sleepless nights of her first wintering against tuberculosis in the south of France early in 1918, and she wrote about the dream in one of her hectically loving letters to Murry. She always coded her anxiety about his taking particular stories too personally by presenting their origins as mysterious, and her note on the composition of this slight piece suggests her underlying agenda in speaking to Murry: "I dreamed it all—about children. . . . Nothing is any good to me—no thought—no beauty—no idea—unless I have given it to you and it has become the property of these wealthiest little proprietors in the whole world Wig & Bogey & Bogey & Wig" (CL 2:66). In a parallel indulgence of childish fantasy, Sun's concentration on the ideal perfection of the make-believe house blinds him not only to the sexuality of his parents but also to the avidity of his sister—who simply wants to eat the leftovers. That he has to be sent away wailing to bed is both comic and pathetic. The dialectic of brother love is here collapsed by the aggression of the sister, who allies herself with the erotic maturity of the parents in wanting to partake of the feast rather than admire it in retrospect.

And so the assertiveness of female desire could destroy the daydream of mutual childhood. By the end of 1914, Mansfield was in frantic rebellion against the masculine abstraction of her retreat with Murry, and her reaction against it was to seek a return to the sexual excitement of earlier days. In a crucial episode during Christmas of 1914, she insisted on acting out a cuckolding of Murry with Mark Gertler so literally that Lawrence and the rest of their circle were shocked and amazed (Alpers, *Life*, 173).[16] Mansfield's diary entries for the final weeks of this first sojourn with the Lawrences illustrate her skepticism about the possibility of a male version of utopia, irritation with Murry's "intellectual mysticism," and sheer sexual tension. She had been receiving passionate letters from Francis Carco, who was stationed near the French front. She actually discussed going to him with Murry, sardonically recording his reaction in her journal: "When once I have left you I will be more remote than you could imagine. I see you and Gordon Campbell discussing the extraordinary time it lasted" (*Journal* 63). Carco offered sensuality, and she abandoned herself to that prospect, joining him in a barracks town near Paris in the spring of 1915. Recording the adventure in "An Indiscreet Journey," she accented the excitement of disguising herself to fool the military authorities. There is little of the helpless child in the narrator here; instead there is the satiric sang-froid of the same kind of adventuress who narrates many of the stories of *In a German Pension*. Moreover, the journal sketches from which this story was drawn were quite explicit about the erotic element, although Mansfield finally noted, "I don't really love him now I know him—but he is so rich and so careless—that I love" (*Journal* 75).

We can discern in this episode the difficulties Mansfield had with intimacy— vacillating between isolation with Murry in a fantasy of childhood regained and public promiscuity with Carco in the excitement of war. Though traveling near a battlefield, however, she moved in the closed circle of her own sensibility in which the actual suffering of the wounded French soldiers seen along the way intruded only as so many touches of local color: "The French Soldiers are pour rire," she commented in an unposted letter to Frieda. "Even when they are wounded they seem to lean out of their sheds and wave their bandages at the train" (*Journal* 74).

Making her way back to Paris, thinking little further of the war, she settled in Carco's apartment and began writing to Murry again in the most loving of terms. Reconciled to him, she nevertheless planned to stay and work in Paris, freed from all distractions. Writing from Paris in early 1915, however, Mansfield described herself again as a lonely child separated from her true love: "No, Ill *not* think of you like that—Ill shut my teeth and not listen to my heart. It begins to cry as if it were a child in an empty room & to beat on the door and say 'Jack—Jack—Jack and Tig.' Ill be better when Ive had a letter" (*CL* 1:158).

Thus her mode of bracketing the Murry relationship by working all alone in Paris could not last for very long, and Mansfield could not escape the worst consequences of the war.[17] When she returned to England in the summer to start up again with Murry, she invited her brother, who had been posted to

London in the army, into their ménage. She spent some happy days reminiscing with Chummie, for her brother's enthusiastic acceptance of his "famous" sister represented a welcome reinstatement into the Beauchamp family. Although at least one biographer suggests that Mansfield was not particularly close to her younger brother (they were, actually, six years apart in age),[18] he represented not only a link with home but an admiring one.

His own letters to Wellington indicate that he had become something of an emissary in her behalf, writing to reassure his parents about her health (he notes her bouts with rheumatism and neuritis), her financial situation, and her relationship with Murry. His first letter mentions running into her at the office of the family solicitor in London; her ignorance of the fact that he was already in London suggests the gap in communication between herself and the rest of the family. But Chummie's tone is boyishly cheerful and reassuring: "We went off together and picture her happiness at seeing one of the family, not having the faintest idea that I was coming over. She is more in love than ever with J. M. Murray [*sic*] which is a thing to be thankful for" (June 11, 1915, ATL). And then in August after visiting the two in St. John's Wood, "I was awfully glad to see how smoothly things were running" (August 25, 1915, ATL). Thus the reestablished link with her brother was a link with her family.[19]

In the fall of 1915, Leslie Heron Beauchamp was killed in France by a defective grenade he was demonstrating to the men under his command. He called upon the tie with his sister in his death: Mansfield reported to her friend Koteliansky that his last words were addressed to her: "'Lift my head, Katy, I can't breathe'" (*CL* 1:200). Mansfield was at first angry and numb, and then she decided that she could not bear her grief in the London she had shared with her brother. She took off for the south of France. The journal entries from her first weeks there are harrowing in their grief. She narrowed the circumference of her physical world, while she expanded her imaginative world to include in hallucinatory detail all the memories of the actual childhood she had shared with her brother. That world served her effort to redeem the past through reworking it in the present, replotting the Oedipal rivalry in such a way as to permit Chummie to be lifted up to breathe again.

Some critics have suggested that Mansfield's art became excessively nostalgic after her brother's death. I believe that her return to the New Zealand childhood in her later fiction is in fact an interrogation of the kinds of regression in which she indulged with Murry and which made them such targets for charges of calculated romantic posturing, such tempting examples of moral hypochondriasis.[20] Granted, the dreamy childishness in stories such as that of Henry and Edna is repellant. But for Mansfield to deal with her own past confusions—paralyzing confusions—and confront a future that would soon be enmeshed in a mortal illness, she *needed* to regress. In this instance, blame is less helpful to interpretation than a return to D. W. Winnicott's more benign view of the psychic uses of the personal past: "The psyche begins as an imaginative elaboration of physical functioning, having as its most important duty the binding together of past experiences, potentialities, and the present moment awareness and expectancy for the future" (*Human Nature* 19).

~

The death of Leslie Heron Beauchamp brought the complex of family and sexual feelings to a fevered pitch of emotional turmoil in Katherine Mansfield's imagination. The record is painfully elaborated in her journal writings from Bandol, in the south of France, right after his death. Her initial numbness of feeling, her self-isolation, her absorption in the private world of memory, and even her brutal hilarity (she had stonily answered a friend who inquired about her brother, "Blown to bits," with no further comment) simulate the symptoms of classic hysteria (Morris 115). But in the context of "normal" mourning, they are not pathological; Bowlby lists four phases in the process:

1. Phase of numbing that usually lasts from a few hours to a week and may be interrupted by outbursts of extremely intense distress and/or anger.
2. Phase of yearning and searching for the lost figure lasting some months or sometimes for years.
3. Phase of disorganization and despair.
4. Phase of greater or less degree of reorganization.   (III: 85)

The last phase incorporates an aspect of Freud's differentiation of mourning from melancholy in its emphasis on return to normal functioning: despite the intensity of this episode in her life, Mansfield returned to a productive life within the standard year. Having already begun "The Aloe," an initial draft for "Prelude," under the influence of mutual celebrations of old times in New Zealand with her brother, she intensified her program of recapturing the past by extending and recasting it, feeling that she "owed" her brother the debt of reestablishing his right to be born and cared for in an emotionally distant family.

At times, Murry was a guarantor of repayment; at times he was a threat to it. She made the link between her husband and her brother a matter of renunciation in a long, Brontësque journal entry just after Murry joined her in the south of France in 1916: "You know I can never be Jack's lover again. You have me. You're in my flesh as well as in my soul. I give Jack my 'surplus' love, but to you I hold and to you I give my deepest love. Jack is no more than . . . anybody might be" (*Journal* 86).

The brother/sister incest taboo had always shadowed Mansfield's feelings about her little brother; now the longing for some ultimate intimacy with the loved usurper became a passionate identification with him. In imagining her brother as a twin who takes over her body, Mansfield exhibits the remnants of a displacement reaction typical of a rejected child's efforts to salvage a sense of self. Erik Erikson has noted such pathology in the loss of such sibling relations among adolescents:

> Because of an early identity hunger, our patients are apt to attach themselves to one brother or sister in a way resembling the behavior of twins. . . . It is as if our patients surrendered their own identity to that of a brother or sister in the hope of regaining a bigger and better one by some act of merging. For periods they succeed, but the letdown which must follow the breakup of the artificial twinship is only the more traumatic. Rage and paralysis follow the sudden insight—also possible in one of a pair of twins—that there is enough identity only for one, and that the other seems to have made off with it. (*Identity, Youth, and Crisis* 178).

Mansfield's reaction to her brother's death involved such a loss of identity— thus the existential panic in her grieving. She spoke to her brother in her journal as if he were there—a part of herself—listening, and she alternated between frenzied writing and complete paralysis:

> Awake, awake! my little boy. A misty, misty evening. I want to write down the fact that not only am I not afraid of death—I welcome the idea of death. I believe in immortality because he is not here, and I long to join him. First, My darling, I've got things to do for both of us, and then I will come as quickly as I can. (*Journal* 86)

In spite of her ghostly conversations with the dead, however, Mansfield can now do something to reassert her own position in the grieving family. She can call into play an ethic of work, of the virtues that Erikson assigns to the successful triumph over adolescent identity confusion.[21] Her sense of competence, her ideological commitment to writing, transform her rebellious will to achieve independence into a familial project. And yet this purposiveness was still to be beset by reversions to images of herself as the helpless child struggling against fate.

The letter Mansfield wrote Murry on Christmas Day of 1915, as she antici-

pated his rejoining her in January, shows how she depended on the ideal of
their mutual innocence to work through her grief (*CL* 1:229–32). More intensely than ever before, she had to imagine that their love was a re-creation
of childish joy. She commences with a salutation that addresses Murry as "my
little King." Then she continues to describe her feeling for him in terms appropriate to the excitement of a child's Christmas morning. "I am so happy
and there are so many candles and angels burning on the tree that you have
planted in my heart that I can hardly write to you." In the midst of her fervor,
though, Mansfield is worried that Murry will be unfaithful when he goes to
spend the holiday at the house of one of their literary friends. She now feels
that they must be totally committed to each other erotically: "Before I write
any more I must tell you something. I hope you don't kiss anybody at Lady
Ottolines. After all I have said—it does sound absurd! But I minded you kissing
even Anne [Drey] 'seriously.' I minded you *really* kissing" (*CL* 1:230). Having
voiced her fears, Mansfield returns to the playful imagery of herself and Murry
as children. Murry's cable has been garbled in a charming way by the French
telegraph operator. His name had come through spelled "MErcy," and Mansfield fastens on this error as a sign that she and Murry are specially guarded
in their innocence: "I feel as though fate did it on purpose to show that she
really does love us and we really are her funny little children." She goes on to
describe the ecstatic feelings she had as she looked at Christmas toys for sale
in the little French town where she is staying: "I nearly bought an elephant or
a dog with one ear standing up, or a *lovely* tea set with roses painted on it &
a sugar basin with a tiny strawberry for the handle on the lid" (*CL* 1:231).
Her allusion to the extraordinary guardianship of fate in this letter may be an
expression of her sense that fortune has dealt hardly with her (her brother had
been dead for two months at the time), but it is also a return to her perennial
theme of the special election of children.

The rapt ideal of brother love was probably the most important aspect of
Mansfield's sense of providential support for her efforts to make recompense
to the dead. It haunted her sexuality with surreal concreteness when Murry
finally came to her in the south of France:

The night before, when I lay in bed, I felt suddenly passionate. I wanted J.
to embrace me. But as I turned to speak to him or to kiss him I saw my
brother lying fast asleep, and I got cold. That happens nearly always. Perhaps because I went to sleep thinking of him, I woke and was he, for
quite a long time. I felt my face was his serious, sleepy face. I felt that the
lines of my mouth were changed, and I blinked like he did on waking.
(*Journal* 95)

Her own being, sustained upon her ambivalent relationship with the loved brother and with all the lovers she had taken in his image, was profoundly threatened by his death, even as she sought to resurrect him through her art. She reports feeling that *he* is unhappy when she is not writing, hearing summonses from him, seeing him in the landscape when she looks out the window in the night. Putting these hauntings to rest, she must reattach herself as well as "Bogey" to the Beauchamp family. The greatest betrayal would be to neglect the work of memory, as she later illustrated so devastatingly in her portrait of a bereaved old man forgetting his son's grave in Flanders, distracted by a fly struggling its way out of an ink blot in "The Fly."[22]

In rebirthing her brother through her writing, however, Mansfield did not return to the *German Pension* mode, which concentrated on the sheer pain and drudgery of culturally required motherhood in which the delivery of children could be detached from the acceptance of them. The need for attachment required Mansfield to embrace an alternate ideology of motherhood which might mediate the resistance of the mother, especially the privileged and pampered mother, through recognition of the blameless imperative of the child's being. Helene Deutsch has suggested that in most cases the woman's self-loving fear of depersonalization in childbirth is displaced by love for her child, "and the idea of eternity inherent in reproduction overcomes her fear of being destroyed. The future triumphs over the present, but only if the past is favorably disposed of" (2:50). This is the kind of paradigm which Mansfield would eventually plot in "At the Bay."[23]

Writing, like childbirth itself, could bring such an obstetrical triumph of the future. Dedicating herself to Chummie, moreover, Mansfield would accommodate the troublesomely inadequate sexuality she had shared with Murry while engaging in the faithful creativity of the imagination. And the hoped-for progeny of this legitimate act of creation would be both the fully embodied narrative of the past and the son she expected to conceive with Murry.

Thus from the melancholy of unbearable loss, Mansfield drew new insight into childbirth and its possible power of reconciliation; she summarized her aims in writing "Prelude": "And you must mean the world to Linda; and before ever you are born Kezia must play with you—her little Bogey" (50). Nevertheless, Mansfield's construction of reconciliation must be framed by a sharp representation of women wasting their creative lives by succumbing to a range of hysterias. Thus "womb madnesses" beset Linda and Beryl, the two sexually active women of the Burnell family, who have neither the love of their children nor the consolations of memory nor meaningful work to do to overcome their fear of being destroyed. This mandate may explain why Chummie is not fully present in "The Aloe" or "Prelude" (Antony Alpers does think, however, that details in the story hint at Linda's pregnancy; *DE* 558). Chummie's birth occurs in "At the Bay," which Mansfield completed in 1921, long after the death of her mother.

~

When Katherine Mansfield turned again to childbirth as a focus in drafting the early version of "Prelude" in 1915, she wanted to slough off the ironic mode and the naturalistic style of her earlier childbirth stories. Thus in her final revision of "The Aloe" into "Prelude," she omitted a parenthetical description of her own birth: "She had come forth squealing out of a reluctant mother in the teeth of a 'Southerly Buster.'"[24] Such a loaded comment was at odds with her effort to remember her own childhood as poetry:

> Oh, I want for one moment to make our undiscovered country leap into the eyes of the Old World. It must be mysterious, as though floating. It must take the breath. . . . I shall tell everything, even of how the laundry-basket squeaked at 75. But all must be told with a sense of mystery, a radiance, an afterglow, because you, my little sun of it, are set. You have dropped over the dazzling brim of the world. Now I must play my part. (*Journal* 44)

One result of this resolve to tell everything is the pellucid detail of childhood perception combined with the rhythms and assonances of a prose designed to sing, as in the morning scene that begins the fifth segment of "Prelude":

> Dawn came sharp and chill with red clouds on a faint green sky and drops of water on every leaf and blade. A breeze blew over the garden, dropping dew and dropping petals, shivered over the drenched paddocks and was lost in the sombre bush. In the sky some tiny stars floated for a moment and then they were gone—they were dissolved like bubbles. (231)

In none of her earlier stories had Mansfield tried so hard, or so successfully, to let the natural setting unfold as a source of mystery unseen and unheard by human senses. This celebration of a childhood in nature required the perfection of a kind of poetic prose which would give a sense of the cyclical repetition of human life within a sad "idea of eternity" which might reconcile the mother to her son.[25] Here, although the bush is "sombre" and the stars dissolve after their brief moment, the continuity is magisterial. It is this kind of writing, foregrounded in the ecstatic avowals of Mansfield's journal, which may deflect critical attention from the complicated analysis of the feminine resistances to the depersonalization of such cyclical births and deaths in "Prelude" and "At the Bay."

But the text of "Prelude" actually begins not with the Wordsworthian sublime but with a scene of the callous rejection of her children by Linda Burnell as she moves to a new home in the country. There is no room for them in the carriage, if Linda is to have room for "the absolute necessities" that she will not let out of her sight "for one instant." Kezia and her younger sister must be remanded to the care of a helpful neighbor until the next cart can take them. Linda expresses her relief in terms that would appall a child psychologist such as John Bowlby: "'We shall simply have to leave them. That is all. We shall simply have to cast them off,' said Linda Burnell. A strange little laugh flew from her lips; she leaned back against the buttoned leather cushions and shut her eyes, her lips trembling with laughter" (219–20). In "The Aloe," it is Linda herself who negotiates with the neighbor to take care of the children, but in the revision of "Prelude," that decision is made by the grandmother. Linda's detachment from the scene in the final version is thus intensified not only by the grandmother's taking the role of presiding presence during the move but also by the heightening of Linda's hysteria in the "trembling with laughter" phrase. Indeed, Linda Burnell is a more active and attractive figure in "The Aloe," where pervasive, self-romanticizing melancholy and invalidism are assigned to a third sister, the mother of the Trout children, who was excised from the cast of characters in "Prelude."

In the mother's departure from their old home at the beginning of "Prelude," her younger daughter is patient with the prospect of the brief separation, but Kezia springs forward to claim a kiss from her grandmother. She is then left at the mercy of the rough neighbor children and eventually escapes them by exploring the emptiness of the Burnells' abandoned house, contriving stories as she does so. Interestingly, Kezia's vulnerability is emphasized in "Prelude," whereas in "The Aloe" she is capable of striking back at the neighbor children by playing a nasty trick on them (*A* 33).

In both versions, however, the reluctant mother's refusal to submit to the needs of Kezia and her sisters is set by this first episode of rejection. Though loosely structured by the progress of the first day at home after the little girls finally arrive and take their first sleep there, the narrative line is divided by shifts from one member of the Burnell family to another—moving among the children, Linda Burnell, the grandmother, and Linda's unmarried sister Beryl. This structure pretends to plotlessness in its associative wandering; certainly there is none of the obvious contrivance of sardonic revelation which motivated so many of the *German Pension* stories (and remained within Mansfield's arsenal for later stories such as "Bliss"). Rather, the theme of desertion is worked through Linda's fear of another pregnancy, Beryl's fear of isolation in the country with no prospects for marriage, and Kezia's fear of death.

Thus in the interweavings of "Prelude" Mansfield's sympathies for the entrapment of women become more mixed than in the *German Pension* stories. It is true that for the most part, however, her treatment of the father, Stanley Burnell, retains the irony deployed against the patriarchal Andreas Binzers of the world. Thus Mansfield's representation retains the edge and clarity of the earlier analyses of women's strategies to undermine and control patriarchy, even as it judges them for the manner of their desertion of their children. The focus in "Prelude" is only glancingly directed towards the male, however; the center of interest is the generational tensions of the women of the Burnell family laboring under the constraints of their roles. Indeed, under the brilliant encasement of the narrative of a day's domestic details in language of exact material and psychological precision, "Prelude" and "At the Bay" together provide a spectrum of cases of feminine aspiration driven underground for relief.

These innovative features of Mansfield's narrative experiments become clear early in the story as the Burnells prepare for their first night in a new house. Kezia, isolated by her mother's rejection of her, has turned to the grandmother for solace. Indeed, she treats the grandmother as a lover, in terms that recall Mansfield's lesbian desire—"Come to bed soon and be my Indian brave," she says (228). Aunt Beryl, the expectant virgin, thinks of another kind of lover as she prepares for sleep. But her longing is thwarted by social constraints that will eventually tempt her to a polymorphously perverse exploitation of her sexuality in "At the Bay":

> Somewhere out there in the garden a young man, dark and slender, with mocking eyes, tiptoed among the bushes, and gathered the flowers into a big bouquet, and slipped under her window and held it up to her. She saw herself bending forward. He thrust his head among the bright waxy flowers, sly and laughing. "No, no," said Beryl. She turned from the window and dropped her nightgown over her head. (229–30)

The mocking, laughing phantom lover is an ambivalently comforting and threatening phallic daydream, playing on Beryl's sexual desire and her fear of being violated. Such tensions make her desperate in her virginity. And her desperation blinds her to the needs of Kezia, upon whom she frequently turns with savage irritation.[26]

Once the confusions among the younger females of the family are established, "Prelude" moves to the father and mother in their lovemaking: "He slipped his arm under her neck and drew her to him. 'Yes, clasp me,' said the faint voice from the deep well" (230). Linda's response to her husband is submerged, almost anonymous, and when he is asleep at last, she has a terrifying dream.

> "How loud the birds are," said Linda in her dream. She was walking with her father through a green paddock sprinkled with daisies. Suddenly he bent down and parted the grasses and showed her a tiny ball of fluff just at her feet. "Oh, Papa, the darling." She made a cup of her hands and caught the tiny bird and stroked its head with her finger. It was quite tame. But a funny thing happened. As she stroked it began to swell, it ruffled and pouched, it grew bigger and bigger and its round eyes seemed to smile knowingly at her. Now her arms were hardly wide enough to hold it and she dropped it into her apron. It had become a baby with a big naked head and a gaping bird-mouth, opening and shutting. Her father broke into a loud clattering laugh and she woke to see Burnell standing by the windows rattling the Venetian blind up to the very top. (231–32)

This dream—more thoroughly surreal than Beryl's fantasy of the lurking male—is a compendium of motifs that posit interrelationships between hysteria, the fear of phallic potency, and the threat of the omnivorous baby.

It is significant that after she makes love with her husband, Linda's dream memory should be of her father. At first that is a pastoral and safe memory, but then her father turns on her, like all representatives of the male sex, and hands her a gift. The gift is a phallus that Linda initially accepts: "It was quite tame." But it is not really tame: it begins to grow as she strokes it—becoming too large for her to cope with and terrifying in the impersonality of its blind smile. By the time she drops it into her apron, it has become—like a variation on the pig in *Alice in Wonderland*—a baby. But the infant is not sweet and tender. Its most threatening aspect is its gaping mouth, opening and shutting as if to devour her. The relationship between eating and childbirth established in the *German Pension* stories thus persists, represented as masculine at its origin.

Linda Burnell wakes from her nightmare of the betrayal implicit in eroticism to the sight of her commonplace husband doing his sitting-up exercises. His glowing health and confidence contrast with Linda's incessant struggle against a biological destiny that she does not want. And after Stanley leaves, Linda daydreams again. All reality now takes upon itself the blind, knowing smile of the well-fed phallic infant bird of her earlier dream:

> But the strangest part of this coming alive of things was what they did. They listened, they seemed to swell out with some mysterious important

content, and when they were full she felt that they smiled. But it was not for her, only, their sly secret smile; they were members of a secret society and they smiled among themselves. (234)

The terror Linda feels as a woman trapped in her body's dreaded potentiality has led her to a form of semiconscious hallucination. The familiar secret smile is always waiting for her behind the objects of her surroundings.[27] Like her husband, who wants a son to round out his family of girls, everything seems to want something of Linda Burnell—"THEY knew how frightened she was," the narrative tells us; "What Linda always felt was that THEY wanted something of her" (234). Finally, then, Linda's anxiety about motherhood is not simply a problem about sexuality; it is a problem with existence itself. She has no rooted duties to help her cope with her existential fears, and in focusing on this lack of purpose Mansfield reveals herself to be a moralist of feminine hysteria.[28]

During her drowsy early-morning reveries in "Prelude," the voices of Linda's children are an intrusion: "They had been turned out after breakfast and told not to come back to the house until they were called" (233). Her children are always in exile because they give Linda no release from reality. Once her children have been reluctantly conceived and born, she must reject them as reminders of her servitude. Traumatized by fear of childbirth, Linda has turned the mothering of her children over to her own mother. When Linda finally comes down to breakfast, she finds her mother busily setting up the new household. When she asks what she might do to help, her mother asks that she watch after her own children. But Linda responds, "Of course I will, but you know Isabel is much more grown up than any of us" (238). Claiming the role of dependence for herself, Linda enacts hysteria as defensive escapism; her lassitude, as her mother gently suggests, is malingering.

The interchange between Linda Burnell and Mrs. Fairfield dramatizes the conflict between the good mother and the bad. Though Linda's own mother can humor her, however, Linda's daughter will not be so patient. Perceiving that a hysterical mother is terrifying, the ever observant child will note the symptoms of her willed invalidism. Mothers and their daughters are inevitable rivals, but they must overcome this rivalry if the younger woman is later to accept her own situation in the cycle of nature. The daughter who has felt her mother join with her in acknowledgment of her own birth and thus generation in general has her anxieties about birth and death mediated by a consoling figure. The aloe that grows in the Burnell's front yard provides the backdrop for the representation of the failure of this mother/daughter scenario in Mansfield's story. When Linda stands before the aloe with her most sensitive daughter in a short episode towards the beginning of "Prelude," Kezia asks her to explain the plant. As Linda gazes on it to give answer, another display of phallic imagery reiterates the ambivalence about birth—or flowering in this case—shown in Linda's dream.

> Linda looked up at the fat swelling plant with its cruel leaves and fleshy stem. High above them, as though becalmed in the air, and yet holding so fast to the earth it grew from, it might have had claws instead of roots. The curving leaves seemed to be hiding something; the blind stem cut into the air as if no wind could ever shake it.   (240)

When Kezia asks if the plant ever flowers, Linda answers with a smile and half-shut eyes, "Yes. . . . Once every hundred years." The indefinite statement and unseeing smile divide Linda from her daughter. She seems barely to recognize Kezia's need for some insight about the mysteries of birth and time symbolized by the aloe. Without some generational assurance of a more positive kind than Linda's smile, Kezia will be left alone in her own fears. Her life as a woman will also be beset by the phallic presence, the "blind" stem, as a threat.

Furthermore, the mother's obvious disdain for childbearing casts the father, and by extension the male principle, as a cruel threat in the eyes of the children. The sense of irrepressible phallic force plays in Linda's complaint against her husband: "If only he wouldn't jump at her so, and bark so loudly, and watch her with such eager, loving eyes. He was too strong for her; she had always hated things that rush at her, from a child" (258). Linda's phobic reaction to dogs is contagious. Kezia has inherited it: her own phobia against dogs—confided to a fatherly storeman early in the story—uses the same imagery as her mother's rejection of Stanley Burnell. "I hate rushing animals like dogs and parrots," Kezia says. "I often dream that animals rush at me—even camels—and while they are rushing, their heads swell e-enormous" (225). Significantly, such a fear of animals is a characteristic reaction of children who have undergone extended maternal separation (Bowlby 2:289). Thus not only Kezia's fears but her dreams reverberate to Linda's hallucinatory phantasms that entertain and justify abandonment of her children.

And with Kezia, separation incites hysteria about the threat of annihilation. This tendency rises to a crisis in the famous episode in which the child witnesses the killing of a duck for the first dinner in the new house. Unlike the other children who witness the act, Kezia screams loudly, demanding that the duck's head be put back on. She is finally consoled by Pat; the handyman who has killed the duck also takes her in his arms. His golden earrings distract and enchant the child, for they signify his crossing the line between masculine and feminine. Kezia's terror of death is thus consoled by foster figures but never by her mother.[29]

Later in "Prelude," Linda stands before the aloe plant again, this time with Mrs. Fairfield. Now, for a moment, the plant presents Linda with a qualified image of liberation. Linda thinks of it as a ship that might take her miles away and protect her from her Newfoundland dog. But her reverie of freedom quickly becomes another argument against her motherhood. She recalls Stanley's lovemaking:

> There were times when he was frightening—really frightening. When she just had not screamed at the top of her voice: "You are killing me." And at those times she had longed to say the most coarse, hateful things. . . .
>
> "You know I'm very delicate. You know as well as I do that my heart is affected, and the doctor has told you I may die any moment. I have had three great lumps of children already." (258)

And yet the aloe cannot be denied, and under the spell of its inevitability, Linda's thoughts become less self-isolating. She makes a grudging admission of her role in the biological cycle: "What am I guarding myself for so preciously? I shall go on having children and Stanley will go on making money and the children and the gardens will grow bigger and bigger, with whole fleets of aloes in them for me to choose from" (258). Linda Burnell thus comes to a limited reconciliation with birth by linking herself with the process of nature which the aloe symbolizes. And though she cannot give herself generously to her children, her grudging surrender to her biological destiny saves her from the near insanity of her morning dreams. Linda turns to ask what her own mother has been thinking while contemplating the century plant. Mrs. Fairfield's response implies a simpler acceptance of the basic tasks of nurture: "'I haven't really been thinking of anything. I wondered as we passed the orchard what the fruit trees were like and whether we should be able to make much jam this autumn'" (259).

Mrs. Fairfield is on familiar terms with nature, and she makes use of its fruits. She need not search out some "idea of eternity" to justify the mode of her existence; indeed, because she feels at one with all of life, "eternity" is implicit in all her acts. Only she among all the members of the family can move beyond incipient feminine hysteria to become a source of comfort for her grandchildren.

～

Linda Burnell's acceptance of the aloe in "Prelude" marks a temporary relief from her hysterical rebellion, but her final release is not imagined until Mansfield returns to finish off the recollection promised to rebirth her dead brother by writing "At the Bay." This sequel to "Prelude," finished in 1921 when Mansfield was aware that her dream of having her own child was impossible, brings the Burnell family together again during a summer's stay at the seaside. Though in narrative form and in the emphasis upon the natural imagery of the setting "At the Bay" continues "Prelude," it also shifts its emphasis. Here Beryl is more at center stage; indeed, the story seems crucially interested in showing the difficult transition from virginal girlhood to sexually mature womanhood through her portraiture. Despite the focus on Beryl, however, Linda Burnell is still very important in "At the Bay." She has finally given birth to the boy that Stanley has always wanted, but she still resents her forced motherhood. In fact, her resentment has become such a subject of conscious soliloquy that her rationale for it, rehearsed in "Prelude," has become an automatic feature of her consciousness. In her major scene, Linda is daydreaming as she sits out of doors with her sleeping infant. As always, she broods upon maternity:

> Yes, that was her real grudge against life; that was what she could not
> understand. That was the question she asked and asked, and listened in
> vain for the answer. It was all very well to say it was the common lot of
> women to bear children. It wasn't true. She, for one, could prove that
> wrong. She was broken, made weak, her courage was gone, through
> childbearing. And what made it doubly hard to bear was, she did not love
> her children. It was useless pretending. Even if she had had the strength
> she never would have nursed and played with the little girls. No, it was as
> though a cold breath had chilled her through and through on each of
> those awful journeys; she had no warmth left to give them. As to the
> boy—well, thank Heaven, mother had taken him; he was mother's, or
> Beryl's, or anybody's who wanted him. (279)

Feeling that she now understands her problem clearly, Linda turns to the infant lying nearby and tells him, "I don't like babies." But a surprise is in store for the reluctant mother. The infant seems so unconcerned, so smiling, that Linda is won over. Her unmaternal confession seems to open her heart to one of her children at last:

> Linda was so astonished at the confidence of this little creature. . . . Ah
> no, be sincere. That was not what she felt; it was something far different,
> it was something so new, so . . . The tears danced in her eyes; she
> breathed in a small whisper to the boy, "Hallo, my funny!" (280)

This unexpected relenting may be related to her production of a male child; Linda has never been so moved by her girl children. But her sudden release also rises from finding that her coldness is unimportant in light of the boy's right to be. The "confidence" of the infant is what intrudes on her self-isolation. She thus makes the necessary accommodation with nature in the form of her son, and that accommodation renews her capacity for more general sympathy.

Later in "At the Bay," Linda's acceptance of the child shows in her charity towards her brother-in-law, Jonathan Trout. Meeting her in the garden later in the day, Trout greets her as "little sister," asserting kinship so that he can pour out his problems to her. If Linda has been caught by the inexorable demands of her sex, he is equally imprisoned by the demands of social convention for men. The garden, which has held the images of threat for Linda, is an object of desire for Trout: "There's this vast dangerous garden, waiting out there, undiscovered, unexplored," he moans melodramatically (293). The now responsive Linda forbears to respond with the kind of irony she habitually applies to the sufferings of the male. She listens in a way that is indeed sisterly.

As Trout continues to talk, the sun begins to set, and Linda sees in it both the threat of a world made for men and the solace of the woman's destiny.

> In the western sky there were great masses of crushed-up rose-coloured clouds. Broad beams of light shone through the clouds and beyond them as if they would cover the whole sky. Overhead the blue faded; it turned a pale gold, and the bush outlined against it gleamed dark and brilliant like metal. Sometimes when those beams of light show in the sky they are very awful. They remind you that up there sits Jehovah, the jealous God, the Almighty, Whose eye is upon you, ever watchful, never weary. You remember that at His coming the whole earth will shake into one ruined graveyard; the cold, bright angels will drive you this way and that, and there will be no time to explain what could be explained so simply.
> (293–94)

The sympathy between Linda and Jonathan, between Linda and the world of men, is always to be qualified by the note of threatening masculinity invoked by the sun imagery of this remarkable passage. Linda glimpses the apocalyptic Hebrew father-god presiding over nature and promising only death and judgment. But Linda no longer cowers before this vision. The threat of nature has changed for her on the day she accepts her son. The passage continues:

> But to-night it seemed to Linda there was something infinitely joyful and loving in those silver beams. And now no sound came from the sea. It breathed softly as if it would draw that tender, joyful beauty into its own bosom. (294)

The maternal image of the sea now replaces the paternal image of the sun, and Linda can turn to her brother-in-law and say, with feeling, "Is it too late, even now?"

Linda's charity is genuine, but it is also fleeting. She can sympathize with a weak man, but she cannot quite forgive her powerful husband's egoism. In the section that follows Linda's session with Jonathan Trout in "At the Bay," we glimpse her again with Stanley Burnell. Full of the insecurities that have made his morning breakfast, earlier in the story, tense and suspicious, Stanley returns home from his day at the office remorseful for having forgotten to bid Linda good-bye. In typical fashion, he is hurt that Linda had not noticed, and in forcing his "sensitivity" upon his wife, he must exaggerate it: "Didn't you realize—you must have realized—I went away without saying good-bye to you this morning? . . . I've suffered for it enough today" (295). Linda indulges Stanley's awkward attempt to reinstate his preeminence in her life, but she cannot refrain completely from irony. During his day of "suffering," Stanley has found time to buy himself a new pair of gloves. Linda notes the fact silently, with a smile as impersonal as the blind, phallic smile that has been a feature of her anxious dreams:

> She pulled one of the large, pale gloves on her own fingers and looked at her hand, turning it this way and that. She was still smiling.
>
> Stanley wanted to say, "I was thinking of you the whole time I bought them." It was true, but for some reason he couldn't say it.   (295)

But resolving the mother's resistance to her children is not an easy or conclusive imaginative act in Mansfield's survey of domestic hysteria. She is interested in the socialization of women to such resistances within the family, and so the concluding episode of "At the Bay" is reserved for Beryl, Linda's younger sister, the expectant virgin—still longing for a lover to take her away from the Burnells. This preoccupation with her own imprisonment has turned Beryl into a self-conscious and posing creature whose fantasies alternate between the desire to remain a child and the urge to become a seductive woman. Caught between these two impulses, Beryl is as vulnerable to hysterical dislocations from reality as Linda has been. We have glimpsed her discontent in "Prelude," but "At the Bay" is even more fully focused upon her internal divisions.

As we have already seen, the expanded seaside society of the Burnells' summer home has put her in contact with Mrs. Harry Kember, a woman whose intimacy fascinates and repels Beryl. Mrs. Kember enjoys watching Beryl's body and encourages her to sexual adventures: " 'I believe in pretty girls having a good time,' said Mrs. Harry Kember. 'Why not? Don't you make a mistake, my dear. Enjoy yourself' " (277). Beryl is flattered by such talk, but as they are swimming together early in the day, she hallucinates the older woman almost as a sorceress, imagining her as a turtle and then a rat. She feels threatened by the poison of the woman's seduction.

As I have suggested, Mrs. Kember is the wicked witch who lures young maidens away into a perverse parody of lesbian desire as sterile narcissism. She has no children of her own; she is courting Beryl for her husband. When Harry Kember does appear in the Burnells' garden at the end of "At the Bay," however, he is not the rescuer Beryl has been dreaming of. Beryl walks out to meet him for a moment, perhaps still under the mesmerizing influence of his wife's courtship earlier in the day. But at the point at which sexual contact might be made, Beryl backs away—shocked by that same image of sexual impersonality which has figured in Linda's dreams. It is the image of the blind, phallic smile: "His smile was something she'd never seen before. Was he drunk? That bright, blind, terrifying smile froze her with horror" (298). Beryl flees from Harry Kember in this last action of "At the Bay," and in doing so she rejects the sterility of perverse heterosexuality. But her rejection is only tentative. She appears again in "The Doll's House" as even more cruelly trapped without a man to rescue her—engaging in furtive love affairs and lashing out at the children in her fear of being caught.

The question posed in both "Prelude" and "At the Bay" is whether the rejected Kezia will inherit the hysteria of her mother and aunt, or whether she can mature into a less neurotic femininity. At the close of "Prelude," we see Kezia playing with Beryl's face cream, furtively, and then sneaking away from it. In "At the Bay," it is Alice the servant girl who encounters the weird temptations of feminine vanity in the comic personage of Mrs. Stubbs with her "fair frizzy hair," her "plump neck," her new photographs of herself, and her photograph of her dead husband (287). Confiding that her husband had died of a superfluity that had been drawn from him—"one and a half pints from 'im at the 'ospital. . . . It seemed like a judgmint' "—she frightens Alice, who also wants to flee. Alice's fear is transferred in the following episode with the children, playing at animal games and thoroughly frightened by the sudden apparition of their uncle at the window.

In Katherine Mansfield's short stories, the woman's acceptance of sex and reproduction is always frightening. But there is a clear sense that the alternative is to flirt with the temptations of the inhuman. Thus in order to come to a limited truce with herself, Beryl must reject the witch's promise of sexual initiation without the responsibility of children. Beryl's episode with Harry Kember wakens her from her daydreams of romance, and she flees: "But Beryl was strong. She slipped, ducked, wrenched free." The moon, not the sun, presides in the short, concluding prose piece that ends "At the Bay."

A cloud, small, serene, floated across the moon. In that moment of darkness the sea sounded deep, troubled. Then the cloud sailed away, and the
sound of the sea was a vague murmur, as though it waked out of a dark
dream. All was still.   (299)

Thus Beryl must remain under a female influence, the moon that wakens
women from the dark dream of hysteria. Mrs. Fairfield, the grandmother, offers
such guidance for all the women of the Burnell family. She is the mythic midwife
who helps her daughters through the agonies of birth and who urges them to
reject hysterical fantasies so as to take responsibility for the next generation.
Mrs. Fairfield's changelessness and imperturbability link her with a simple acceptance of nature that neither of her daughters can manage completely. As a
final comment on the anxieties of sex and birth, Mansfield thus provides a
vision of eternally recurrent nature which both troubles and consoles.

~

Katherine Mansfield worked intensively on "Prelude" and "At the Bay" after
her brother's death. On the evidence of "The Aloe," some fragments of which
were probably completed before her brother's death, it seems that she may have
originally intended to write her reminiscences of New Zealand with an emphasis on the domestic comedy in the Burnell women's interactions. There is
a rejected scene in the early draft which shows Linda Burnell with her sisters
at tea and which plays like drawing-room comedy. And the episodes with Alice,
the servant girl, are mainly sketches of comic relief. But the death of Chummie
changed the direction of this draft, causing Mansfield to plot the way the interrelationships between the most significant female members of her family
inflected her own tendency to hysteria. Under this interpretation, Mansfield's
elimination of the episode that was to include Linda's other sister was not a
matter of simplifying the genre painting but a result of her design to establish
the plot of the hysterical mother's inscription within the psyche of the child.
Thus Beryl must become the pivotal child/woman hysteric, absorbing Linda's
hallucinations, engaging in at-risk behavior, transferring anxiety to Kezia, and
feeling profoundly dissociated from herself.

We have seen that Mansfield's journal for the winter of 1915 directly addresses her dead brother, committing herself to recording their childhood together. And this working out of memories of her childhood is accompanied by
her own longing for children. During the time of mourning through laying out
the New Zealand stories, she wrote Murry of a haunting dream:

I dreamed that I had a baby (Virtue always rewards me with this elfin
child) and Grandmother was alive. I had been to sleep after it was born

& when I woke it was night & I saw all the people in the house lying on
their backs asleep too. And I was sure my baby was dead. For a long time
I was too frightened to call anyone—but finally called to Grandmother &
she came in and said nonsense, child he's getting on beautifully (as
though "he" were a cake in the oven.) She brought him in to reassure
me—a charming little creature in a flannel gown with a tuft of hair. So I
got up and kissed Grandmother who handed me the baby and I went
downstairs & met you in the street.   (CL 1:207)[30]

The pattern of relationships between the child, the grandmother, and the husband can be discerned in this letter as a template for Mansfield's reminiscences
of her childhood. From the time she left New Zealand, she imagined her grandmother to be presiding over her life, and the presence of this self-assured
woman returns to comfort her dreams when she mourns the death of the
brother who was as a son to her, and as she looks to the possibility of carrying
life forward in his memory. These reparative sources of her New Zealand narratives are made even more explicit in a strange address Mansfield wrote to
her dead brother in early 1916:

The Aloe is lovely. It simply fascinates me, and I know that it is what you
would wish me to write. And now I know what the last chapter is. It is
your birth—your coming in the autumn. You in Grandmother's arms under the tree, your solemnity, your wonderful beauty. Your hands, your
head—your helplessness, lying on the earth, and, above all, your tremen-
dous solemnity. That chapter will end the book. The next book will be
yours and mine. And you must mean the world to Linda; and before ever
you are born Kezia must play with you—her little Bogey. Oh, Bogey—I
must hurry. All of them must have this book. It is good, my treasure! My
little brother, it is good, and it is what we really meant.   (Journal 98)

Katherine Mansfield's reenactment of the history of her family thus gives the rejected girl child the opportunity to rejoice "that a man is born into the world."
And she rejoices not because the birth of a brother has at last satisfied the patriarchal Beauchamp insistence for a son to validate the generative cycle. She rejoices
because the existential rights of the baby mandate his recognition; he must mean
"the world" to his mother. In Mansfield's scheme, the remembered grandmother
stands in the background, holding the child in her arms, quietly signifying the
consolations of birth by serving it in her old age, modeling a generational network
of interdependence. Birth, then, cannot finally be rejected as an insult to independence. The acceptance of it differentiates woman's willed creativity from surrender to womb madness. "The next book will be yours and mine."

CHAPTER 6

"*Je ne parle pas français*"

Tuberculosis and the Modalities of Perception

ON NOVEMBER 9, 1918, several days after she had gone to visit Katherine Mansfield and two days before the armistice was declared ending the Great War, Virginia Woolf described in her diary the changes that the initial bout with tuberculosis had wrought in her friend and main rival in writing:

> Katherine was up, but husky & feeble, crawling about the room like an old woman. How far she is ill, one cant say. She impresses one a little unfavourably at first—then more favourably. I think she has a kind of childlikeness somewhere which has been much disfigured, but still exists. Illness, she said, breaks down one's privacy so that one can't write—The long story she has written breathes nothing but hate. Murry & the Monster [L.M.] watch & wait on her, till she hates them both; she trusts no one; she finds no "reality." (*Diary* 1:216)

Although a source of their wariness about each another was their mutual inability to assess "how far" she was ill, Woolf's description of Mansfield shrewdly consolidates a number of the themes of the fatal disease that inscribed Mansfield's body and mind from the instance of its first unmistakable manifestation in a terrifying coughing up of blood on February 19, 1918, until its cessation in a fatal pulmonary hemorrhage on January 5, 1924. Mansfield lived on for almost six years in the debilitated state Woolf first encountered in the fall of 1918.

During this time, Mansfield wrote most of the fiction that has made her work an inescapable model for the modern short story; she wrote "Bliss," "The Doll's House," "At the Bay," "The Garden-Party," and "The Daughters of the Late Colonel" while she was desperately ill. "Prelude" is the only major New Zealand story written before tuberculosis turned her into an invalid. During her illness, Mansfield also wrote for Murry's *Athenaeum* more than a year's worth of reviews that form a body of criticism on the nature of the fiction of her day.[1] Moreover, since she was apart from Murry and her friends for a great deal of the time, she wrote letters and journal pieces enough to fill several volumes and to make her one of the most notable writers of personal prose in this century. Since her writing tends to flow so effortlessly and energetically, with a surface that is so controlled and a tone that is so vital, it has been easy to dismiss her work as "facile." It is therefore all the more important to consider the cost it exacted from Mansfield's vitality.

Annotating Woolf's description can dramatize the physical actuality of the conditions of her work. Being "up," for example, implies that Mansfield had to spend much of her day in bed. Moving her body about a room was an exercise of will over fatigue. Loss of weight changed her face from that of an incipiently buxom young woman to the ethereal, worn visage that has made it as evocative an icon of the woman writer of the twenties as are the photographs of Virginia Woolf. The isolation of her fatality had indeed "disfigured" those designs for the future which had motivated her through the writing of "Prelude"; she would not have children, though even in the worst of 1918 she hoped that the cessation of her menstrual period betokened pregnancy.[2] Isolation did not, however, bring the privacy needed for writing, for Mansfield found herself ever more dependent upon others to maintain the physical conditions necessary for her work. The requirement of special treatment also presented the demand for additional money to pay the medical bills, and Mansfield's penury—casually embraced as a feature of bohemian life early on—became an obsessive worry during her last years.

Finally, the frustration of utter dependency combining with the constant inspection of the body for illusory signs of returning health took a toll on her temperament—one that had been destabilized by the earlier crises that we have already surveyed. Thus she became a connoisseur of corruption, physical as well as psychological. Her trust in the stability of a normative "reality" ebbed and flowed, frequently leaving her in an address to life suspended between bitter, satirical "hatred" and hectic joy. In a notable assay of the sources of her art, she declared in a famous letter to Murry from the depths of her new illness in 1918:

> Ive two "kick offs" in the writing game. *One* is joy—real joy—the thing that made me write when we lived at Pauline [after Chummie's death], and that sort of writing I could only do in just that state of being in some perfectly blissful way *at peace.* Then something delicate and lovely seems to open before my eyes, like a flower without thought of a frost or a cold breath—knowing that all about it is warm and tender and "steady." And *that* I try, ever so humbly to express.

Katherine Mansfield,
1915. (ATL)

Katherine Mansfield's
passport photo, 1919.
(ATL)

Katherine Mansfield at Villa Isola Bella, 1920. (Ida Baker Collection, ATL)

The other "kick off" is my old original one, and (had I not known love) it would have been my all. Not hate or destruction (both are beneath contempt as real motives) but an *extremely* deep sense of hopelessness—of everything doomed to disaster—almost wilfully, stupidly—like the almond tree and "pas de nougat pour le noël"—There! as I took out a cigarette paper I got it exactly—*a cry against corruption* that is *absolutely* the nail on the head. Not a protest—a *cry,* and I mean corruption in the widest sense of the word, of course.— (*CL* 2:54)

The immediate occasion for this remarkable self-description was Mansfield's anxious explanation of the inspiration for one of her most disturbing stories, *"Je ne parle pas français."* She seems to have feared that Murry might read too personally the plotting of the story—which revolved around the abandonment by her fearful lover of a vulnerable young English girl to a French pimp in a country and city where her ignorance of the language will leave her unable to mediate her situation. Soon after she had become ill, Mansfield herself was hurried abroad to the French Riviera by her doctors, and on the way she was exhausted by the wear and tear of a country at war, becoming increasingly conscious of having been left alone by Murry in this ordeal. As Antony Alpers has shown, she wrote the story on a variety of sheets of paper, on the trains, in the hotel, in a flurry of frantic creativity. The manuscript evidence indicates that much of her writing was done on the fly, in bits and pieces. Illness drove her to extremities of contrivance in getting her writing done (*DE* 559). In her worry that Murry will read the story as an accusation, then, Mansfield overexplains the story in her account to him, but she also provides a general outline of her reaction to a kind of disaster which is "corrupt" in its irrationality, its cruelty, and its overturning of all faith in the future. The disease is a betrayal that embodies all the other betrayals of her life.

In this chapter it is necessary to investigate the way the corruption of the body—the hidden infection that had finally erupted in terrifying manifestations—impinged upon Mansfield's most desperate articulations of her situation in her fiction. I want to suggest here that Mansfield's experience of acute tuberculosis, of the endless diagnostic examinations she had to undergo to confirm its presence and chart its progress, and of its grim prognosis—all drove the narrative strategy in her second "kick off" as exploited in her experimental *"Je ne parle pas français."* I contend that that story reflected tuberculosis, as perhaps none of her others did. Its setting in Paris implies the contagion of the poor in the great city; the fragility of its isolated heroine points to the demographics of tubercular fatality for young women during the war; and, most important, the self-absorbed introspection of its narrator, Raoul Duquette, provides access to the self-concern of the stricken invalid—alert to the slightest nuance of internal meaning, impervious to other human or moral demands, and suffused by a profound sense of self-infection.

In letting Raoul Duquette speak out of his corruption, moreover, Mansfield listens to herself. She hears the crackle of the breath that pulls no air, the murmur of the heart that barely beats, and the pounding of a pulse that fails to give the body heat. Lodging these metaphors in her allegory of a demented mind, like Poe before her, she shocks even herself. But she also confronts the worst and then moves on to the most creative period of her short career. Like the late Anatole Broyard, she seems to have found that her illness gave her life, her writing, a deadline (4). Ultimately, however, I contend that in the process of living her illness, she skirts the precocious self-analysis involved in the diseased preoccupations of the aesthetes—for Raoul Duquette is above all an aesthete—to ally herself with Chekhov, the physician-writer who also died of tuberculosis.

~

The epidemiology of tuberculosis in the second decade of the twentieth century is marked by two contrary scientific attitudes. On the one hand, the isolation of the bacillus announced by Robert Koch in 1883 had seemed to promise rapid progress against the spread of a disease that swept away young adults and before 1890 "was rivalled among illnesses only by the venereal diseases and insanity" (Smith 1). Indeed, the germ theory of diseases helped to institute numerous public health measures designed to retard the spread of tuberculosis, even though there were indications (such as the lack of interfamilial infection in many cases) which undermined a general medical acquiescence to the theory of contagion. The French, for example, were reluctant to take extreme measures to quarantine consumptives, whereas the Italians had insisted on "isolation and fumigation procedures" since the nineteenth century (Smith 33).[3] Despite Koch's brilliant laboratory work, however, it was becoming clear even in the early twenties that the whole story of tuberculosis was not simply that of an invasion of the body's organs, especially the lungs, by an alien bacterium. Statistical studies began to indicate that tuberculosis was a social as well as a bacteriological disease; it was affected decisively by environment.

The bacterial theory eventually led to measures of public sanitation that instigated public legislation on such behaviors as spitting and washing hands in food service and on public procedures such as pasteurization of milk and inspection of the food supply. F. B. Smith suggests that the emphasis on asepsis in the antituberculosis drives of the twenties and thirties was at the source of the new emphasis on the smooth, washable surfaces and the uncluttered spaces of modernist interior design (121–22). The environmental theory added to these measures of antisepsis an emphasis on public nutrition, well-ventilated public housing, and the benefits of outdoor exercise, natural foods, and regular vacations. Indeed, one of the classic preantibiotic studies of environment and health, René and Jean Dubos's *The White Plague* (1952), showed that although bacteriology promised help in the fight against tuberculosis, "the hereditary constitution, the physiological state, the nature of environment, and all the stresses and strains of life [were] of paramount importance in determining whether infection [would] manifest itself in the form of progressive disease" (128). The miracle drugs streptomycin, PAS, isoniazid, and rifampicin were, however, just on the horizon at the time of the Dubos book; within a half-dozen years they would offer a definitive cure for the disease and shut down hundreds of sanatoriums.[4] As proponents of the social construction of tuberculosis point out, however, modern chemotherapy simply accelerated the close of an epidemic that was already waning as a result of healthier lifestyles in Europe and North America.[5]

The victory over tuberculosis was not, then, another story of miraculous scientific discovery eliminating a major scourge, though there were elements of that story in what actually happened. But as modern histories of medicine have become more cognizant of the multiplicity of forces in cure, and less a string of hagiographies of famous doctors, the history of tuberculosis has been problematized. It is now seen to have been caused not only by bacteria but by a congeries of forces—possibly including genetic disposition and allergic sensitivities but certainly involving the physical and mental environment of individual patients. Even as early as 1918 a study by the Medical Research Committee, *An Inquiry into the Prevalence and Aetiology of Tuberculosis among Industrial Workers, with Special Reference to Female Munitions Workers,* revealed that the percentage of young women (fifteen to thirty-five years old) dying of the disease increased significantly in the cities and towns of England during the war years. It was not only the stress of war work which made young women susceptible; it was lack of air and sun, poor nutrition, crowding in urban housing, and general anxiety. Thus while young men died on the front, young women at home lived within the shadow of lung disease: in Britain, 1.3 per 1,000 died of tuberculosis in 1914, and that increased significantly to 1.65 per 1,000 in 1918 (Smith 222). In the London area, phthisis (as the last stage of tuberculosis was then called) was the leading single cause of death for women in their late teens and twenties, accounting for more than 45 percent of the fatalities in 1916 (Medical Research Committee 16). Thus, although munitions factories provided access to "real" employment to women (L.M., for example), they were dangerous places, and work in them was a hazard to general health.

Although, as Gilbert and Gubar have shown, some masculine evocations of the Great War from the front envied the healthy woman safely pursuing her new freedom at home as "an apotheosis of femaleness, a triumph of women who feed on wounds and are fertilized by blood" (*Sexchanges* 262), the statistical truth—in which Katherine Mansfield was a figure—was that the war took its toll on women at home, killing them off in significant numbers through tuberculosis and its corollary complications in the influenza pandemic of late 1918.

The 1918 study of wartime tuberculosis for women expressed its social and economic truth in stark, Darwinian terms: "We know that, in the mass, the robust die at a lower rate than the weaklings, that also the rich die at a less rate than the poor" (Medical Research Committee 7). Given the fact that Katherine Mansfield started out the decade in a robust state of health and was, if not rich, at least not destitute, a number of her biographers have unknowingly adopted the simple germ theory of her tuberculosis, attempting to designate some personal carrier for the bacillus that infected her. Knowing what we do about the environment of the disease, however, we need not hypothesize about whether Murry himself (he was turned down for the army because of suspicious lungs), D. H. Lawrence, Mark Gertler, or the child she took in for the summer in Bavaria was the source of her initial infection. What is quite clear is that tuberculosis was part of the bohemian way of life which Mansfield chose to live in London.[6] From the time she went there, she lived an erratic schedule with meals on the fly, an addiction to cigarette smoking,[7] and irregular sleep. Going back and forth to the Continent, she associated with artists who had varying histories of disease, and she unknowingly subjected herself to the general debilitation and contagion involved in travel. She and Murry moved from one cheap flat to another in London and in Paris; in one such move, for example, they had to fight off an infestation of bedbugs. And finally, Mansfield's infection by systemic gonorrhea in 1911 rendered her vulnerable for the rest of her life; its effects possibly masked early symptoms of tuberculosis in her case. Mansfield had been subject to bouts of "pleurisy" since the time of her living with William Orton, and since tuberculosis is a disease of activity and arrest, it is possible that such episodes, as well as periods of general fatigue and malaise, could have had their origin in tubercular infection.

In addition to all these clinical possibilities, the seriousness of Mansfield's illness may have been masked by a mentality in Mansfield's subculture which tolerated the nineteenth century's glorification of consumption as an extended metaphor of tragic romantic lyricism. There is a litany of the heroes of the disease in nineteenth-century lore: in opera the lady of the camellias in *La*

Traviata and Mimi of *La Bohème*; in literature the saintly Helen Burns of *Jane Eyre,* and the rebellious Nikolay Levin of *Anna Karenina*; and in famous lives Keats above all, but also Chopin, the Brontës, Marie Bashkirtseff (whose diary Mansfield read in New Zealand), A. J. Symonds (another fin-de-siècle prose model), Rilke, Modigliani (Beatrice Hastings' lover), and Kafka.[8] Mansfield was aware of this heritage, for when she reported her first hemoptysis (coughing of blood) in a letter to Murry from France, she emphasized its significance by alluding to Keats—"When I saw the bright arterial blood, I nearly had a fit" (*CL* 2:79–80).[9]

At this crisis point Mansfield began to think of the long-term implications of the disease, urging Murry to keep himself warm and to eat well. In her journal, she was more open about her terror: "Oh, yes, of course I'm frightened. But for two reasons only. I don't want to be ill, I mean 'seriously,' away from Jack is the first thought. 2nd, I don't want to find this is real consumption, perhaps it's going to gallop—who knows?—and I shan't have my work written. *That's what matters.* How unbearable it would be to die—leave 'scraps,' "bits" . . . nothing real finished" (*Journal* 129). The question was no longer, then, whether Mansfield had tuberculosis; the question was what phase of the disease she was experiencing and how much longer she had to live. The answer must come from expert medical examination in a period in which the etiology of the disease might be known but its assessment was still highly problematical.

According to a 1939 textbook, *Pulmonary Tuberculosis in Adults and Children* (Miller and Walgreen), the definition of the stages of tuberculosis was relatively difficult to discriminate clinically—even after the institution of the tuberculin test for sputum and the x-ray of the chest, two modes of diagnosis which were still in a rudimentary state when Katherine Mansfield became ill.[10] The discrimination of phases, however, was particularly important because it could inform the physician about the best course of treatment. Since tuberculosis is an intermittent disease, the outbreak of fever, night sweats, coughing, and general malaise can betoken either a mild development or a massive change in the lungs. For one thing, the body's reaction against the infection frequently involves a walling off of the site of the outbreak in a tubercle, or encapsulated node, which might render the infection dormant for years. In the last stage of tuberculosis, called phthisis because of its characteristic feature of "wasting" the body, the "exacerbation of some of these localized, often long-latent, lesions in the lungs" activates the movement of the bacteria through the bronchial passages and into the general blood and lymph system of the body. Using the wonderfully dramatic vocabulary of descriptive medicine, the 1939 textbook speaks of the spread moving "very gradually, insidiously, and more or less continuously, or . . . abruptly, acutely, and interruptedly" (13).

In the eruption of the disease, not only are the lungs affected, but there are possible complications in ulceration of the gastrointestinal tract, anorexia caused by metabolic dysfunction, joint inflammation, and the infiltration of lymphatic glands, especially in the neck area. All of these complications—which Mansfield suffered—can take years to unfold, but the end result, the "terminal phthisis phase," is a "fatal end." "We observe this in chronic consumptives whose resistance has become exhausted in the course of a long-protracted disease, or even in patients with latent or arrested lesions flaring up in association with some severe crisis in their physical, social-economic, and mental well-being" (Miller and Walgreen 16). Mansfield's initial worry was about her possible situation within this third stage—"galloping consumption"; in fact, her first hemoptysis probably involved a flareup that was only a prelude to further encroachments of the disease, marked by severe weight loss, fever, and final exhaustion six years later. That she held on so long is remarkable, for she never seems to have been in significant remission during this time. By contrast, D. H. Lawrence—whose health Mansfield worries about in 1919 (*CL* 2:304)—was clearly tubercular during the war years but held on until 1930. Mark Gertler was in and out of sanatoriums through the 1920s and again in 1936. His suicide in 1939 would have been, at least in part, a delayed result of tuberculosis.

The insidiousness of the progress of tuberculosis had implications for the success of its treatment because the sudden alleviation of symptoms, or the continuation of them at only a chronic low-grade level, could lull patients into believing themselves well and behaving accordingly. That is why the diagnosis of the stages of the disease was such a matter of concern. To what extent had the infection spread in the lungs? Were there large areas of cavitation? Or had active infection finally been caseated by the white blood cells into a cheeselike substance that would either block the lungs or finally soften into liquid form that might be expelled through coughing and expectoration? Or had the body successfully encased the lesions by fibrosis or calcification, essentially walling off the alien effects? Such developments would inhibit lung capacity, to be sure, but the end result would be some level of viability.

Sputum tests could confirm the presence of the bacillus, and x-rays might calculate the progress,[11] but the seriousness of the total prognosis must be decided by the physician's two most important diagnostic tools—the case history and those procedures for attending to the body's internal signs which had been contrived by specialists in lung disease during the nineteenth century.[12]

The case history involves the physician in the novelist's art, for it requires an eye for obscure material clues allied with an ability to interpret the patient's total life story:

Realizing the marked tendency of tuberculosis toward latency and its tendency to masquerade under a great variety of trivial ailments or other misleading conditions, we must not overlook any symptom or complaint of the past. The correlation of preceding events, often widely separated in time, and the localization of their focal symptoms will aid us in piecing together the story of the evolution of the tuberculous process in the individual in question. (Miller and Walgreen 27)

Under this kind of mandate, it is no wonder that excellent clinical practitioners have had a facility for listening attentively and minutely to the story of a patient's life and even becoming masters of narrative themselves; significantly, the creator of the detective story was trained as a physician.[13] The ability to read the illness's whole story was a feature of Mansfield's trust in her relations with physicians: sympathy and narrative emphasis were always desiderata in her continuing search for an adequate doctor. She was very impressed with her first doctor because he read Tolstoy. Of course, this search for sympathy could also be a form of denial, and it may well be that Mansfield neglected the biological side of her disease through her emphasis on defining it as the culmination of her lifelong illness of the spirit. Always a contriver of illness narratives, deeply implicated in her own mother's illness story, Mansfield searched her own symptoms with her doctors to discover a positive denouement. And when the doctor's plotting failed to fit her own design, she placed upon herself the entire mandate of cure.

She became involved with the reporting of her various doctors' emphases and conclusions to an anxious Murry. Many of her letters to him are inventories of her symptoms, and though she withheld the most serious ones, she reported carefully the implications of each physical change. She could, as we have seen, be comic about bodily symptoms. A doggerel verse that she sent to a woman friend apologizing for missing a New Year's party in 1919 illustrates her gift for making light of her pain when describing it to mere acquaintances:

> After my Plan
> For New Year's Day fell through
> I gave up hope
> Of catching a rope
> Which would land me down near you.
> Since then Ive been
> (Pulse one sixteen
> Temperature one o three)
> Lying in bed
> With a wandering head

And a weak, weak cup of tea.
Injections, chère
In my derrière
Driven into a muscular wad
With a needle thick
As a walking stick—
How *can* one believe in God!
Plus—pleurisy
And je vous dis
A head that went off on its own
Rode a circular race
That embraced every place
I ever shall know or have known.

(CL 1:222–23)

The gallantry of this kind of humor was very hard to sustain day by day within the domestic circle, and it was Murry and L.M. who heard the other, more bitter and plaintive version in Mansfield's letters.

Beyond the case history, the standard diagnostic procedure for tuberculosis involved close physical examination that included the classic operations of "inspection, palpation, percussion, and auscultation" (Miller and Walgreen 37).[14] One of my reasons for emphasizing these procedures of discernment is to adjust Michel Foucault's emphasis on the clinical "gaze" in his brilliant analysis of the history of late-eighteenth-century French medical practice. Characteristically, Foucault extrapolates generalizations about individual mentalities from a fragment in the culture's approach to disease, in this case by way of the specular and socially open nature of the French clinic's public display of the patient. I want to suggest here another kind of mentality derived from the altogether more private, inward modality of *listening* to the patient's chest. In the case of tuberculosis, inspection and palpation, operations on the surface, are secondary to auscultation and percussion, sonar penetrations of the interior. Because of the privacy and intimate silence of auscultation and percussion, I believe, the patient's knowledge of his or her sickness is likely to operate in a mode of interior wariness.[15] Thus Foucault's analysis may lend itself more readily to forensic kinds of ailments (madness, hysteria, tumors) available to the audience of the clinic than to the kind of ailment which requires a doctor to come close to the body and listen to the dullness or hollowness of the sounding board of the chest cage. He must also listen through the stethoscope for faint crackling sounds of the oxygen exchange at the pulmonary ends of the alveoli, for telltale wheezes at inspiration, or for murmurs around the heart.

And he may ask the patient's cooperation in taking various depths of breath or whispering softly so as to trigger the ventriloquism caused by the hollowness, the excavation, made by disease within the ribs. Such listenings require delicate discriminations, extreme patience, and intimacy with the sufferer.[16] In the close space between the doctor and patient, the stakes being so high, there can be no modesty, no withholding of the body as an instrument of its own revelation, but although the examination is an unveiling of the body, its technique is private. Thus in describing her first examination for the "pleurisy" that began her career in tuberculosis, Mansfield notes that "that man has just been—the doctor—& thumped away" (*CL* 1:344). Then a week or so later, she has to report on more ominous diagnostic sounds: "He says that left lung of mine that had the *loud deafening* creak in it is 'no end better' but there is a SPOT in my right lung which 'confirms him in his opinion that it is absolutely imperative that I go out of this country & Keep out of it all through the future winters'" (*CL* 1:356).[17]

In tuberculosis, then, specularity gives way to sonority as the source of diagnostic signification. In accordance with that transition, or so it seems to me, Mansfield's sense of herself in her journal and letters shifts from self-imaging to self-listening. The dramatic confrontations with images in lighted mirrors seem less significant than the audition of noises from the alien outside world of the healthy, or the howling of night winds which troubles profound insomnia, or the cough and wheeziness of her own body—the inspiration and suspiration of what she called her "puff."

In June 1918, Mansfield endured one of the worst periods of her illness in a resort hotel off the coast of Cornwall. She had just returned from the stay in the south of France, excited by the fact that her divorce had been granted and that she and Murry could marry at last. But the marriage day had been disappointing; Murry had never really held her and indeed had surreptitiously wiped his lips with a handkerchief after they kissed. So frightened was he by her appearance upon her return from France that he had arranged for her to go away again to build up her health. Mansfield's cataloguing of her sensations in the sickroom of this second retreat illustrates the invalid's habit of listening for sounds to interpret as the sights of the room, quarantined by illness, remain inert in their deadness of detail:

> *Friday, June 21* What is the matter with to-day? It is thin, white, as lace curtains are white, full of ugly noises (e.g. people opening the drawers of a cheap chest and trying to shut them again). All food seems stodgy and indigestible—no drink is hot enough. One looks hideous, hideous in the glass—bald as an egg—one's feet swollen—and all one's clothes are tight.

And everything is dusty, gritty—the cigarette ash crumbles and falls—the marigolds spill their petals over the dressing table. In a house nearby someone is trying to tune a cheap piano.   (*Journal* 138)

The presence of a mirror in this scene is interesting because it must be avoided. The glass can only be glanced at; its reflection is too ghastly to be sustained. And touch is deactivated as well; there is a low-level sensation of the body, but its discomforts are at a steady state. Sounds are the sensory data that the invalid can interpret and enlarge into meaning outside the body; they place her within an ongoing world and call upon her ability to listen within the perceptual field to generalize the nature of that world. Proust, a great authority on the invalid's dependence on sound, has worked out the perceptual equation:

> And I settled down again to listen, to suffer; when we are kept waiting, from the ear which takes in sounds to the mind which dissects and analyses them, and from the mind to the heart, to which it transmits its results, the double journey is so rapid that we cannot even detect its course, and imagine that we have been listening directly with our heart.   (*Cities of the Plain* 95)

Proust's analysis tends to linger over each phase in his reception of sensation; Mansfield's decodings in her spontaneous writing are, however, immediate and impetuous. There is a story behind every sound, usually of the cheap realities of transient life. But in her formal stories of the stay-at-homes, Mansfield shows that such noises may bring in the only interest of a wasted day; her neurasthenics are so bereft of vitality that they are extrasensitive to noise. Thus noise may intensify the sense of suffering by contrasting the feeble world of the sick person with the vital world outside.

Another passage from Mansfield's jottings in the lonely Cornwall period of her early illness shows how the presiding modality of sonance in her experience of illness intensifies her articulation of the sick person's isolation. Although Murry's *Journal* edition reproduces this passage as prose, Philip Waldron notes that it actually appears in the manuscript as verse, entitled "Malade":

> The man in the room next to mine
> Has the same complaint as I.
> When I wake in the night I hear him turning.
> And then he coughs.
> And I cough.
> And after a silence I cough.
> And he coughs again—
> This goes on for a long time

> Until I feel we are like two roosters
> Calling to each other at false dawn
> From far-away hidden farms.
>   (*Journal* 139; Waldron 16)

Mansfield thus lives a silent, inward private life, except for the sounds her body makes. But this personal silence is, like the doctor's, an attentive listening to the interior alarms of progressive disease punctuated by echoes from outside. Here, the answering cough of a fellow sufferer is no less poignant for the comic image of the answering rooster which Mansfield attaches to it. The cough displaces the mirror as the source of her identity, and in one letter she comments that she has *become* her cough.

Moreover, since one of the classic symptoms of acute tuberculosis is the labile alternation of moods (Miller and Walgreen 31), the inner listening becomes a psychic as well as a somatic application of diagnostic technique. Like the body's temperature, which in tuberculosis tends to be low in the morning, rise in the afternoon, drop again, and then erupt in night sweats, the psychic register is so unstable as to require incessant gauging. Mansfield recorded such soundings in the letters that she wrote to Murry, the moods of which ascended and fell like the lines on a fever chart. Thus in a coruscating letter from Cornwall on May 27, she writes of the agony of her isolation, vows the intensity of her love for Murry, accuses him of betrayal of her suffering through insensitivity, vows her love again, and finally ends with a plea for quiet: "So now, please God, let us be calm again. *I will not be sad.* Let us be calm. Let our love keep us quiet & safe—like two children in a great big quiet field—sitting there hidden in the flowers & grasses" (*CL* 2:198).

Such violent swings involved listening to her querulous inner voice as well as her reverberating body, and the two auscultations blended in a number of her stories of self-enclosed invalids who cannot find the quiet field of childhood. When these stories target the corruption of the central character, there is likely to be more emphasis on the material clues of the psychic disease and less on its history. The result is a kind of clinical ventriloquism which amounts to authorial mockery of the character. "Bliss" is such a story, and so is the story of Monica Tyrell's terrible morning in "Revelations." The latter story introduces Monica's neuroticism through showing her extraordinary sensitivity to the sounds of life outside as her maid comes into her bedroom at the beginning of the story. In this cry against the corruption of women, Mansfield contrasts the hypersensitivity of the false invalid with the genuine illness of the daughter of Monica's hairdresser, who has died during the night. Monica must flee this site of genuine illness at the end of the story and take herself off to a fashionable restaurant for lunch. Mansfield expressed the connection between death and moral corruption even more explicitly a year later, writing to Murry about being cheated while she was staying on the Italian Riviera: "Oh, it is agony to meet corruption when one thinks all is fair—the big snail under the leaf—the spot in the childs lung—what a *wicked, wicked* God! But it is more than useless to cry out. Hanging in our little cages on the awful wall over the gulf of eternity we must sing—sing—"(CL 3:37).

～

Mansfield wrote *"Je ne parle pas français,"* the first story of her new illness, in the early winter of 1918 while she was feeling abandoned by Murry on her way to the south of France. She had gone to Paris and then made a nightmarish train trip to Bandol, the scene of their time together in 1915 when she had written out the grief of her brother's death. But she found everything changed by the war, herself unrecognized by old friends, the soldiers on the train threatening, her hotel dingy, and its proprietors unpleasant about her cough. Unable as yet to accept fully the seriousness of her illness and its requirement for days of absolute rest, she was in a state of continuous frustration. And yet she wrote.

She was aware that the story was a dangerous one: reassuring Murry, she wrote, "I hope youll see (of course, you will) that Im not writing with a sting. Im not indeed!" (CL 1:56). The question of the sting in Katherine Mansfield's satirical stories is of long standing: some of her critics have found the modernist astringency of stories such as *"Je ne parle pas français"* to be a welcome relief from nostalgic sentimentality in her more lyrical stories. Other critics are uncomfortable with such vengeful cynicism and prefer the more subtle emotion of her memories of childhood. My own inclination is to find *"Je ne parle pas français"* more valuable as a technical experiment that was profoundly influenced by illness than as a satisfying sample of her art at its best. Indeed, the defensiveness in her letter to Murry strikes a false note that rings through the manipulations of blame in the story itself, for it is clear that Mansfield did write with a sting. The story itself reveals her personal animus in two of its major features: the setup of the vulnerable young woman as a blameless victim of male carelessness, and the relentless homophobia—a displacement of her anger at the treacherousness of the straight male—loaded against Raoul Duquette.

Nevertheless, Mansfield exercises the powers of her enforced silence and her attendant clinical awareness in revealing the corruption of a man who seeks to quiet it by always talking. She lets the central character speak for himself, forcing the reader to listen intently for clues to interpretation. Mansfield had narrated many of the *German Pension* stories in the first person, to be sure, but she had never dramatized the narrative voice as a critical character in its own telling.[18] I don't want to stretch the clinical metaphor too far, but I hazard the suggestion that the narrative voice in this story represents the muffled sonority of illness which turns the monologue from a communication with an auditor (whose status is never dramatized in the story) into an internal echo in which the speaker's sense of himself as diagnostician reverberates back into a verdict about his own essential disease. The voice of the degenerate thus speaks his disease in isolation.

At the beginning of "*Je ne parle pas français,*" Raoul Duquette is sitting in a low café, watching the passersby, his observations underlaid by the incessant murmur of the self which sounds in a kind of ventriloquistic diagnostic stream:

> And the moment of hesitation as to whether I am going to be fooled just before I chalk that squiggle, and then the other moment of hesitation just after, as to whether I have been, are perhaps the two most thrilling instants in life. Yes, they are, to me. (351)

Duquette goes on in such a manner for several pages before he reports recently coming across the phrase "*je ne parle pas français.*" That banal sentence triggers a physical and emotional frisson that inspires him to tell his story in a mode that claims its fevered introspection as a special gift of temperament:

> There! it had come—the moment—the *geste*! and although I was so ready, it caught me, it tumbled me over; I was simply overwhelmed. And the physical feeling was so curious, so particular. It was as if all of me, except my head and arms, all of me that was under the table, had simply dissolved, melted, turned into water. Just my head remained and two sticks of arms pressing on to the table. But, ah! the agony of that moment! How can I describe it? I didn't think of anything. I didn't even cry out to myself. Just for the one moment I was not. I was Agony, Agony, Agony. (353–54)

Such anatomical precision in Duquette's rehearsal of the onset of his crisis emphasizes the immediacy of the connection between his psyche and his body; but the body here is dislocated into a diagrammatic disjuncture of head, arms, and remainder. Before he attaches his own interpretation to the impulse to respond to an incident in the past, the somatic details must be recorded. They imply a psychological suffering that is like physical pain but in hysterical exaggeration. Not content with letting the physical reaction tell its own story, then, Duquette applies his version: "And up I puffed and puffed, blowing off finally with: 'After all I must be first-rate. No second-rate mind could have experienced such an intensity of feeling so . . . purely'" (354).

The perennial theme of childhood is present in the story, but innocence is displayed as its most pathological perversion. Mansfield thus exhibits the way a character can lose the essential health of his childhood, misusing his longing for some lapsed state of innocence as a cover for extreme cynicism. Childhood, in this version, is the source of moral infection, and the memory's encasement by aesthetic pretension here cordons off a festering locus for further toxicity. "About my family—it really doesn't matter. I have no family; I don't want any. I never think about my childhood. I've forgotten it" (355). In such a representation, Mansfield is figuring the negative version of her own nostalgia when its reference is the immature ego rather than the effort to repair through memory. Indeed, she provides in the abandoned young woman of the story a childlike victim to vindicate the narrative animus against its own patient.

The phrase has reminded Duquette of his lost love for an English man named Dick Harmon. When Harmon had returned to England after their first intimate episode together, Raoul was bereft: "I felt hurt. I felt as a woman must feel when a man takes out his watch and remembers an appointment that cannot possibly concern her, except that its claim is the stronger" (362). Allying himself here with the figure of the rejected woman, Duquette describes the charming young girl Harmon brought with him when he finally returned to Paris. Her name was "Mouse," and that diminutive gives a sense of her vulnerability to the two conspiratorial males. Unable to carry through an elopement with her, however, Harmon had left her alone with Duquette in a hotel on the very day of their arrival, depending on Raoul to manage the situation for him. The abandoned Mouse had welcomed his help: "'Yes, you're very kind. Yes. Do come to-morrow. I shall be glad. It makes things rather difficult because— . . . *je ne parle pas français*'" (376).

Duquette never returned to help Mouse, and the implication is that she was drawn into the vortex of the Parisian street life that Duquette serves not only as an aspiring avant-garde writer but as a procurer. Far from finding his vagrant memory of Mouse a symptom of moral disease, however, Duquette reads it as a source of aesthetic wonder that reassures him of the essential soundness of his sensibility.

Duquette is also gay, and it is a measure of the power of Mansfield's homophobia when she is under emotional or physical threat that she portrays homosexual preference as an aspect of moral corruption. The male homosexual seems the epitome of betrayal here because his interest in the female is never erotic, always distanced and proprietary—"between men." *"Je ne parle pas français"* thus carries the anger of the woman who sees herself as a medium of exchange in its homophobia.[19] Insofar as *"Je ne parle pas français"* is an illness story, however, the illness is not homosexual but heterosexual. Originally, Raoul Duquette has been corrupted by heterosexual experience proffered by a seducing washerwoman, and greedily taken, too early in childhood. An earlier version of the story shows that the most vivid detail of the erotic experience was cut when the story was first printed commercially. The censored version suggests what has happened in general physical terms: "She took me into a little outhouse at the end of the passage, caught me up in her arms and began kissing me. Ah. those kisses! Especially those kisses inside my ears that nearly deafened me" (356). But this censored version leaves out the sentence that refers to the most significant action of the seduction: "And then with a soft growl she tore open her bodice and put me to her" (*DE* 281).[20] Such explicitly lurid details are rare in Mansfield's fiction, but in the case of Raoul Duquette, she wanted to confront the body sharply. Here again, however, her mimicry of the case history monologue betrays the maternal by showing its abuse as a source of dehumanization in her narrator; Mansfield has turned away from her own celebration of the foster mother's breast in "How Pearl Button Was Kidnapped."

Further, in the final paragraphs of the monologue, when Raoul rises to leave the café, his story now unfolded, the uncut version makes his profession as pimp brutally clear by indicating his specialization in producing virgins (Mouse herself?) for old men:

> And so on and so on until some dirty old gallant comes up to my table and sits opposite and begins to grimace and yap. Until I hear myself saying: "But I've got the little girl for you, *mon vieux*. So little . . . so tiny. [And a virgin.]" I kiss the tips of my fingers—["A virgin"]—and lay them upon my heart. "I give you my word of honour as a gentleman, a writer, serious, young, and extremely interested in modern English literature." (*DE* 299. Bracketed material not available in American edition of stories.)

Thus Duquette reenacts his own defloration in sponsoring that of virgin women.

What motivates Raoul Duquette in "*Je ne parle pas français*" is less his sexual perversity than his early discovery that his somatic indoctrination could help him to rule people through his own sharp knowledge of their weaknesses. "I became very languid, very caressing, and greedy beyond measure," he says of his seduction, "And so quickened, so sharpened, I seemed to understand everybody and be able to do what I liked with everybody." Raoul's innocence, lost as a child, is lost forever—"From that very first afternoon, my childhood was, to put it prettily, 'kissed away'" (356). Having no childhood, he can provide no context for his case history; this is illustrated in the nullity of the titles of the books he has written, *False Coins, Wrong Doors, Left Umbrellas*. But more significantly, Raoul has begun to glory in his own lack of selfhood, presenting it as a positive artistic achievement. It makes him, he believes, especially interesting, especially clever. At the beginning of the story, he states his views on the "human soul," proclaiming that he does not believe in the organic self, that his observations of the types in the café are simply amusements:

> I don't believe in the human soul. I never have. I believe that people are like portmanteaux—packed with certain things, started going, thrown about, tossed away, dumped down, lost and found, half emptied suddenly, or squeezed fatter than ever, until finally the Ultimate Porter swings them on to the Ultimate Train and away they rattle. (350–51)

But the love for Dick Harmon has made Raoul a "case" himself as well as the connoisseur of other people's cases. After confessing all his perversities to Dick during their early friendship, Raoul remembers his regained innocence: "And there sat the man I had confided in, singing to himself and smiling. . . . It moved me so that real tears came into my eyes. I saw them glittering on my long silky lashes—so charming" (361). Even in the process of giving himself away, then, Raoul must notice himself as an object of contemplation. Thus his perversity lies more in his distance from the complications of human destiny than in his sexual pathology. He believes himself to be the ultimate clinician who sees everything, even his own reactions, as disguises for some deep irrationality. Mouse attracts him because she is real, vulnerable, isolate, perhaps even ill (she carries a muff to keep herself warm and caresses it several times in the hotel room). But he will not submit himself to her predicament. He must play the role he has become, even as he draws the reader into its plot: "Of course you know what to expect. You anticipate, fully, what I am going to write. It wouldn't be me otherwise" (376).

There is a subtle power in Raoul's clinical objectivity, and Mansfield recognizes it as terrifying even as she engages it. She knows that his delusion lies in his failure to realize that even the most self-searching patient can *become* his illness, and only that. Duquette gives the reader the minute particulars of his dress, his room, his personal appearance, and his efforts to impress the minor literary world of Paris. He *has* become a painted invalid in his own richly detailed life. Thus he describes his ride with Harmon and Mouse from the train station to the hotel where she will be deserted: "Away we jolted and rattled like three little dice that life had decided to have a fling with" (367). Seeing fate in such a way, Raoul envisions human behavior as awkwardly mechanistic rather than mysteriously willed. At the end of the uncensored version of the story, Duquette considers the possibility of sleeping with the café's proprietress as he leaves. It is a sign of how corrupted his perceptions are that his impulse is thwarted by a sudden clinical conclusion about her body: "Would she be pale like that all over?" he asks himself. And then he answers, "But no. She'd have large moles. They go with that kind of skin. And I can't bear them. They remind me somehow, disgustingly, of mushrooms" (*DE* 299). Under such a gaze, he can absolve himself of responsibility or care and thereby spend his existence in exploring his own pathology and that of the other patients in his clinic. His stance is, therefore, purely specular; he never listens to his own narrative and therefore he can never assess his own history.

Duquette takes on the cheerfully despairing view of the incurable. Human life, under his view, is a random and meaningless series of bodily and emotional poses. In dramatizing the character who is nothing but a collection of symptoms, Mansfield articulates her own mistrust of the narrative technique that can mimic the strategies of clinical objectivity with no thought to cure. It was this aspect of the artist which she feared most, even while she knew that as a writer, she must be an echo, in some sense, of what she herself surveyed.

~

Mansfield's turn in *"Je ne parle pas français"* was a turn into exploration of the disease of the intellectuals—a terminal self-consciousness that picks up and hordes every clue about the self but which has no power to set the symptoms within a total case history.[21] To use, more approvingly than she does, Sydney Janet Kaplan's notion of Mansfield's divided allegiance to Oscar Wilde and Anton Chekhov, I assert that Mansfield turns from the endless "clinical" self-diagnosis of Wilde in this story to the more "medical" practice of Chekhov in the stories she wrote after her problematical experiment. Her cry against corruption in *"Je ne parle pas français"* is a dissection of the self-listening of the condemned, and the effectiveness of the story lies in her letting Duquette tell his own history without understanding it. She wants common understanding after this tour de force, more than precocious catalogue of defect. The distinction I am making here has its parallels in the criticism of medical practice which has become standard in recent years as patients have asked for more from their doctors than laboratory tests and invasive diagnostics. As Edward Shorter has pointed out in his study of the interaction between doctors and patients, the tendency started by the rise of "pathological anatomy and the germ theory of disease" in the 1880s was to make modern medicine a system of diagnosis, not cure (*Bedside Manners* 78, 75). This process replaced healing as the main focus in patient relations; Shorter, like other medical historians and critics, has called for a renewal of the doctor's more ancient, more risky task of a sympathetic understanding of the whole case which leads to interaction with the patient in cure. Indeed, Shorter sees modern healing to lie not so much in miracle cures as in the "psychotherapeutic power of the consultation" (252).

In Mansfield's own clinical approach to Raoul Duquette, the power of the cure lies in dissection and surgery rather than in the kind of informed and generous "consultation" between narrator and the object of narration made available in much of her third-person fiction. Like Eliot in one of his early first-person narrative poems, she imagines a totally clinical vision, "the evening . . . spread out against the sky / Like a patient etherized upon a table"[22] The positioning of the object of the modernist gaze can reflect an image that is grotesquely passive, dehumanized, resistant to interpretation. And Mansfield's later satirical portraits of the avant-garde all show them as "cases" who have either accommodated themselves to the limitations of their sick roles or exaggerated their own labile sensitivities. Mr. Peacock in "Mr. Reginald Peacock's Day,"[23] Monica Tyrell in "Revelations," and Bertha Young in "Bliss" are hypochondriacal children who mistake moral and physical self-diagnosis for innocence regained.

Given her clinical expertise, Mansfield's problem as a writer was to use her capacity for observation as more than an exercise of power over the anesthetized characters in such stories. As one medical sociologist suggests, medicine exists in a context of "three types of forces: systems of meaning, norms, *and* power" (Kleinman 45). So also does writing. Mansfield could exercise the power of her control of telling sensory detail, but her problem in "*Je ne parle pas français*" was how to assert her own system of meaning without enforcing the intolerant norms of homophobia. In her depressions, she did assert such meaning—fearlessly and sharply, condemning mockery, as she does in rendering Duquette's devastating final gesture of disengagement through his disgust with the body's imperfections.

Elizabeth Bowen comments of her clinical method, "Katherine Mansfield, we notice, seldom outlines and never dissects a character: instead, she causes the person to expose himself—and devastating may be the effect. The author's nominal impassivity is telling. I should not in the main call her a kind writer, though so often she is a pitiful one" (xxii). Although Mansfield accepted as part of her talent the impulse that could create a story such as "*Je ne parle pas français*," she did not consider such probing as her greatest strength. She would continue investigating the corruptions of innocence, but she wanted to drain stories with such obvious villains and victims of what Elizabeth Bowen has called "transferred self-pity" (xvii). She went back to the mode of first-person pathologizing only once again in her fiction in the slight melodrama "A Married Man's Story"; but essentially she seems to have learned what she could from "*Je ne parle pas français*" and then turned back to the fictional work of the physician rather than the pathologist.

If Mansfield's answer to the "kick off" of satire in herself was to consciously pursue the role-playing of limited characters, she distrusted too great a distance from common human feeling in her objectivity. Writing to S. S. Koteliansky in praise of his and Lawrence's translation of Ivan Bunin's "The Gentleman from San Francisco," Mansfield states the case against such hardness no matter how brilliant:

> Bunin has an immense talent. That is certain. All the same—there's a limitation in this story, so it seems to me. There is something hard, inflexible, separate in him which he exults in. But he ought not to exult in it. It is a pity it is there. He just stops short of being a great writer because of it. Tenderness is a dangerous word to use, but I dare use it to you. He lacks tenderness—and *in spite of everything*, tenderness there must be. (*CL* 2:173)

What she requires more and more as she becomes more fatally ill is the listening power of Chekhov. Thus she included in a list of passages that she copied from Chekhov's letters in 1919:

> The immense majority of people are nervous: the greater number suffer, and a small proportion feel acute pain; but where—in streets and in houses—do you see people tearing about, leaping up, and clutching at their heads? Suffering ought to be expressed as it is expressed in life— that is, not by the arms and legs, but by the tone and expression; not by gesticulation, but by grace. (*Journal* 174)

But how was Mansfield to achieve this tonal "tenderness" and "grace" herself without falling into the dangers of sentimentality? And how could she square her reiterated requirements for elimination of the "personal" in her stories with her demand that the artist not be humorless, inflexible, separate? The answer was, of course, the other "kick off," the joy that was even more intensified by her illness than her satire was. Like the patience that she had to cultivate in order to submit to the care of friends and strangers during her illness, the joy was frequently strained. The complications, and gender, of such care are the topic for the next chapter.

Using the heuristic of medical diagnosis, we may say that Mansfield presents Duquette in a way that provides a plethora of overt symptoms but finally ignores his case history.[24] Her experiment in first-person narration is an exercise in the structure of examination she herself has submitted to by doctors who understood her life, and those who didn't. Thus she is aware that any such examination is fraught with what Henry James called "the terrible *fluidity* of self-revelation."[25] Self-examination is always liable not only to misdiagnosis but to revealing unacknowledged secrets to a more clinically alert hearer. Listening to the spoken and the unspoken, Mansfield worries again about the success of this complicated venture, "Oh God—Is it good? I am frightened. For I stand or fall by it. It's as far as I can get at present and I have gone for it, bitten deeper & deeper & deeper than ever I have before" (*CL* 2:54).

CHAPTER 7

"I prevented you from living at all"

The Gender of Care

THE INTERPRETATIONS of the medical case history and the creative life come together in the designation of Mansfield as a patient. In medical sociology, the term *patient* incorporates the notion of affliction and of seeking a cure. As a matter of fact, the progress of bacteriology and of surgical intervention in modern medicine has led to a contemporary expectation that the patient be socially and ethically obligated to submit to regimes of treatment (and more recently of prevention).[1] In becoming a "patient," however, Katherine Mansfield resisted the partnership between social coercion and inner passivity which so often complicates illness. While seeking to understand the peculiar status of the chronically ill, she also sought to avoid their pathos. At the same time as her illness forced her isolation, it also drew her into a wider community of the sick—into intimate contact with servants and nurses, into solidarity with fellow sufferers, and finally into the search for a community in which she could either get well or die well.

Had Katherine Mansfield been less resistant to the heroics of her need to respond to fatality by writing, she might have acted more wisely. She suffered her diseases, however, in a period before the benefits of the bacteriological regime of twentieth-century medicine were fully established. Pediatrics, gynecology, obstetrics, and internal medicine in the second decade of the twentieth century were far from exact sciences, and where a medical practice newly invested with the surety of microbiology could not bring immediate relief, "experts"—from engineers with x-rays to holistic gurus—stood ready to promise miracle cures. In the absence of effective medical help, then, Mansfield sought her own knowledge, insisting after each setback that the final outcome must lie in some harmony of soma and psyche. Setting up one regimen after another as each collapsed under the progress of her disease, she invariably planned moral as well as physical rejuvenation. In this imagination of her illness, then, she recapitulated her moralizing of her health which had been a habit from her early childhood guilt about surviving her baby sister, her adolescent medicalizing of her transgressive bisexuality, and the incessant meditation in her satirical stories on the ethical implications of feminine "splitting" in hysterical role-playing.

Mansfield's answer to moral problems was to act; her famous defense of D. H. Lawrence by boldly confiscating a volume of his poems that were being abused by a sneering group of erstwhile friends at the Café Royale is a case in point.[2] In a state of physical weakness, however, any act requires practical assistance, and one of the main challenges of terminal illness for active people is the acceptance of care. Mansfield's need for aid in living with her disease brought the issue of her dependency into sharp focus. Such dependency was especially frustrating because it arose at a time when she seemed to have mastered her insecurities as a writer and to take advantage of a rhythm of success in her writing. Working through the death of her brother, she seems to have broken through the writing block that unsettled her sense of her vocation after the publication of *In a German Pension* in 1911. The publication of "Prelude" in 1917 seemed to put her doubts securely behind her, and indeed, all the indications of Mansfield's biography point to her determination to begin to live and work on her own in the fall of 1917. She had rented a studio flat in Chelsea and lived apart from Murry, going back to publishing some sketches in the *New Age* and gathering new friends in the Bloomsbury circle. Meanwhile, L.M. had taken work in a munitions factory and seemed resigned to establishing her life without her friend. Mansfield's sudden collapse under rampant consumption in December 1917, possibly triggered by a cold she caught in nursing Murry, who was himself ill at Garsington, redirected her trajectory back again to dependence.

Beset by his own recuperation and his work in the War Office, and then later preoccupied with establishing his literary career, Murry showed himself unequal to the task of caring for Mansfield. Several times during her six years of illness, he dropped his work to join her in her places of recuperation, but he could never "enter into it," as she told him in a letter after a particularly bleak visit to her in January 1920: "That I shall *never* understand. Even when we sat there at evening & I said can you imagine what this is like when one is alone & ill & L.M. away? *Still* you would not see" (*CL* 3:191). In contrast, L.M. dropped everything to come to Mansfield when she imagined the situation of her sick friend alone in wartime France in the spring of 1918. Despite Mansfield's premonitory horror when her friend appeared as an anxious helper, she finally had to turn to L.M. as factotum, nurse, and "wife."[3]

That Lesley Moore stood always ready to suspend her own life to perform the service of care was both a convenient asset and a continuing irritant to

Katherine Mansfield and John Middleton Murry, 1913. (Mrs. M. Middleton Murry Collection, ATL)

Mansfield. Some of her most hectic railings against her illness came in the form of castigation of L.M. as an angel of death rather than an angel of mercy. It is in this aspect of her illness that Mansfield's defects of egoism and role-playing, her failures of generosity and sympathy, her defensive reaction against lesbian love came to the surface. The irritability in her acceptance of L.M.'s ministrations reached a pitch of hatred which has unsettled a number of her critics and biographers, leading them to accuse Mansfield of a failure of sisterhood.[4] Such judgments, however, fail to take account of the panic that almost inevitably engulfs the terminally ill. The stages of shock, denial, anger, depression, and bargaining which precede the acceptance of fatality have now been studied by experts in thanatology and have dissipated the expectation that dying be enacted in an uncomplicated exercise of stoic fortitude.[5] The psychology of Mansfield's last years seems to have followed a pattern that can now be explained as an aspect of her illness, as she herself suggested in efforts to repair the wounding effects of her own changes in mood. Thus in an unpublished letter to L.M. in 1922, she confided, "I am not at all well yet—terribly nervous and exacting and always in pain—but I'll get over it. But I need you and I rely on

Katherine Mansfield and John Middleton Murry, 1922. (A. Alpers Collection, ATL)

you—I lean hard on you—yet I can't thank you or give you anything in return—except my love. You have that always" (ATL).

The forced sisterhood of her bodily reliance on a naive, pathetically devoted, déclassé woman aroused all of Mansfield's defenses, but in calmer moments and over time, her reliance on L.M. also inspired a profound contemplation of human interdependence. Thus in a number of late stories, Mansfield gave as her last testament a portrayal of the burden of chronic and terminal illness on those who had to care for the dying. In these stories, she saw women's caretaking as marked by those characteristics of helplessness which ally gender dependence with other forms of powerlessness—poverty, class, and age. However chaotic her transient reactions in her personal situation, Mansfield's need for care generated stories that dramatized a new solidarity with the poor, the dispossessed, and the old.

Gradually, then, she plotted her narratives less on the romance of childhood and its betrayals and more on the indignities of older women, whose fate involved their accommodation with their loss of power and presence. But even as she surrendered her dream of marriage and family as the source for care—

Katherine Mansfield (right) *with her cousin Connie Beauchamp* (left front), *Mrs. Dunare* (center), *and Jinnie Fullerton* (back), *1920*. *(ATL)*

resigning her reliance on either Murry or her father for personal comfort and financial security—she still made several attempts to penetrate the self-enclosure of the masculine sensibility. In "The Man without a Temperament," she imagined more sympathetically than she had ever done before the heroic boredom of a healthy man attached to a sick woman. Her greatest testament to care, however, was "The Daughters of the Late Colonel," in which she imagined the total self-sacrifice of two simple spinsters who had spent their lives tending a querulous, sick old man.

~

According to Michel Foucault, "the natural locus of disease is the natural locus of life—the family: gentle, spontaneous care, expressive of love and a common desire for a cure, assists nature in its struggle against the illness, and allows the illness itself to attain its own truth" (*Clinic* 17). Such an idealized notion

Lesley Moore [Ida Constance Baker] (right) *and Dorothy Brett* (left) *with Katherine Mansfield, 1921. (ATL)*

of the family is at variance with much of the social history of tuberculosis, as well as with the psychological reality of families whose reactions to terminal illness can be as angry and denying as those of the patient. With a disease as contagious as tuberculosis, the patient has to be physically segregated. Moreover, when the disease is obviously contagious, family members are apt to find ways to distance themselves as Murry did from Mansfield in his turning from her kiss on their wedding day to wipe his lips with a handkerchief. Katherine Mansfield hoped for the kind of familial environment of cure envisioned by Foucault; indeed, her illness intensified her idealization of the family as a locus of support. But the realities of her condition violated such expectations, isolating her from the familial sources of her identity even as she wrote about them in retrospection.

The regime of care for tuberculosis in 1918 militated against the patient's recourse to the family. Generally, doctors recommended removal to a sanatorium for consumptives, a place "of hope deferred" (Smith 97). If the sanatorium was not feasible, doctors recommended finding some alternate locale that would afford almost total bed rest, fresh air, and a diet that emphasized milk, eggs, and meat on an almost forced-feeding schedule. For those who could afford it, travel to a better climate, either by the sea or in the mountains, was strongly advised. Only the very wealthy could afford such travel in a family entourage,[6] and so for most sufferers tuberculosis meant exile from loved ones and familiar friends. The poor were segregated in forbidding public institutions, while those with middling incomes went to modest health resorts, trying to "get well" on their own—hiding their fever, weight loss, and, when possible, their coughs.[7]

It is no wonder, then, that victims of tuberculosis resisted the "truth" of their disease. They might find themselves regimented in authoritarian institutions in which all vital activity was forbidden, contact with friends and relatives was cut off, sexuality was suspended, and failure to recover was viewed as something of an insult to science. Even the more systematic sanatoriums that became the refuges of tubercular patients in the England of the 1920s and 1930s could not offer cure, but rather a prolonged illness with many relapses. F. B. Smith's excellent study of the sanatoriums in Europe between 1850 and 1950 unfolds a history of unredeemed grimness in which patients were dehumanized by therapeutic routines that absorbed funding that might well have been better spent in alleviating the conditions for the majority who "shuffled out their lives at home" (130).

Mark Gertler, a member of the early Lawrence-Murry circle (and at one time a possible lover of Mansfield's),[8] entered one of these sanatoriums in Mundesley, Norfolk, in the 1920s.[9] His letters to S. S. Koteliansky speak the pathos of the artist cut off from sympathetic human contact and from his art in his treatment for tuberculosis. One long account of his stay in the sanatorium after a sudden hemorrhage in 1925 gives a firsthand description of the trials of such sequestration for an artist:

> Letters—in a place like this are indispensable—Here one becomes an isolated atom—Revolving alone and silent like some pole star—Letters alone break down the barrier—and remind one that there *are* some interesting people in the world, and that one has some sort of contacts after all—So please write. I sit at a table—during meal times—with five other people—I force down a good deal of food including quantities of milk, and meanwhile sweat with horror at the proximity of these people—No doubt they are nice and I shall like them in time—But just now they bore every nerve in my body. . . . They have allowed me to start work—I work from lunch

to tea, and . . . out of sheer boredom I have started a little picture by artificial light—So then I shall also be able to work after dinner—It is wonderful what resources boredom will put one to—To be working again
makes a great difference—At once I am placed into a world that matters—a life that counts and has reality—For the Hum-drum world as it
is, and its people are unreal and Hazy to me—I mean rather that their
lives are so purposeless in the *real* sense of the word—that they become
to me unreal—Though in the flesh they exist of course only too much so
alas. (Sept. 18, 1925, ATL)

Gertler left Mundesley in December, but he had to return again in 1929. He
fought a recurrence of the disease through the thirties, and it seems certain that
the recurrent isolation in illness contributed to Gertler's suicide in the late thirties. D. H. Lawrence was another of the tuberculosis victims among Mansfield's
friends who refused treatment in a sanatorium and who, like her, traveled
widely in pursuit of a moral health that would work a bodily cure.

Lawrence's denial of his own disease seems to have been threatened by
Mansfield's example; in a note added to a letter to her in 1919, he wrote om-
inously: "I wonder if you are not so well again, that you have not written"
(*Letters* 3:324). But after his famous falling-out with Murry in 1920, he sent
her a famously vindictive letter; Mansfield reported its contents to Murry: "he
spat in my face & threw filth at me and said 'I loathe you. You revolt me stewing
in your consumption. The Italians were quite right to have nothing to do with
you'" (*CL* 3:209). Among the many features of temperament Mansfield and
Lawrence shared were their outrageous projections of their anger on others as
they wrestled with the grim prognosis of their disease. Lawrence sought a reconciliation of sorts by sending Mansfield a postcard from Wellington in August
1922, with the single word "Ricordi"; on that same day Mansfield made her
last will and requested that Murry give Lawrence a book from her library in
remembrance.

Those who chose to confront their illness as Mansfield and Lawrence did,
outside the sanatorium—in the genteel tattiness of rest homes in Cornwall, the
south of France, Italy, or the Swiss Alps—might also find themselves dependent
upon the care of strangers, viewed suspiciously by healthier residents, and subject to a variety of sanitary measures designed to ward off infection. Mansfield's
one venture into the Italian Riviera in 1920, for example, was complicated by
the traditional Italian treatment of tuberculosis as a contagious disease that
required quarantine of the sufferer and extreme measures of decontamination.
Mansfield's letters reveal the fact that she could not keep a servant when she
was in Italy and that the manager of her hotel in San Remo asked her to leave

and then sent her a bill for the fumigation of her room (Alpers, *Life*, 298–99). Lawrence's reference to the Italian rejection of Mansfield thus illustrates a point of difference in the cultural styles of treatment for tuberculosis. Mansfield's travels eventually led her to the Swiss mountains, where that style was more scrupulous but less acceptable because of its chilly efficiency. As Antony Alpers has pointed out, during her stay in Switzerland in 1922, she probably spent some time in the same hotel as Rainer Maria Rilke (352), but her restless awareness that she was not getting well eventually drove her back to France for the last months of her life.

Life in recuperation for Mansfield and all her fellow sufferers either in sanatoriums or among the scattered stopping places on the Continent involved a variety of dodges to forage for needed foods, especially in wartime Europe. Mansfield's letters to Murry are punctuated by reports of her food intake, inventories of supplies, rehearsals of small victories over rationing, calculations of what things were costing, and accounts of the lamentable cookery of servants and, later, of L.M. She was also constantly in need of small personal necessities that she requested of her women friends—warm underclothing, specially comfortable outerwear, and cigarettes (Mansfield was grateful to Virginia Woolf, for example, for a gift of good cigarettes). Money to pay for doctors, drugs, and landladies was a constant theme, one that Murry finessed with the smallest of loans to his wife and careful merchandizing of her stories. The couple kept their finances separate even after they married.

Finally, Mansfield's isolation—like that of Gertler—made her almost totally dependent on letters from home to keep her from despair, and her sense of being cut off from life was exacerbated by the insecurity of communication by mail or wire, especially during the war. In the almost daily letters that Mansfield wrote to Murry while she was in the exiles of her illness, her most agonized accusations of his desertion were inspired by the failures of his letters to reach her. The most pressing fear of the dying is dying alone.

In the light of the choices of other victims of consumption such as Gertler and Lawrence, then, Katherine Mansfield's efforts to find interim substitutions for life in a sanatorium should be viewed more temperately than Murry could see them. She was doing what other sufferers tended to do, making the best compromises that she could devise in the hope that she might find some way to live in spite of the disease. Thus she made her first foray to the south of France in the winter of 1918 as a temporary expedition. When she returned to England in the spring to marry Murry (the divorce from George Bowden having finally been granted), she was so emaciated that he insisted that she spend the summer in a convalescent seaside hotel in Cornwall. After a summer of excruciating isolation there, attended by a motherly landlady named Mrs.

Honey and a helpful artist friend, Anne Drey, she returned to take up residence with her husband in their long-desired house in Hampstead. Her health declined so badly in London that she fended against another exile by attempting to organize the house as a private sanatorium. A note to Murry outlining this plan in the early fall of 1918 shows the dimensions of her anxiety about the failure of her recuperation. The theme of familial care as the foundation for her personal independence as well as her recovery is notable in her strategizing:

> I confess that these last days my fight with the enemy has been so hard that I just laid down my weapons and ran away, and consented to do what has always seemed to me the final intolerable thing i.e. to go into a Sanatorium.
>
> Today, finally thinking it over, and in view of the fact that it is not, after all, so much a question of *climate* as of *régime* (there are very successful sanatoria in Hampstead and Highgate)[10] I am determined, by my own will, to live a sanatorium life *here*.
>
> (1) Father shall have built for me a really good shelter in the garden where I can lie all day.
> (2) He shall also give us two good anthracite stoves.
> (3) I shall buy a complete jaeger outfit for the weather.
> (4) I shall have a food chart and live by it.
> (5) This new servant releases Ida [L.M.] who has consented to give her whole time to me—as a nurse.
> (6) Sorapure shall still be my doctor. I shall have a separate bedroom *always and live by rule*. You must have a bed in your dressing room when the servant comes.
> (7) I shall NOT WORRY.
>
> You see, Jack, for the first time today I am determined to get well as Mother would be determined for me. If we are depressed we must keep apart. But I am going through with this and I want you to help me. It CAN be done. Other people have done this in Hampstead. Why not I?
>
> Anything else, any institutional existence would kill me—or being alone, cut off, ill with the other ill. I have really taken my courage up & Im not going to drop it. I *know* its possible. (CL 2:292)

The very form of Mansfield's resolve, the methodical listing of her necessities, indicates her growing awareness of the extent of her illness even as she bargains with its fatality by imagining it as a serious battle that requires only organization and discipline for the winning. Negotiating with her denial by now assenting to her illness, Mansfield engages in a contract with the truth of her disease, promising a reform of her old habits of disorganization, poor eating, and anxiety in return for health. The family of her childhood is to sanction her program in the way it had always done—her father financing it and her mother's memory providing the disciplinary moral support. Significantly, when she asks her husband for help in carrying out her plan, and perhaps in her delusion, she asks only that he not intervene with his own emotional problems. It is also significant that L.M. makes an appearance in the plan as a nurse whose loyalty is beyond question.

The Hampstead battle plan was not workable. For one thing, Mansfield could not keep herself from engaging with the various friends who came up to Hampstead to see her. She had to flee to the Continent once again, returning to Hampstead in the summer of 1919. But then Murry's hopes for establishing the *Athenaeum* as London's leading literary magazine required that she serve not only as his hostess but also as the journal's main book reviewer. Thus it was in the year after she had given up the experiment with Hampstead as a sanatorium that Mansfield had most of her important conversations with Virginia Woolf. And thus she wrote her brilliant weekly reports on contemporary fiction (both in Hampstead and later in France again) until her weakness forced her to beg off in December 1920. She wrote most of her best-known stories in the years of her direst illness, between January 1918 and July 1922.

The comparison of Virginia Woolf's conjugal situation with her own was painful. Whereas Leonard Woolf managed, perhaps dictatorially, to shield his wife from the distractions of outside life when she was suffering her bouts with mental illness, Murry did not have the same unswerving dedication, nor did he exercise the same will to protect Mansfield. Against all common sense, for example, he staged a party at their home when he became the well-paid editor of the *Athenaeum* in the summer of 1919. Mansfield held forth as hostess, exhibiting what Antony Alpers has described as "her remarkable ability to live on her nerves for special occasions" (*Life,* 292). At one point during Mansfield's failed experiments in trying to survive in Hampstead, she finally faced the fact that she must go into a sanatorium. But Dr. Sorapure agreed that the move would kill her spirit, and so she kept to the notion of surviving through self-discipline on her own.[11]

The geography of Mansfield's illness situated her in an extremity of ambivalence between a need for independence and a desire for the kind of familial reassurance invoked by Foucault; she maneuvered in every way to find an intermediate locale that would allow her to remain in touch with her marriage to Murry while providing the refuge advised for her health. The stay on the Italian Riviera in the fall of 1919 was the most miserable of her whole experience, and Murry's arriving for Christmas of 1919 only added his own anxiety to her despair. As Virginia Woolf noted, seeing her the following summer in

Hampstead, she seemed changed after that episode, realizing that Murry could never be her caretaker.

> Then I said, "You've changed. Got through something"; indeed theres a sort of self command about her as if having mastered something subterfuges were no longer so necessary. She told me of her terrific experiences last winter—experience of loneliness chiefly; alone (or only with "Leslie Moor" alias Ida Baker) in a stone house with caverns beneath it into which the sea rushed: how she lay in bed alone all day with a pistol by her; & men banged at the door. Sydney [Schiff] wrote *"Stick it out"* twice, underlined. Murry sent a balance sheet of his accounts: came at Christmas with plum pudding & curd cheese; "Now I'm here, its all right." Then she went to him for assurance; didn't get it; & will never look for that particular quality again. I see what she means, vaguely. (*Diary* 2:45–46)

It was out of that revelation that Mansfield wrote "The Man without a Temperament," in which she imagined not only the limitations of the men upon whom she had relied but also the burdens they were compelled to bear. In the story, she presents Robert Salesby, an amalgam of her husband and her father, so sympathetically that he seems an innocent victim of his wife's illness.[12] For once in this rare exercise of assuming the male subject position, Mansfield is able to present the caretaking man without irony; rather, his downright masculinity is shown as a victimized foreground upon which his wife displays the delicate enthusiasms of her invalidism. She is the one who cannot enter into his sacrifice as he plods on among the strangers in their convalescent hotel, longing for home. Tactfully, Mansfield also registers his sexual deprivation as he goes to his bed, observing her sleeping, corpselike, in her own:

> He sees her through the nets, half sitting, banked up with pillows, her white hands crossed on the sheet. Her white cheeks, her fair hair pressed against the pillow, are silvered over. He undresses quickly, stealthily and gets into bed. Lying there, his hands clasped behind his head . . . (340)

Mansfield's recognition of the intractable otherness and loneliness of Murry's masculinity helped her to appreciate the tensions in her parents' marriage, to forgive her father to a limited extent,[13] and finally to see her own strength as the proper sustaining force in her life.

From the time of writing "The Man without a Temperament," Mansfield was confirmed in the fact that she must manage whatever recuperation available to her on her own, with the help of L.M. And so Mansfield's eventual recognition of the possible fatality of her disease sent her into a burst of writing against time. She got through the early months of 1920, returned to Hampstead for the summer, and then retreated again to the south of France in the winter of 1920–21. Murry quit the *Athenaeum* in early 1921 in order to join Mansfield in Italy again, but their relationship was strained by her realization that he had been having an affair in London. She decided to move to Switzerland in May, and he moved with her for a trying time together which lasted into January 1922. Then she suddenly went to Paris to take a last-resort x-ray treatment. That initially hopeful and then debilitating course of treatment lasted through the early months of 1922 but in the summer, she suddenly suspended it and returned to London to find out about a philosophical system of living promulgated by P. D. Ouspensky. In the fall of 1922 she joined the commune set up outside Paris by George Ivanovich Gurdjieff to pursue a holistic, primitivistic way of living.

There were several reasons for Mansfield's pursuit of health outside the sanatorium, only at the last to latch on to the promise of Gurdjieff's "Institute for the Harmonious Development of Man." First, she continued to wrestle with the denial that accompanies any fatal diagnosis. Her sudden transition from relative health to imminent death outstripped her ability to concentrate on the fact that she was as sick as she was; even though she had intimations of imminent death from the time of her first hemorrhage, she also had periods of relative remission when she could indulge in daydreams of total recovery. Nevertheless, when she left for her second winter abroad, she had written her first will and left it with Murry. Even so, she would soon be sending him ecstatic previsions of having children after she recovered. As Elisabeth Kübler-Ross has noted, such hopefulness is not a form of delusion but a necessary resource for the dying. As for her rejection of entering a sanatorium, it must be remembered that Mansfield had already experienced the regimented life in a health spa[14] when her mother packed her off to Bavaria in 1909, and so she knew the banality of the environment, the hypochondriacal intrigues of its patrons, and their preoccupation with the minutiae of their symptoms; she could hardly be willing to undergo such an experience again.

Indeed, Dr. Sorapure's initial advice to avoid a hospital existence had encouraged her to think of her creativity as the energy that kept her alive: "I had also a letter from Sorapure today which really boxed it. I mean, he said it was only my 'indomitable will'(!) which kept me alive this last year, & he is sure I shall now get absolutely well and 'grow into your dream of achievement.' This, of course, makes me feel *cicatrisé* all over and also rouses my pride. I *will*." (*CL* 3:10). Thus, while she complied with doctors' orders to some extent— she agreed that she had to spend most of her time at rest—she also contrived to set up each place of exile as a place for writing. Her best defense against dying became her work. The Foucauldian "natural locus of life—the family" would be available to her only in the New Zealand memories she could summon up in the stories of her childhood which she wrote during her illness: "At the Bay" with its representation of Linda Burnell's accommodation with childbirth may also have echoed Mansfield's accommodation with mortality.

~

Although the constant movement in search of a healthy place to work may seem the most dramatic feature of Mansfield's struggle with tuberculosis, it should not hide the continuing parade of therapeutic indignities that were pressed upon her by one doctor or another in a series of questionable remedies. One way to dissipate the romanticizing of her disease and thereby reveal the truly heroic dimensions of her struggle is to inventory day-by-day occasions of trial. Her triumph was not, after all, the kind of romantic process which Murry evoked in his description of her death at the end of his edition of her letters to him, "that process of self-annihilation which is necessary to the spiritual rebirth, whereby we enter the Kingdom of Love" (*LKM* 701). A close reading of all her letters for the particulars of her illness provides a catalogue of "minor" complications that tend to be derealized by such language.[15]

In a sample, from early 1918 through 1919, Mansfield's letters speak of "night coughing and sweating" (*CL* 2:11), "weight loss" (*CL* 2:17), an ache in the left lung (*CL* 2:22), spitting blood (*CL* 2:79), the cessation of her menstrual period—"I have never seen Aunt Marthe *since that Sunday afternoon*" (*CL* 2:137), pleurisy, anemia, "spinal rheumatiz" (*CL* 2:241), and "acute neuritis in [her] arm and shoulder" (*CL* 2:286). And during this initial year of her disease she underwent treatments that further debilitated her, among them strapping of her chest so that she could hardly breathe, injections of strychnine which gave her a high fever, and electric shocks. She consulted at least four doctors, all of whom rendered the same diagnosis but each of whom advised separate treatments and varying prognoses. Writing to Virginia Woolf in early November 1919, she commented on the parade of doctors she had consulted, drawing a memorable image of their invasion of her privacy: "Why *are* doctors so preposterous? I see them in their hundreds, moving among sham Jacobean furniture, warming their large pink hands at little gas fires & asking the poor visitor if this will come off or pull down—curse em" (*CL* 2:288–89).

She took the various medicines, and she worried about the bills from the doctors and the chemists. Her cough was controlled by hydrobromic acid (*CL* 3:85) and possibly by codeine, and although there is no sign that she became addicted to such drugs, she must have required a great deal of them; she tended to turn down Veronal. In terms of her own self-doctoring, she also took iron and other tonics, took Guiacol (phenol) for inflammation (*CL* 3:41), and rubbed her lung with "Capsoline," recommending to Murry a powder called "*irénine*" for "neuralgia or rheumatism or any pains of that kind . . . its absolutely INfallible" (*CL* 3:222–23). In one fanciful letter to Anne Drey, with whom she was apt to exchange the comic details of bodily distress, she ruefully described her amity with her air cushion:

> I am out of bed sitting on my aircushion on the sofa. About *aircushions*. I hear the Chinese are never without them. They make them of rice paper, paint [them] with lovely designs, fold them up small—And then whenever you go for a walk or a picnic and want to sit down on a stone or a piece of *hard grass* you just shake out the little packet, blow it up, sit on it & there you are. A home from home! . . . This last little characteristic, in my present "état de genoudefemmedechamberisme" makes me long to join their flag. (*CL* 2:290)

The letters of the following years continue the list of specific afflictions and home remedies as well as the exercises of the many doctors she consulted at home and abroad. In 1919, she writes that she can barely walk: "My leg is so swollen I can only hop today" (*CL* 3:13). It is a sign of improvement when she reports, "I can *whistle* again" (*CL* 3:18). But the degrading side effects continue: both her hands are bandaged (*CL* 3:28), her eyes have become all bloodshot (*CL* 3:29), her sight has begun to fail and she needs glasses, her joints are painful, and her lung "creaks like a Sam Browne belt" (*CL* 3:61). She has sessions of palpitations which she calls a "heart attack" (*CL* 3:170), and she has an almost constant backache and "chronic neuritis in [her] lower limbs" (*CL* 3:205–6). At this juncture her hip is almost immobile. She seems to have had tinnitus that contributed to sleeplessness, nightmares, and possibly hallucinatory voices during her worst times alone in Italy. She is very much aware that some of her outbursts might be psychologically based, that she might be suffering a kind of madness brought on by her afflictions.

Early in her illness, she lost her menstrual periods, possibly because of emaciation, and when the menses returned, she became anemic and began taking cod liver oil—one of the universal tonics of the time. Alpers suggests that some of her intense irritability may have been caused by the hormonal imbalance of her irregular periods (*Life* 303). Her most efficacious course of treatment seems to have been in the winter of 1920–21 when she stayed with her affluent cousins in Menton; there she received the best of care in a luxurious rest home and then in their villa. But even so, the treatment was intrusive and almost overwhelming: "Every morning the Swiss masseuse is to give me a friction all over to aid my awful circulation" (*CL* 3:191). Then several months later she was getting injections of iodine every other day for two weeks; with her habitual wit about her trials, she wrote to Murry:

> I am taking a sun-bath cure on Doctor Bouchage's advice and at 8 o'clock the sun streams on my bed and nearly burns me. It's a very wonderful treatment. I believe in it. I'm also having those confounded iodine injections which make me an appallingly tired girl. But I believe in them, too, so I must put up with the feeling. . . . I am having the iodine every other day for a fortnight. By that time I shall have to hang like a bat when I'm not walking. Like the poor Lord, who had no place to rest his head, I've no place to rest my derrière. (*LJMM* 575)

It might seem from the number of doctors she saw and the cures she tried that Mansfield indulged in doctor shopping, a tendency familiar in terminal (and hypochondriacal) patients. Her comments on the treatments in 1920 emphasize the need for her to *believe* in them. But worse than doctors who sincerely assured her that she could get well were the doctors who offered too much hope and then withdrew it. One such physician was a Dr. Ansaldi in Italy, whose cheerful prognostications gave Mansfield a fortnight's hope that she was getting well, but on his second visit the truth came out: "Don't *count* on him. Hes a charlatan. He owned yesterday that the reports he gave me were because 'I saw dis lady wants vot you call sheering up' " (*CL* 3:130–31). Mansfield still looked for a doctor she could believe in; as Kübler-Ross has observed from working with many terminally ill patients, "Even the most accepting, the most realistic patients left the possibility open for some cure, for the discovery of a new drug or the 'last-minute success in a research project.' . . . It is this glimpse of hope which maintains them through days, weeks, or months of suffering" (123).

Although Mansfield valued the hopeful personality of her doctors highly, she was alert to new developments in the treatment of tuberculosis. She went to Switzerland to see about the Spahlinger cure. And her final major indulgence in an experimental cure was her submission to x-ray irradiations by Dr. Manoukhin in Paris the spring before she died. She did gain some weight from these expensive treatments and had a short burst of last hopefulness from that, even though she also seems to have suffered some of the symptoms of radiation sickness. Such bizarre treatments were recognized in a medical world that seemed willing to try anything (Smith 146), and about Manoukhin she reported that her father had read of his treatments in the *Lancet* and that he worked in the Pasteur Institute. In the light of the dawning truth of her illness and the medical controversies about how to treat it, her attempts were not necessarily exercises in denial, no matter how desperate they seemed. She was one of the multitudes of tuberculosis patients who were caught up in trying to find something to believe in between the era of romantic resignation and the triumph of positive science. In July 1919, she entered in her journal a satirical verse (titled "Tedious Brief Adventures of K.M.") about the scientific pretensions of her current doctors:

> A Doctor who came from Jamaica
> Said: "This time I'll mend her or break her.
> I'll plug her with serum;
> And if she can't bear 'em
> I'll call in the next undertaker."
>
> His *locum tenens*, Doctor Byam,
> Said: "Right oh, old fellow, we'll try 'em
> For I'm an adept, O,
> At pumping in strepto
> Since I was a surgeon in Siam."
>
> The patient, who hailed from New Zealing,
> Said: "Pray don't consider my feeling,
> Provided you're certain
> 'Twil not go on hurtin',
> I'll lie here and smile at the ceiling."

As the verse continues, the patient is pumped with "five million, then ten," but the experiment fails, sending all the "strepto" to her feet and thus crippling her. And so she ends up as a beggar on Hampstead High Street, "In a box on four wheels / With a whistle that squeals; / And her hands do the job of her feet" (*Journal* 129–30).

The prevision of being totally deformed by her treatments is comically masked here, as are so many of Mansfield's fears in such versifications. Luckily, she was ill before the heyday of surgical intervention to collapse the lung through pneumo-thoracic surgery, which required insertion of a needle to regulate the air from the most affected lung in order to let it rest.[16] And she died before the horrifying decades of radical surgery—loosening the rib cage or removing the phrenic nerve that controls the diaphragm or ligating pulmonary vessels or cauterizing lesions—turned sanatoriums into surgical arenas for practitioners of heroic medicine (Smith 136–47). Compared with such measures, her therapeutic efforts may seem conservative and sane.

The one major surgical intervention in Mansfield's disease occurred in March 1921. She had written to L.M. (who was away in England closing up the Hampstead house during this crisis) describing the infection of a gland in her neck which was "a great deal more swollen for some reason. The blood goes on tapping squeezing through like a continual small hammering and all that side of my head is numb. Its a vile thing" (unpub. letter, Mar. 8, 1921, ATL). Several days later, she had to go to the office of her current French doctor to have the gland aspirated; Murry accompanied her. She described the experience to Sydney Schiff, again with a characteristic wry explicitness about the scene of her suffering:

> Since receiving your letter Life has driven me through dark little doorways, down underground passages which ended this week in one of those white tiled rooms with glass shelves, a fine display of delicate steel, too many wash basins, a frosted windy glass & a narrow little black sofa with steel grips for the patient to cling to. Here the surgeon & my doctor decided to risk it and plunged about 2½ inches of hollow knitting needle into my neck & withdrew it. Success triumphant.   (Unpub. letter, Mar. 16, 1921, ATL)

Her vivid description of this episode, which Murry left out of his edition of her letters, only implies the fearfulness of the procedure by describing both the obscurity of the clinic and its forbidding instrumentation. The notation of the "steel grips for the patient to cling to" barely lifts the veil on the horror of her pain as well as on her habituation to sessions with doctors who would punish her body with their instruments of "delicate steel." This surgical episode is especially significant in showing the extent of Mansfield's bodily affliction, a fact that I have emphasized in order to set both the emotional turmoil and the sustained creativity of her illness in the context of her concrete bodily experiences. But the operation on her gland is also significant in its illustration of the economic dependency on Murry which was always a feature of her suffering.

Since L.M. was not with Mansfield during this crisis, Murry was her only companion; he accompanied her to the surgery. And the trip itself was almost as painful as the operation, for it dramatized Murry's characteristic limitations in understanding Mansfield's situation. Mansfield was always short of funds in her illness, too proud to ask Murry for help and then furious that he wouldn't come through without her telling him. She constantly worried that her father would take away her allowance of three hundred pounds, without which she could not manage at all: at this very time, she was embarrassed that she had an overdue bill with her beloved Dr. Sorapure in London. Indeed, Alpers contends that the reason that she wrote a number of relatively ephemeral magazine stories in 1920 and 1921 was to earn enough to pay her medical bills (*Life* 416). She had supposed that Murry might pay for some incidentals while he was visiting her, but she reported to L.M. that after they returned home from her horrendous bout with the swollen gland, he presented her with a bill for half the cab fare and half the tip:

> But fancy not paying your wife's carriage to and from the surgery! Is that simply extraordinary or am I? I really am staggered. I think it is the meanest thing I ever heard of. It's not the fact which is so queer but the lack of fine feeling. I suppose if one fainted he would make one pay 3d for a 6d glass of sal volatile and 1d on the glass. That really does beat Father. (*LM* 159)

The two men of her family upon whom Mansfield hoped to rely in her illness simply could not respond adequately, and their failure to provide was a besetting concern for Mansfield during her final illness. Confiding this small detail of conjugal life to L.M. indicates a new note of feminine camaraderie in their relationship. Later in the year she wrote in open appreciation, "If I were to tell you how I've missed you even you might be satisfied!" (*LM* 171).

Murry took every release that Mansfield offered as genuine because it enabled him to stay in London at work in the great world of journalistic literature while she fretted in exile. And he indulged her ideal hopes for cure by rationalizing his saving all his money as an investment in their future home. In some desperation Murry did finally quit the *Athenaeum* to come to Mansfield in the south of France and move with her to Sierre in the Swiss Alps. But the inevitable end was becoming more clear, and Mansfield was moving further away into the final phase of her dying. When Mansfield decided to make one last try at the new x-ray treatment, she used her last hundred pounds for the "last chance." Significantly, she borrowed another hundred pounds from a woman, her cousin Elizabeth, Countess Russell, to make her final flight to the Gurdjieff Institute.

∼

Antony Alpers, Katherine Mansfield's most generous biographer, has asked: "How does someone who has no religious faith and is only thirty-one 'accept' the imminence of death?" (*Life* 301). In the light of the record of the cascading side effects of her illness and its treatment, that simple question may be the most important one to pose about Katherine Mansfield. My answer is that she did come to accept her death within her writing, for her journal and letters record a number of luminous statements of resignation which interweave with her despair in each of her crises, especially her final ones. It is not just forced resignation that beckons her acceptance, however, for the kind of acceptance observed in dying patients is not a comalike anesthesia but an acknowledgment of the inevitability of the end and with it an ability to go through whatever remains without fruitless resistance or anger that others live and enjoy. I believe that Mansfield reached this state before the time assigned to it by most accounts of her life, that is, before she removed herself to the Gurdjieff Institute. She reached it, however, in difficult stages that involved reversions to childishness, rebellion, and rage. Nevertheless, there seems to have been an accession to self-sufficiency—reflected in "The Man without a Temperament"—after her agonizing episode in Italy when Murry's coming to help proved to be a useless exercise in misunderstanding. A next phase involved her acceptance of the care of L.M., even against her desire to be free of L.M.'s clumsy ministrations. Indeed, some of her irrational anger at L.M. must be read as an attempt to locate the threat of her illness within a tangible agent, a scapegoat. But I discern a final stage in which she made an effort to detach L.M. (and Murry) from herself. In this detachment, she recognized the tyranny of her own death and sought to defend her friend from dying through it as well.

The truth is that in all the wanderings of her illness, Mansfield had needed L.M. more than she could admit. L.M. was the last remnant of family she possessed; she answered Robert Frost's definition of home as a place where "they have to take you in," and though Mansfield abused her, she could always turn to L.M. in times of trial. Having left her family of women behind in New Zealand, she especially needed a sisterly woman friend in England. From the commencement of her liaison with Murry, the lesbian desire in such friendships had to be rejected, but it was replaced by the desire for the familiarity of women—for sharing memories, experiences of the body, observations of the absurdity of the male. Throughout her life Mansfield had been attracted to "literary" women such as Beatrice Hastings, Frieda Lawrence, Ottoline Morrell, and Virginia Woolf, but they were too outré to perform the traditional services of female kinship. Often their intellectual aggression seemed artificial and shallow to Mansfield; they aroused her own competitiveness. In short, they were not simple people.

And so in all her troubles, Mansfield came back to L.M. or to other women who, like her, could replicate the protection she remembered from her grandmother. In her various refuges from tuberculosis, then, she formed attachments to motherly or sisterly women who would devote themselves to making her comfortable. In addition to L.M., she formed important female ties with Anne Drey, the artist who had befriended her in Cornwall; Dorothy Brett, another artist whose power among the Bloomsbury intellectuals was diminished by her deafness; two maiden cousin converts to Catholicism, Connie Beauchamp and Jinnie Fullerton, who had made themselves financially secure through running a rest home in London and who took her into their villa on the French Riviera after the Italian fiasco; and Elizabeth, Countess Russell (writing under the name Elizabeth von Arnim), whose presence in a nearby chalet in Switzerland gave Mansfield's sojourn there the intimacy of blood kinship. In making such attachments, Mansfield sought the female "culture of solace" which Edward Shorter has remarked as the place where the misery of womanhood found understanding before the advent of modern medicine made doctors effective healers rather than unsympathetic disciplinarians of the female body (*History* 192). With the exception of Elizabeth, the women who could offer such solace may have struck Mansfield as pathetic in the limited range of their sophistication, but in them resided the most genuine selflessness she could imagine. Her reconciliation with L.M. marked an acknowledgment of her need for them and an opening up from her isolation to include those people who had stayed with her during her worst moments. Thus in 1920 she wrote to Murry:

> My feelings towards Lesley are absolutely changed. It is not only that the hatred is gone—Something positive is there which is very like love for her. She has convinced me at last, against all my opposition that she is trying to do all in her power for me—and that she is devoted to the one idea which is (please forgive my egoism) to see me well again. This time she has fed me, helped me, got up in the middle of the night to make me hot milk and rub my feet, brought me flowers, *served* me as one could not be served if one were not loved. All silently and gently too, even after all my bitter ravings against her. (*CL* 3:178)

The acknowledgment of L.M. and women like her was accomplished in several of the stories Mansfield wrote in early 1921. These include "Miss Brill," "The Life of Ma Parker," and "The Daughters of the Late Colonel." James H. Justus has remarked upon "the poetics of poverty" (16) in these stories, noting that "by momentarily transcending the isolated self and its agonies" in them, Mansfield produced "stories stripped of the psychic excesses of her own desperate life" (22).[17] An illness reading of the stories shows the way these women share the deprived physical state of the chronically ill. Mansfield tends to describe their physical deprivations as the very aspects of their experience which make them caretakers. Thus Miss Brill is grateful for the comfort of her worn fur as she sits like an invalid in the sun in the Jardins Publiques: "The air was motionless, but when you opened your mouth there was just a faint chill, like a chill from a glass of iced water before you sip" (549). And Ma Parker, telling her "literary" employer of the death of her grandson, remembers his death within the sensation of her own permanent pain: "To take off her boots or to put them on was an agony to her, but it had been an agony for years. In fact, she was so accustomed to the pain that her face was drawn and screwed up ready for the twinge before she'd so much as untied the laces" (484–85). These women serve with no acknowledgment except Mansfield's telling of their stories, and Mansfield worried that her representations of their lives would be tainted by her reputation as a writer of "pretty little" stories of small failures (unpub. letter to Countess Russell, n.d., Russell, Box 7).

But Mansfield's most important act of reconciliation with her dependence on female caregivers was "The Daughters of the Late Colonel," which she was intent on having read as a gesture of homage rather than satire. I read the story here as paying a tribute of expiation to the female servants of her illness, even as she records the absolute nullity of physical death and the fading of the presence of the dead in memory. The story thus embeds its tribute within scenes of death which confront the irrevocability of dying.

That she had in mind a general tribute to the service of obscure women's lives is clear from Mansfield's remark on the models for the sisters in a letter to an old family friend, in which she identified her two maiden cousins and several other women friends, as well as L.M.: "To write stories one has to go back into the past. And its as though one took a flower from all kinds of gardens to make a *new* bouquet" (unpub. letter to Charlotte B. Parkins, ATL). But it was L.M. who presided over the story, for her halting attempts to express to Mansfield her own poetic revelations were the seed of its conception, and she was there during the hectic composition of its second half, waiting with tea and egg sandwiches to celebrate when Mansfield finished after midnight on December 12, 1920. In a journal entry of 1922, Mansfield remembered writing the story as a race against death: "I was so terribly unhappy that I wrote as fast as possible for fear of dying before the story was sent" (*Journal* 287).[18]

Thus "The Daughters of the Late Colonel" is more a death than an illness story, and it meditates upon death along a register of representations that face not only the stark ending of the Colonel's life but the slow process of internalized dying which servitude has wrought upon the women who serve him. There are actually, then, three deaths in "The Daughters of the Late Colonel," each representing an aspect in the sick person's dying which concerns not only her own fate but that of her nurses.

The initial death is that of the late Colonel Pinner, whose funeral has already been held at the beginning of the story but whose memory haunts his two frail daughters' comically reverent superstitions about his continuing power over them. Mansfield presents that death with devastating emphasis on the unremitting ire of the patriarchal body fighting against its last moment:

He lay there, purple, a dark, angry purple in the face, and never even looked at them when they came in. Then, as they were standing there,

wondering what to do, he had suddenly opened one eye. Oh, what a difference it would have made, what a difference to their memory of him,
how much easier to tell people about it, if he had only opened both! But
no—one eye only. It glared at them a moment and then . . . went
out. (467)

Death here is the angry cessation of material vitality, a turning off of a light,
and no more.

In this stark description, Mansfield registers the hard fact of the transition
from being to nonbeing without recourse to the memorialization of sentiment.
Though Con and Jug are visited, awkwardly, by the local vicar, it is clear that
their father's wrathful death deprives them of religious solace. Indeed, Mansfield's own refusal to take refuge in the conversion to Catholicism urged on
her by Connie Beauchamp and Jinnie Fullerton may be mirrored in her depiction of the failure of the benefits of clergy to cope with the hard facticity of
death. This religious vacancy is lightened in the story by the sisters' embar-
rassment at the thought of receiving "a little Communion" right there in the
drawing room. Constantia worries that the piano is too high for an altar, and
Josephine worries about being interrupted by the doorbell.

Further, the Colonel's resistance to dying causes his daughters endless anxiety about their father's blaming them, for burying him and then for locking
his clothes in a closet—"one of those amazingly bold things that [Con had]
done about twice in their lives" (472). In narrating the daughters' bizarre reactions to their father's death, Mansfield acknowledges the need of the living
to be done with a servitude that has turned them into foolish old maids who
wonder if they should dye their nightclothes black to prove the sincerity of their
grief. Locking the father's clothes away is commensurate with a second burial
of him in the coffinlike wardrobe. The daughters expect retribution, but Mansfield emphasizes their realization of the finality of their father's death by recording the fact that "nothing happened. Only the room seemed quieter than
ever, and bigger flakes of cold air fell on Josephine's shoulders and knees. She
began to shiver" (472).

The fears of the sisters are the only remainders of lives lived out in service
to the father, and their relationship with their own hired servants—Nurse Andrews and Kate the serving maid—plays out the will-lessness that is their in-
heritance. Thus they watch in helpless horror as Nurse Andrews violates their
own feminine norm of self-sacrifice by eating butter and expecting jam for her
blancmange. And when they try to gather their forces to decide about dis-
missing Kate for general insubordination and suspected disrespect, they find
that they cannot quite make up their minds. The encounters with these ag-

gressive "professional" servants are among the most Dickensian comic passages in Mansfield's stories.[19]

As in Dickens, however, in Mansfield the comedy is inflected by pathos. This pathos is accented by the daughters' later panic at the music of a barrel organ outside, for one of their most important services to their father had been to silence all intrusions. Forgetting that their father is dead and will no longer rage at such sounds of street life shows how stifled their sensory experience has been in their service to an invalid. Having served and been left behind, the daughters must now think of the past and the future. The music from the street inspires their reveries on the long duration of their service, and their roaming memories bring a second death into the story, the death of their mother. Her death is reenacted in the fading of her photograph caught by a movement of sunlight that has accompanied the penetration of the street music into the parlor:

> When it came to mother's photograph, the enlargement over the piano, it lingered as though puzzled to find so little remained of mother, except the ear rings shaped like tiny pagodas and a black feather boa. Why did the photographs of dead people always fade so? wondered Josephine. As soon as a person was dead their photograph died too. (481)

Although their mother had been killed by a snake, the phallic serpent of their father's career in Ceylon, her loss has been so gradual that the sisters only now begin to realize that it initiated their own deaths by placing them in lifelong servitude to their father, cutting them off from marriage and from all other life outside his governance. Mansfield had suggested in her inscriptions of the deaths of her little sister and her brother into her writing that the only form of human immortality available to console the loss of life is memory recorded in words or in photos, but in this story even that kind of memory fades as a last resource of staying alive. The writing in the letter that had been the single overture to either of them in years gone by had become so faint by the steam of the hot water jug on which it had been placed that "they couldn't even make out to which of them it was addressed" (482). And now the spot of unknowing sunlight which caresses everything in the parlor with equal beneficence and equal disregard also fades the photo of the mother. Warm and bright though it may be, it is the agent of death: "As soon as a person was dead their photograph died too."

Left in a house of dead parents, it is Constantia who meditates on the possibility of transcendence in the mute revelations of nature—a transcendence that might warrant suffering and service through its promise of something real beyond her limited circumstances after all:

She remembered the times she had come in here, crept out of bed in her nightgown when the moon was full, and lain on the floor with her arms outstretched, as though she was crucified. Why? the big, pale moon had made her do it. . . . There had been this other life, running out, bringing things home in bags, getting things on approval, discussing them with Jug, and taking them back to get more things on approval, and arranging father's trays and trying not to annoy father. But it all seemed to have happened in a kind of tunnel. It wasn't real. It was only when she came out of the tunnel into the moonlight or by the sea or into a thunderstorm that she really felt herself. What did it mean? What was it she was always wanting? What did it all lead to? Now? Now? (482–83)

This passage of aspiration, with its submerged imagery of being buried alive in a tunnel of daily concerns, introduces the last death in the story, the shared death of Con and Jug. As Mansfield confided to the novelist William Gerhardi, the story resolves itself upon the death of the two sisters: "All was meant, of course, to lead up to that last paragraph, when my two flowerless ones turned with that timid gesture, to the sun. 'Perhaps *now*. . . .' And after that, it seemed to me, they died as surely as Father was dead" (*LKM* 389). The paralysis of the two has become permanent, and they cannot think of what they want to say to each other. Despite Con's questioning, each is left with a nameless loneliness like that of Laura Sheridan in "The Garden-Party" or Bertha Young in "Bliss." The sisters face their reality as women who are already as faded as their mother's photograph, and they find it empty. They want to speak to each other, to say "something frightfully important, about—about the future and what . . ." They grope for a pronouncement commensurate with their revelation, but they cannot find the words. The only life left is the spot of sun, which at the end of the story thwarts any human resurrection in its indifference to memory.

Despite the comedy of some of its episodes, there is no satirical mimicry of the dying sisters in "The Daughters of the Late Colonel," and the ending does not seem to be the cruel last-minute twist that is a trademark of Mansfield's stories of the revelations for more privileged women. The narrator plays over the aging nurses of the dead man with a tender solicitude for their dying. She sifts the minutiae of their lives to reveal the important fact that they have earned some charity because of the simplicity of their familial sacrifice to a life of care. She commented to Gerhardi in defense against the reviewers' having accused her of "sneering" at Josephine and Constantia, "There was a moment when I first had 'the idea' when I saw the two sisters as *amusing*; but the moment I looked deeper (let me be quite frank) I bowed down to the beauty that was hidden in their lives and to discover that was all my desire" (*LKM* 389).

Mansfield's acceptance of her own death did not become a form of simple serenity after the writing of "The Daughters of the Late Colonel" by any means. The story's complexity does not promise dying as a simplicity of acceptance; dying is too hard a fact. Mansfield returned once again to the hard fact of death in the fragments published posthumously as "Weak Heart." In that story, communication between the invalid and her survivors is thwarted. "Edie Bendel's" humble mother cannot command "a word of sympathy, of understanding" from her dying daughter (681). And in the last scene, her bereaved young lover leaves her funeral, calling for her as he enters the house where she had played the piano in defiance of her invalidism:

> But cold, solemn, as if frozen, heavily the piano stared back at Roddie. Then it answered, but on its own behalf, on behalf of the house and the violet patch, the garden, the velvet tree at the corner of May Street, and all that was delightful: "There is nobody here of that name, young man!" (683)

Thus Mansfield imagined that the living would hear no echo of the dead, that the endurance of nature would be all that remained.

Just as she retained a sense that mourning would pass in the natural course of things, so Mansfield sensed that servitude to the dead must come to an end. And that end might be forced and painful. Indeed, her gratitude for the feminine service she needed did not signify that she became ever more forbearing as her own death approached. Like the late Colonel, in whom she may have written some of her own irascibility in illness, she could be demanding and harsh with L.M. And, as her disease progressed, she tended to withdraw from both L.M. and Murry. Her previsions of real death may have made her manner of cutting off and cutting out of her old life severe. But her detachment was no longer frantic, and its severity contained in part the motive of relieving her mourners of their burdens.

Her move to La Prieuré thus seems to have been both a last attempt at life and a preparation for death. Before leaving London for the institute, she filed a formal will, leaving instructions to Murry "to publish as little as possible and to tear up and burn as much as possible" of her personal papers: "He will understand that I desire to leave as few traces of my camping ground as possible" (quoted in Alpers, *Life*, 366). Although the strictures against preserving her in her most intimate writing seem punitive, they also testify to a desire to absolve her husband from the record of the tyranny of her illness. At the end, then, Mansfield gave her survivors leave to lock away the reminders of her long illness so that they could resume their own lives.

And Mansfield was especially interested in setting L.M. free from her bondage of caring for a sick and querulous woman. Pained at her friend's total devotion, she did not want to leave her to the kind of internal death suffered by the Pinner sisters. Her last communications were written in brutal charity. She tried to explain her motive in her final letters from the Gurdjieff Institute, which distanced her from L.M. even in their last requests for parcels of clothing and other necessities. Though she could not quite sever the tie, she attempted to remedy its worst effects by concerning herself with her friend's future. She wrote in November, "But you do see that our relationship was absolutely wrong now? You were identified with me. I prevented you from living at all. Now you have to learn and its terribly hard" (*LM* 218).

Spes Phthisica and the Lyric

THROUGHOUT this study, as a recurring formulation that unites the medical with the aesthetic, I have invoked a link between Katherine Mansfield's illness and writing which reflects Michel Foucault's suggestion that the clinical recognition of mortality and its causes can give rise to a "lyrical experience," a sense of the "obstinate, yet reassuring fact of . . . finitude" shared by the doctor and the poet alike as experts in the knowledge of death (*Birth* 196).[1] To be sure, imminent death may concentrate the imagination decisively, but I do not want to suggest here that Mansfield wrote out of fear—in panic and terror. It seems, rather, that no matter how clear the inevitability of her death as her final disease progressed, her writing derived from an intensifying center of purpose *within* her illness. Her finitude was a "fact" that perhaps reassured by its refusal to succumb without a fight. More important, Mansfield seems to have found reassurance in facticity itself, in the plenitude of the external world to which her illness gave her extraordinary access.

Without succumbing to the romantic theory of tuberculosis as a "spiritual" disease, I have suggested that Katherine Mansfield used the ailing body in which she found herself to imagine and record experience with an unusual attention to the unnoticed details of everyday existence. She seems to have steadied herself upon these details, and in this application of physical sensation to psychic equilibrium, I believe that she exercised an imaginative form of "proprioception," which Oliver Sacks has defined as "that continuous but unconscious sensory flow from the movable parts of our body (muscles, tendons, joints), by which their position and tone and motion is continually monitored and adjusted, but hidden from us because it is automatic and unconscious" (42).[2] Ordinarily, our bodies engage in proprioception without conscious effort, but Sacks' story of "Christina," a young woman who lost that sense through a rare neurological catastrophe, emphasizes the courage as well as the imaginative ingenuity in adjustment by patients whose bodily damage requires a conscious relearning of the flowing grace of normal functioning. Damaged patients must understand their illness if they are to adjust to its deprivations,

Observing communal dancing at the Institute for the Harmonious Development of Man, Versailles, 1922(?). From left to right: Gurdjieff, Katherine Mansfield, Mme. Julia Ostrowska, and unknown. (Courtesy of James Moore)

sometimes regaining the flow of their humanity only under the influence of long-forgotten music.

I make the analogy between the patient who must learn to hold herself in place and the afflicted artist, not to recall the Freudian concept of illness as the source of sublimation that gives rise to art, but to reiterate the notion of Mansfield's art as the result of an engagement of the total sensorium under the pressure to become conscious of its range in active struggle against dying. She confided to one of her sisters in a letter of 1922 that her sense of place had become both implicated in and transmuted by her suffering, and she made the confession of her attachment to the material world in images that accent the modest physicality of her own remains:

> How hard it is to escape from places. However carefully one goes they hold you—you leave little bits of yourself fluttering on the fences—little rags and shreds of your very life. But a queer thing it is—this is per-

sonal—however painful a thing has been when I look back it is no longer painful or more painful than music is. In fact it is just that. *Now* when I hear the sea at the Casetta [the Italian villa where she had felt most isolated in her illness exile the year before], it's unbearably beautiful. (Unpub. letter, Mar. 7, 1922, Berg).

In the process of her constant self-examination and its growing sensitivity to "sensory flow," then, and as the clinical manifestations of her final disease became more apparent, I believe that Mansfield sought to project the bodiliness of the self at a new degree of intimacy in her fiction, even as she managed to represent the materiality of the world—the "obstinate yet reassuring fact of finitude"—outside that self by expanding her already unusual command of imagery, prose rhythm, and spoken language in recollections of the crises of her life which became no "more painful than music is."

Whether or not there is a "genius" that is peculiar to victims of tuberculosis may remain an unanswerable question,[3] but it seems clear to me that in her representation of the material world as framed by mortality, Mansfield manifested something of *spes phthisica*,[4] the hectic savoring of "beauty that must die" which marked the romantic lyricism of tubercular poets such as Keats. Her fears that she might cease to be gave way to a steady contemplation of the finitude of the phenomenal world whose temporality inspired her emotion in re-collecting its smallest rags and shreds even as she projected the end of the future. Over and over again, the letters and journal entries of her illness years restate the hope that her words would be a stay against time. Thus she wrote to Mrs. Belloc-Lowndes in the summer of 1921: "I've seen the best man in Switzerland and he says I still have a chance. But I don't feel in the least die-away. Illness is a great deal more mysterious than doctors imagine. I simply cant afford to die with one very half-and-half little book and one bad one and a few . . . stories to my name. In spite of everything, in spite of all one knows and has felt—one has this longing to *praise life*—to sing one's minute song of praise, and it doesn't seem to matter whether its listened to or no" (unpub. letter, Texas).

The mode of Mansfield's praise was the epiphany, a characteristic modernist expression that George Steiner has described as the confrontation with "the facticity of death, a facticity wholly resistant to reason, to metaphor, to revelatory representation" (140). In resistance against the modernist loading of all its faith into that moment, however, Steiner finds the epiphanic representation of time nihilistic—"an epistemology and ethics of spurious temporality" (126). Steiner's nostalgia for a philosophical/theological basis for consonance between "word and world" underestimates the fact that the ontological satisfactions of facticity may coexist with the modernist's rejection of transcendence. The significance of the moment in Mansfield's writing will not be made manifest through systems or in plotted narratives that inevitably imply causality. The causality of Mansfield's stories is the causality of contingency. Milan Kundera explores this kind of causality in *The Unbearable Lightness of Being* when he comments on the fortuities, or coincidences, that are composed into "motifs" both by characters in novels and by people in life. The "beauty" is like music composed "even in times of greatest distress" (51–52). The music of the slight perceptions that trigger epiphanies is an echo of time past made meaningful by a future that cannot be planned; it is an echo of significance which can only be played upon the instrument of the present, and it is therefore lyrical more than narrative in expression. As the unanswerable questions at the end of "The Daughters of the Late Colonel" suggest, Mansfield's modernist confrontation with death through the staging of the moment of revelation did not yield any final answer. But it posed the question in a fugue of memory and projection, registering the present as the only available repository of implication.[5] As she wrote of Chekhov to Virginia Woolf, "What the writer does is not so much to *solve* the question but to *put* the question. There must be the question put" (CL 2:320).

For Katherine Mansfield, as for Virginia Woolf, the creativity of women was inflected by illness. As madness haunts the writing of Virginia Woolf, physical disease haunts Mansfield's fiction. For Mansfield, illness threatens not by driving women to suicide—an end of time—but by insidiously infecting them with the narcissistic self-absorption of invalidism—a waste of time. Both Virginia Woolf and Katherine Mansfield maintained that women's writing would have to work through such debilitating threats by expressing women's experience in all of its temporal confusions. Mansfield wrung out her epiphanies through the afflictions of a woman's body, but despite her own case history, Mansfield rarely wrote her illness directly into her fiction. Like Woolf, she had an ideal of narrative art as pure expression, unburdened by the special pleading of the writer's circumstances or by the regimenting abstraction of political or philosophical ambitions. This reliance on the present of the epiphany did not, however, embody a belief that the experience represented by her words was merely a surface materiality—what Ronald Schleifer has described as the material "metonymics" of modernism and postmodernism (4, 66)—marshaled ironically as a last resort against the facticity of death.

There was, of course, plenty of irony in Mansfield's fiction, but I believe that it was a tonic irony marshaled in defense of the authenticity of the epiphany. One of her last completed stories was "The Fly," one of her most ruthless satires upon the pretensions of the patriarchal father. It tells of "the boss" who, being reminded by an old retainer of the death of his son in the war, has every intention of spending an hour in solitude mourning the boy. But as he settles at his desk, he is distracted by the effort of a fly to recover from having fallen into the ink pot, and in playing with the creature's struggle, he finally causes it to die. He then tries to remember what he had been doing, but he cannot bring back the thought of his dead son. The piercing recognition in this story is that memory, the only memorial for the dead, is subject to lapse. Critics have belabored the symbolic possibilities in "The Fly," and biographers see in it Mansfield's anger against her father, who had lately remarried and who seemed to reject his daughter's achievements.[6] Placed with her other final stories, however, "The Fly" enacts Mansfield's own main terror about death, her brother's and her own, that their lives should be forgotten. In the fragmentary "Six Years After," the dead son reproaches his mother, "Don't forget me! You are forgetting me, you know you are!" (641). But the mother strives to hold the memory of the dead against her own voyage into darkness; she battles the ephemerality of the moment, unlike the boss, who fritters away his remembrance in the clutter of his self-endowed memorials—the new furniture of his office, his desk, his pen. His memory fails because it has been plotted as a dramatic episode: "The boss covered his face with his hands. He wanted, he intended, he had arranged to weep" (531). The memorializations of women are spontaneous; they remain in the passing perceptions of dreams or of fleeting daily reminders. As the old woman who mourns her canary in Mansfield's very last story says of the sadness in life, "It is there, deep down, deep down, part of one, like one's breathing" (605). Thus Mansfield's irony is gendered rather than general. The "hatred" (she used that word about herself in a marginal comment when she was writing "Six Years After") remained as one of the main "kick offs" in her writing. It has a specific object, however, in the carelessness of self-important authority.

Both Woolf and Mansfield launched their careers as writers under the brave flag of the freedom of women to write in expressive proclamation of the female self, and although each risked the trivialization by philosophical authorities for her efforts, in a different way, each was haunted by the image of the woman of genius as threatened by the finally fatal dissipation of her ambition to give voice to her experience through a lapse of confidence in its reality. Sounding Virginia Woolf's theme of the need for a writer, especially a sick writer, to have money and a room of her own—and the support of friends to help her along— Mansfield wrote to Murry in the dark days of 1919, "I wish I were a great deal more self-supporting. Its a thousand times harder for me to write reviews here where I have no one to talk things over with—Im 'out of it' and see so few papers & never hear *talk*. I have to get into full diver's clothes & rake the floor of the unprofitable sea. All the same *it is my life: it saves me*" (CL 3:73–74). And then the next day, pulling her resources together out of despair, she writes about the memories that form the core of her past and her hope for the future, "It is all memories now—radiant, marvelous, faraway memories of happiness. Ah, how terrible life can be! I sometimes see an immense wall of black rock, shining, in a place—just after death perhaps—and *smiling*—the *adamant of desire*. Let us live on memories, then, and when the time comes, let us live so fully that the memories are no nearer than far-away mountains" (CL 3:76).

The final question is how, in illness and in art, Katherine Mansfield managed the contradictions between her insight into the fragmentation of the self as the dependent subject of multiple roles and social determinations and her conviction of possessing a "self that is continuous and permanent" and so conscientious enough to exert the will to write even in isolation. It has been a running contention of this study that the conviction of selfhood is not only an intuitive and enabling artistic presumption but also an essential foundation for resistance to the threat of disease. In thinking about the hope, however feverish, which has traditionally been associated with the final stages of tuberculosis, I have come to believe that memory is the essential element in the psyche which turns subjectivity into identity. Mansfield's own meditation on the survival of the self is couched in an account of its organic development and of the use of consolidating the self through writing down its phases—creating, as she says, a "rage for autobiography" (*Journal* 205). Oliver Sacks' accounts of the identity destruction that is the main psychic damage done by neurological amnesia show how important a role memory plays in providing the patient a sense of the continuity and meaning of his life. One pathetic case is that of "Jimmie G," a victim of amnesia whose memory is intact up to the age of nineteen and who therefore has always a sense of who he *was* but not who he *is*. An even more tragic case is that of "Mr. Thompson," a man whose Korsakov's syndrome has removed all memory function; this patient has no sense of what he ever was and so spends his days fabricating and narrating perpetually new stories about himself. In a sense, this man might seem to be the model of postmodern subjectivity, unhitched from the illusion of continuity and in constant and immediate contact with the flux of his desire. But in a profound sense, the man is sick; he cannot work or love because the rush of stories, and frantic attempts at stabilizing himself through them, occupy every waking minute of his day. His day is full of discourse, and there is no rest.

Mansfield's resource in the daily presence of her death was the restorative identity of memory recorded, relived, proprioceptively. Her experience of pain gave a sharp edge to her representation of physical sensation—breathing, eating, feeling the warmth of a cup of hot water on cold lips, searching out a spot of sun. These were the writerly instruments of her illness; with them she managed to live through her dying. Her acknowledgment of the limitations of the time available to her orchestrated her representations into a lyric art that made peace with the transitoriness of her moments while asserting their pattern in a life that mattered.

Introduction

1. Jeffrey Meyers first revealed Mansfield's gonorrhea, and he spends some time on her illnesses in *Katherine Mansfield: A Biography*. In *The Life of Katherine Mansfield*, Antony Alpers reluctantly confirmed this long-suppressed biographical fact. Claire Tomalin gives the most extended interpretation of the effects of the venereal infection and general bodily decline in *Katherine Mansfield: A Secret Life* (75–78), and C. A. Hankin makes some references to Mansfield's illnesses in *Katherine Mansfield and Her Confessional Stories* (166 ff). Although each provides more biographical detail than I do, none of these biographical studies has attempted a thoroughgoing reading of illness as a governing context for Mansfield's fiction. See Wilhelmina Drummond, "A Psychosocial Study of Katherine Mansfield's Life," for a simplified survey of the "psychosocial" development of Mansfield which emphasizes the New Zealand sources of her dislocations and achievements.

2. See Kate Fullbrook for a reading that accents Mansfield's "final hanging back" from the possibility of a unified self (*Katherine Mansfield*, 19). But Clare Hanson predicts a shift from such emphases in a post-Lacanian feminist criticism that may "have to focus again on questions of power, strength and authority in women's writing: this in turn may offer some vindication of the ways in which Katherine Mansfield held on firmly, in theoretical terms, to her own complex position of author-ity in language" (introduction to *Critical Writings*, 20).

3. John Eakin's review of theorizing about the nature of the self as articulated in autobiographical writing has helped my thinking about Mansfield's autobiographical self-defining in the light of the limits of the deconstructive brand of poststructuralist theory (*Fictions*). Fierce antagonism to the kind of Anglo-American ego psychology which I invoke here energized Jacques Lacan's project—and provided some of the clearest moments in his exposition of his "return" to the Freud of the unconscious: see "The Freudian thing" in *Écrits*.

4. That such "illness" authors as Elaine Scarry and Oliver Sacks do not discuss the "body in pain" as an always gendered body seems a significant oversight. Mansfield certainly had a sense that women experienced the body, and its pains, in different ways than men did.

5. The distinction is Morris's (*Culture,* 75). Pushing against the biochemical interest in pain only as sensation, Morris emphasizes the cultural interpretations that give pain its perceptual purchase within the patient's suffering. For a sensible effort to shift from the poststructuralist "denaturalization" of the body (à la Judith Butler) into a sense of "our incarnate yet indeterminate bodies" (à la phenomenology), see Bigfoot, "Renaturalizing," 60.

6. Carol Gilligan is highly critical of Erikson for his omission of the feminine in his account of adolescent and midlife development. I think that she underestimates the force of Erikson's recurring emphasis on generativity as a "virtue" in his developmental scheme. Thus, although she does cite Erikson as the only psychologist who notes the troubling disjuncture between a "masculine" morality of justice and a "feminine" morality of care, she continues to classify him with much more masculinist theorists such as Freud and Kohlberg (*Voice,* 103–5).

7. Quoted in Greenberg and Mitchell, *Object Relations,* 200. The accusation of "immaturity" was a feature of formalist criticism of Mansfield's stories; see, for example, Hynes, "Katherine Mansfield," 556, 560.

8. Susan Sontag describes American pop psychology searches for adjustment along these lines in her essay on Norman O. Brown (*Against Interpretation,* 258–59). There is also a "paranoid" strain in medical history which envisages various diseases as constructions of medical megalomaniacs in service of the drive to subjugate the female, the child, and the madman. See Foucault's *Madness and Civilization,* and for a radical, and horrifying, indictment of the male control of female health and childbirth, see Barker-Benfield's *The Horrors of the Half-Known Life.*

Chapter 1: "'Ah! Ah! Ah!' called the grandmother"

1. For example, C. A. Hankin glosses the photo episode as one in which the anxiety of sibling rivalry is softened by a moral indignation (*Katherine Mansfield,* 218–21). Photography of dead infants was a memorial ritual in late-nineteenth-century New Zealand. I am grateful for verification of this practice by the curator of photographs at the New Zealand National Library. A recent newsletter of the Katherine Mansfield Birthplace Society mentions the photograph as of "Mansfield's Granny Dyer and her dead sister Gwendoline" ("'New' Doll's House," 1).

2. D. W. Winnicott surmises that "a baby under two years cannot be properly informed about a new baby that is expected, although 'by twenty months or so' it becomes increasingly possible to explain this in words that a baby can understand" (*Playing,* 21).

3. Florence Nightingale speaks of diarrhea "merging into cholera" (*Notes,* 63).

4. The main desideratum for the use of breast milk in feeding children is, of course, its nutritional value. *Sharland's Settler's Guide* pays particular attention to the importance, and risk, of infant nutrition: "An infant with quick and healthy digestion, can pass through its infantile period without disorder; but, on the contrary, one that has inherited weak organs of digestion will not pass many days of

its early life without betraying its predisposition. It is, therefore, the duty of all about to become parents, to study attentively the management of infants and children" (22).

5. For a history of "artificial feeding" or "bringing up by hand," one of the major challenges for nineteenth-century pediatrics, see Wood, "Artificial Feeding," 21–29.

6. In her famous *Book of Household Management,* Isabella Beeton mentions that the wet nurse could have "occasionally a piece of sago, rice, or tapioca pudding" (1024). Elsewhere, in giving a recipe for sago soup, she remarks that the beaded flour drawn from the sago palm is frequently used "as a restorative diet" (79).

7. Hankin mistakenly dates the departure at "only a few weeks after the birth" (*Katherine Mansfield,* 5). Antony Alpers has assured me that she waited until the eleventh or twelfth month (telephone interview, August 1989).

8. Beeton's *Book of Household Management* seems a reliable source for New Zealand practice, since it was widely read in English-speaking countries. The New Zealand books of family maintenance which I have read in the National Library in Wellington tend to be general in nature, with only an occasional mention of tropical diseases. There is a general emphasis on fresh air and cleanliness, prescriptions that may have had their origins also in an English source, Florence Nightingale's *Notes on Nursing.*

9. Bowlby has shown that the child's response to maternal separation becomes a matter of anguish after the seventh month or so, increasing in intensity into the third year (*Attachment and Loss,* 2:51–53). The effects of such early separations from the mother are decisive in formation of identity but can be mediated by the presence of a substitute attachment figure.

10. Claire Tomalin so interprets her invalidism (*Katherine Mansfield,* 9).

11. See Beeton, *Household Management,* 1020–22. I am not sure that Beeton's catalogue of family servants in English households can be applied to the New Zealand setting. Nevertheless, it is clear that Annie Beauchamp expected to be waited on immediately after her daughter's birth.

12. Alpers notes that Mansfield began to have nightmares after Gwen's death, even though he surmises that her mother's leaving her "may have hardly affected her" (*Life,* 3–4).

13. Quoted from an unpublished manuscript by Hankin (*Katherine Mansfield,* 8). I generally follow Hankin's dating of early and unpublished fragments.

14. I take this contrast from the very helpful survey of object-relations theory by Greenberg and Mitchell (*Object Relations,* 19).

15. Winnicott's clientele included numbers of working-class children, especially in the program he organized for displaced children during World War II.

Chapter 2: "They discuss only the food"

1. "Progresses" is perhaps too suggestive of design here; we have the uncompleted story in the fragments of its drafting over eight or nine months. As Margaret Scott, Mansfield's most expert editor, observes, "*Juliet* is not so much an unfinished novel, as notes towards a novel" (*TLR*, "Juliet," 5).

2. Quoted by Claire Tomalin from an unpublished memoir by Marion C. Ruddick, "Incidents in the Childhood of Katherine Mansfield," in the ATL (*Katherine Mansfield*, 13).

3. Alpers says it was in the *Idler* (*Life*, 113), but my own xeroxed copy from the ATL designates otherwise.

4. The native identity of these women is so submerged that it might be missed by readers unfamiliar with New Zealand Maori culture: allusions to ferns and feather mats and the women's "log house" point to the racial contrast set up in the story. Hankin notes the ethnicity of the women in an analysis that also places the story in the context of Mansfield's alienation from her family (*Katherine Mansfield*, 78–84). Mansfield's identity as a New Zealand writer has recently been canvassed by New Zealand critics, especially Lydia Wevers, in Rhoda Nathan's collection of critical essays. Wevers sees the motif of the kidnapped child as a frequent one in colonial fiction; and in "Pearl Button" kidnapping is a liberation ("Kathleen Beauchamp," 46–47).

5. I base this appropriation on Lacan's formulation in "The Meaning of the Phallus" (*Feminine Sexuality*, 74–85). In this context I also sense elements of the "real," that category that is so elusive in Lacan.

6. Margaret Scott has noted that many of the events in "Juliet" prefigure events in Mansfield's own life (*TLR*, "Juliet," 6–7), in this case her well-founded worries about pregnancy resulting from her earliest heterosexual liaisons.

7. Patricia Moran reads Mansfield's body-image conflict as a rejection of the maternal woman, whose flesh images the humiliation of fecundity ("Unholy Meanings"). This reading seems to me to neglect presiding images of the male as devourer as well as Mansfield's ultimate reconciliation with food, and though it brilliantly analyzes Mansfield's disgust with L.M. as an appetitive woman, it overlooks the possibility that Mansfield rejects her friend's voracity because she identifies it with male aggression. See also Fullbrook, *Katherine Mansfield*, 77–84.

8. In setting up Mansfield's allowance, Harold Beauchamp mandated her reporting to his agent in London once a month. The agent relayed regular bulletins about her health back to Wellington. The letters are preserved in the ATL.

9. The similarity with Frank O'Connor's "My Oedipus Complex" is striking and suggests that although O'Connor criticized Mansfield severely (in *The Lonely Voice*), he may have learned a thing or two from her.

10. The bracketed phrase appears in Alpers' edition (*DE*, 121), which retains the original phrasing rather than the alterations made by Murry for his collection

of the stories. Murry's changes seem to have been designed to placate Harold Beauchamp.

11. Mansfield herself was not content with this ending, finding the episode in the lane "scamped" (*Journal*, 266).

Chapter 3: *"Your lovely pear tree!"*

1. John Middleton Murry later seemed intent upon masking the subject of homosexuality by calling Mansfield's journal entries of this period "overwrought and hectic" (*Journal*, 4). Phillip Waldron's survey of the manuscripts discusses Murry's suppression of details that suggest her "less conventional sex life" ("Mansfield's *Journal*," 12). Despite extensive coding, I think it is clear that Mansfield's lesbianism did involve "a commitment of skin, blood, breast, and bone" as demarcated by Catherine Stimpson ("Zero Degree Deviancy," 364). The breast desire I outline here may not have been operative in Mansfield's affair with "Maata," the Maori girl she loved. I am inclined to think that the more genital eroticism with Maata may have been instigated by Mansfield's supposition of the greater passion of the native girl. Her love for Maata would have been, therefore, doubly transgressive. My discussion of Mansfield's bisexuality here owes greatly to discussions with Alice Falk and Bill Scroggie at Indiana University and Michelle Kuchta at Marquette University.

2. In assigning the etiology of Mansfield's lesbianism to pre-oedipal identifications, I follow the paradigm that Nancy Chodorow suggests in *The Reproduction of Mothering*, though I would qualify her assertion that "lesbian relationships do tend to recreate mother-daughter emotions and connections" (220) by emphasizing that the form of Mansfield's lesbianism derived more from maternal deprivation than connection. Although I agree with Sydney Janet Kaplan that one benefit of such an approach to lesbianism is its avoidance of applying moralizing psychological labels such as "perverse," "infantile," and "regressive" to lesbian experience (*Origins*, 36), I would be uncomfortable with any conclusion that Mansfield's case might be "typical" and therefore serve as an explanatory model. I need hardly emphasize that variations in sexual behavior are so numerous and multifaceted that generalizations about causes are always suspect; I will be content here to describe only the complex pattern that Mansfield herself enacted.

3. Not surprisingly, they also reinvoke Oedipal images of male gluttony and cannibalism, as a number of critics have noted. I discuss the oral imagery of pregnancy in Chapter 4.

4. Name provided in the O'Sullivan and Scott edition of the *Letters*.

5. But see Eve Kosofsky Sedgwick, *Epistemology of the Closet*, for a discussion of the intellectual and political difficulties of such dating of points of origin and transition (44–48).

6. These designations are established by Esther Newton in "The Mythic Mannish Lesbian."

7. Henry James' *The Bostonians* is, of course, plotted by these stereotypes.

8. See Gilbert and Gubar's discussion in the chapter "Cross-Dressing and Re-Dressing: Transvestism as Metaphor" in *No Man's Land*, vol. 2, *Sexchanges*, especially their noting of the "wardrobe of selves" affected by modernist women—like Mansfield—who were more drawn to costume than to cross-dressing (327).

9. Throughout their correspondences Mansfield wrote detailed notes to L.M. with instructions about the color and cut of her clothes, absolving herself of concern with them only at the very last in a note from the Gurdjieff Institute: "Send the green skirt. But please don't write to me any more about clothes. I do not want any and I do not want to talk or think about them *at all* (*LM*, 216).

10. Mansfield's extemporizing with her gender identifications could seem a radically subversive feminist act, especially if viewed within the postmodern critique of gender identities; Judith Butler posits gender as "an identity tenuously constituted in time, instituted in an exterior space through a stylized repetition of acts" (*Gender Trouble*, 140; her emphasis). For Mansfield, however, such stylization was rejected even as it was enacted; she perceived her tendency to masquerade as unhealthy, diseased.

11. Bowden to Andrew Moore, Berkeley, Calif., Feb. 27, 1919, ATL.

12. Though I do not find Mansfield's behavior exemplary, I see no point in choosing sides in the Hastings/Mansfield enmity as John Carswell seems compelled to do in his otherwise very useful book on the pair (*Lives and Letters*).

13. Helene Deutsch has been rightly criticized by contemporary feminists for her rigid emphasis on masochism as the determining feature of feminine gender choice. Nevertheless, the clinical content of her study of the psychology of women remains a rich source of understanding. In her discussion of gender choice, especially, her notation of prostitution fantasies in young girls may help to explain some of Mansfield's turn to heterosexuality with a vengeance in reaction against her father (*Psychology of Women*, 1:268 ff.).

14. Sedgwick discusses Wilde's sentimentality and its mirror reversal of "sentimental/anti-sentimental" in gay male culture in *Epistemology of the Closet* (141–57). I believe that Mansfield was herself involved in such a conflict in her final rejection of Wilde in favor of Chekhov, which Kaplan, however, sees as something of a "reconciliation with the patriarchy" (*Origins*, 199).

15. Paula Bennett mentions the pearl among clitoral images in her study of the female sexual imagery of Emily Dickinson (*Emily Dickinson*, 154, 167) and in a more general survey ("Critical Clitordectomy," 254). *The Woman's Dictionary of Symbols and Sacred Objects* notes, among other significations, that of the androgyne in Greek and Indian myth systems (Walker, 517–18). There was a late Victorian pornographic "Journal of Facetiae and Voluptuous Reading" called *The Pearl*. A piece entitled "Song: Translated from the Hindustani" in one issue refers to the "pearl shell" of the woman's desire (62). Moreover, the stories of sexual surprise which make up the narratives in this kind of book always move from the couple to the triangle in erotic combination. See Magalaner for a doubtful asso-

ciation of the Bertha-Pearl-Harry triangle with that of Mansfield-Murry-L.M. ("Traces").

16. As Margaret Scott has pointed out in editing the fragments of this early novel, "Pearl Saffron" was originally given the name "Vere" after Mansfield's close friend Vere Bartrick-Baker. I know of no autobiographical source for Mansfield's fascination with "Pearl." That it has a symbolic relevance seems clear from the nature of other name changes in the text: "Juliet Wilberforce," for example, becomes "Juliet Night" (*TLR*, "Juliet," 5–6).

17. *Sexchanges*, 355–56. My analysis of the signification of "Pearl" here has benefited from discussions with Alice Falk.

18. I owe this suggestion to Susan Gubar.

19. See Dunbar for a discussion of shifting subject positions in the story. In a reading that figures the story almost as a cubist painting, Dunbar reads the shapes of Bertha's arrangements of fruit in the story as symbolizing breasts ("Bertha," 131).

20. "Bliss" has been one of the most interpreted of Mansfield's stories, and Bertha's sexual orientation has frequently provided the crux for critical disagreements. Judith S. Neaman, for example, sees the image of the pear tree as both biblical and Shakespearean in origin and thus reads the story as one of innocence tested and lost ("Allusion"; Neaman also gives a useful survey of critical points of view, which I will not rehearse here). My own reading is closest to that of Helen F. Nebeker ("The Pear Tree").

21. Virginia Woolf's reaction against the story may have been based upon this treacherous doubleness in the narration (*Diary*, 1:79).

22. Kaplan assesses this turn as a kind of betrayal by succumbing to homophobia (*Origins*, 26). I believe that it involved a necessary rejection of preciosity even as it embodied less admirable resolutions of gender conflict.

23. Although Sir Harold Beauchamp was never called "Harry," so far as the biographical record shows, the name "Harry" seems too close to the name of Mansfield's father to be coincidental.

24. Tomalin makes the association between Mansfield's experiences with Edith Bendall and the episode, citing incidents in the life of Lawrence and Frieda as a convincing basis (*Katherine Mansfield*, 37–38).

25. And lesbian coding (Stimpson, "Zero Degree Deviancy," 371).

26. She also called him "Adonis" in her self-critical diary entry on her love for women quoted above.

Chapter 4: "Fatal—so fatal!"

1. Susan Gubar reads the image of birth in Mansfield's writing as a positive "revision" of woman's creativity rather than a "revulsion" against the "monstrosity" of her situation as artist ("Birth"). Gubar's analysis best suits "Prelude," but

Mansfield worked to that story through *In a German Pension*, where self-revulsion and rejections of feminine maternal solidarity are the presiding themes.

2. I also agree with Tomalin's suspicion that Mansfield's pregnancy began several months earlier than the other biographers contend (*Katherine Mansfield*, 66–68). See Alpers, who positively asserts that Mansfield got pregnant *after* her marriage to Bowden (*Life*, 92).

3. Information received from Professor Sherry F. Queener, director of the Graduate Program, Department of Pharmacology and Toxicology, Indiana University Medical Center, Indianapolis, Ind. Most biographers assume that Mansfield took the Veronal as a sleeping potion.

4. *Psychology of Women;* see also 2:134–40. For a discussion of mythic "eating fears," see 2:43–50.

5. L.M. mentions several incidents in her memoir (*LM*, 58 ff.). For a brilliant analysis of food imagery and sexuality, see Magalaner, "Traces of Her 'Self' in Katherine Mansfield's 'Bliss.'"

6. Antony Alpers has told me that one of the reasons Annie Beauchamp went to England after Mansfield's marriage was to check out Bowden's motivations. The family believed him, and the Trowells, to be fortune hunters. They also suspected Murry, and so Harold Beauchamp never settled any long-term property on his daughter even though he kept up her allowance (telephone interview, August 1989).

7. It is also possible that Mansfield's spa treated venereal disease: see Decker, *Freud*, 52–54.

8. Alpers protests that the pregnancy could not have been in a late stage because such a stillbirth would have required a medical report, and none is on record in Wörishofen (*Life*, 98).

9. Tomalin bases such a conjecture on Mansfield's sudden break with Sobienski and her subsequent report to a woman friend of a "white discharge" through the summer of 1910 (*Katherine Mansfield*, 73). The question that shadows this surmise is the extent of Mansfield's promiscuity after the affair with Trowell. Tomalin is relatively sympathetic with Sobienski's confusion about Mansfield's behavior at this time, but I am concerned with the veiled racism in other accounts, Murry's among them, which characterize him as a "Pole." It may be that this Slavic otherness is what makes him the prime candidate as the source of Mansfield's venereal infection.

10. Segments of this section and the chapter to follow have been taken from my own analysis of Mansfield's childbirth stories in the 1978 *Modern Fiction Studies* special issue on Mansfield (Burgan, "Childbirth Trauma"). I have revised that analysis heavily in light of contemporary psychoanalytic and feminist theory.

11. The most complete study of the narrative strategies of Mansfield's early stories can be found in Saralyn R. Daly's *Katherine Mansfield*. Although this 1965 study is formalist in its approach and thereby distrusts failures of "technical balance" (40), it offers shrewd readings of Mansfield's individual stories.

12. For the most charitable accounts of this issue, see Schneider, "Mansfield and Chekhov," and Franklin, "Plagiarism." Kaplan reads the issue in terms of Mansfield's guilty appropriation of the father's language (*Origins*, 199–200).

13. Celeste Wright ("'Secret Smile'") has been the first to analyze the signification of this trope in psychoanalytic terms.

14. Martin Green has analyzed the influence of the German emphasis on the *Mutterrecht* at the turn of the century, concentrating on its manifestations in the fiction of D.H. Lawrence. De Beauvoir is a stringent critic of this ideology as an enslavement of woman in the ideal: "Hence the fact that while being 'physical,' she is also artificial, and while being earthy, she makes herself ethereal" (*Second Sex*, 582).

15. Tomalin (*Katherine Mansfield*) takes for granted that Mansfield's general health problems from 1911 to 1917 were due to venereal disease. As I suggest in Chapter 7, she may also have been ill from tuberculosis during this time. The gonorrhea symptoms could have masked those of t.b.

16. For feminist analyses of the masculine medical discourse of women's gynecological diseases in the late nineteenth century, see Rich, *Of Woman Born*, as well as Poovey, "'Indelicate Character.'"

17. Using manuscript sources, Gillian Boddy has recently confirmed the possibility that this is a pregnancy story ("Notebook Draft," 109).

18. I am not sure what to make of the pearl imagery here, except to say that the moment so described is one that recalls genital sexuality—possibly evoking an ethereal orgasm as a refuge from the sexuality that has led the young woman to the doctor's examining table.

19. This story seems so similar to Hemingway's "Hills Like White Elephants" that the possibility of influence must be considered.

20. Alpers has done the best job of sorting it all out (*Life*, 122–24).

21. Another of Mansfield's stories, "A Dill Pickle," records the unknowing complacency of a male lover who has left the woman with no explanation. Although this fine story is not necessarily an illness story, Alpers believes that it derives from Mansfield's affair with Francis Heinemann, who may have gotten her pregnant (*Life*, 119, 122).

22. Ehrenreich and English (*Her Own Good*, 131 ff.) and Morris (*Culture*, 105 ff.) discuss the authoritarian cast of S. Weir Mitchell's American "rest cure."

Chapter 5: "Lift my head, Katy, I can't breathe"

1. In this discussion I have relied heavily on Phillip R. Slavney's *Perspectives on "Hysteria,"* an account that manages to give a full view of the biology and symptomology of the illness without neglecting the patient's agency in its behavioral detail and, most important, its insertion in a "life story" that can yield to a variety of therapeutic interpretations. Slavney is one of those physicians who sees the patient as "a *self*—an entity aware of its existence, continuity and coherence; an entity that assigns values, makes choices, and gives reasons" (165).

2. Cited by Morris, *Culture*, 113.

3. See *In Dora's Case* (Bernheimer and Kahane, eds.) for a collection of critiques of Freud's failures in this founding case for psychoanalysis.

4. See, for example, the semimedical diagnosis of Frank O'Connor, that Mansfield—driven by homosexual leanings—was caught in a "permanent adolescence" that has all the earmarks of hysteria (*Lonely Voice*, 131). Virginia Woolf remarked in trying to assess her total effect after her death, "In casting accounts, never forget to begin with the state of the body" (*Diary*, 2:228).

5. Temoshok and Attkisson cite this 1958 formulation as "the most popular behavioral description" in their 1977 survey ("*Hysterical Phenomena*," 147–48). Slavney concludes that the designation of "hysteria" has become so controversial that other words will have to be found—but for the same congeries of symptoms (*Perspectives on "Hysteria*," 190).

6. In this regard, my interpretation of the movement from "Prelude" and "At the Bay" is consonant with the general trend of interpretation by Hankin (*Katherine Mansfield*) and Magalaner (*Fiction*).

7. I am aware of invoking Proust in this statement. The similarity of their interest in the past has been remarked by many critics, notably Hankin (*Katherine Mansfield*, 210). I would emphasize as well the similarity of their mental and physical states as obstacles to be overcome through their writing.

8. According to Catherine Clément, women's writing is the writing of the sorceress and the "hysteric, whose body is transformed into a theater for forgotten scenes, relives the past bearing witness to a lost childhood that survives in suffering (Cixous and Clément, *Newly Born Woman*, 5). And Luce Irigaray asks, "Isn't hysteria a privileged place for preserving—but 'in latency,' 'in sufferance'—that which does not speak?" (*Sex*, 136). See also, for example, Hunter, "Hysteria," 113–14.

9. Teresa de Lauretis critiques as "heterosexual presumption" any thematizings of the woman's body which "relocate woman in Nature, beyond Meaning and Death, and the female body in *hysteria* rather than in history" ("Female Body," 266).

10. See Krohn, *Hysteria*, 174–192, for a description of hysteria in Victorian times as an aspect of feminine cultural repression.

11. These two episodes provided Lawrence with the foundations for his working out of the four-part relationship of two couples in *Women in Love*.

12. Virginia Woolf had long heard of her, but they met relatively late, in 1917. For an account of their interactions as writers, see MacLaughlin, "Uneasy Sisterhood."

13. For a description of his editing of the *Journal* to emphasize her otherworldliness, see Gordon, *Katherine Mansfield*, 32. ´

14. Murry's idealization of Mansfield continued after her death in grotesque ways. For example, Violet le Maistre, his second wife, not only made herself a twin to Mansfield by changing her hair style to Mansfield's cut, but she named her daughter after Mansfield (calling her "Weg" for short). Violet le Maistre also rejoiced that she too contracted tuberculosis; she remarked to Murry: "[Now you can] love me

as much as you loved Katherine" (quoted in Lea, *John Middleton Murry*, 144). Katherine Middleton Murry's loving account of her father's childish weakness in coping with his abusive third wife, Betty, is painful reading. See *Beloved Quixote*, especially p. 59, which quotes Murry's journal entry in which he confides, "I always felt, quite simply, that Violet's daughter was Katherine's daughter." Her brother, Colin Middleton Murry, remembered his father's weakness with less adulation: see *One Hand Clapping*.

15. In her essay "Katherine Mansfield's Piece of Pink Wool," Ruth Parkin-Gounelas reads "Something Childish" as containing a repressed feminist analysis of Edwardian capitalism, designating its sentimentality as "only half the picture" (500).

16. No one has suggested that Gertler might have been the source of her tubercular infection, though Claire Tomalin has theorized that Lawrence may have been the source (*Katherine Mansfield*, 163). In the light of all the environmental variables involved in full-blown tuberculosis, such speculations seem uselessly specific—as we shall see in the next chapter.

17. Mansfield's main criticism of Virginia Woolf's *Night and Day* (*Novels*, 112–15), and the source of her extremely reserved review of the novel, was that it proceeded as if the war had never happened (*CL*, 3:82).

18. Alpers (*Life*, 186) also attributes part of Mansfield's mourning for Chummie to guilt for her own vexed relations with her family.

19. The letters from Chummie, as from her sisters, her Aunt Belle, and the family solicitor, all betray anxiety about Mansfield's health and state of mind, sending good news whenever possible to her parents. After her son's death, Annie Beauchamp wrote to a friend, "You will be glad our darling Leslie was the means of bringing poor old Kass *right* into the fold again" (quoted in Alpers, *Life*, 193).

20. This has been the term used for the male presentation of hysteria. Aldous Huxley mercilessly skewers Murry's childishness and hypochondria in the character of Denis Burlap in *Point Counter Point*.

21. See, for example, his statement on mature identity which lists "a 'conflict-free,' habitual use of a dominant *faculty*, to be elaborated in an *occupation*; a limitless *resource*, a feedback, as it were, from the immediate *exercise* of this occupation, from the *companionship* it provides, and from its *tradition*; and finally, an intelligible *theory* of the processes of life" (*Identity and the Life Cycle*, 118). The emphasis is Erikson's, and it highlights his insistence on work as an aspect of cure.

22. This story matches in sardonic anger against patriarchy Wilfred Owens' image of the generals as Abraham sacrificing his son. One of Mansfield's most analyzed stories, "The Fly" has never been evaluated in terms of her ethic of memory (see Conclusion).

23. See Gubar for a more general, full reading of "Prelude" and "At the Bay" in terms of this "axis in which female definitions of creativity hinge" ("Birth," 25).

24. O'Sullivan's edition of "The Aloe" provides a useful side-by-side printing with "Prelude" (*Aloe with Prelude*, 33).

25. Sylvia Berkman's study still gives the best account of Mansfield's Wordsworthian mode (*Katherine Mansfield*, 12–13).

26. This irritation is reiterated in "The Doll's House" when Beryl castigates Kezia for admitting the poor children into the garden.

27. Celeste Wright was the first critic of Mansfield to note the psychoanalytic interest of her images and to explicate the meaning of the smile as well as the lunging dog in Mansfield's stories.

28. See Murray, *Double Lives*, for a reading that sympathizes with Linda Burnell as representing the only model available for women in the patriarchal grip of New Zealand society of her day. This "political" categorization of Mansfield's women seems to me often misguided as to where the center of Mansfield's critique of women's lives actually lies.

29. Other readings of this episode emphasize the oral/phallic significations (see, for example, Moran, "Unholy Meanings," 119), but I think that the death itself needs to be recognized. Kezia's separation fears are fears of ultimate annihilation.

30. The editors of Mansfield's letters note the similarity of the description of the grandmother and the baby in this dream with the account of the death of Gwen (*CL* 1:208, n. 1).

Chapter 6: "Je ne parle pas français"

1. In her introduction to *The Critical Writings*, Clare Hanson has given the best assessment of the importance of Mansfield's critical contributions to women's writing in modernism. See also Magalaner (*Fiction*) for a shrewd survey of Mansfield's reviews.

2. The disappearance of "Aunt Marthe" was a cruel physiological joke, possibly caused by Mansfield's severe weight loss. When her period returned later, she suffered a bout with anemia.

3. Herzlich and Pierret point out that the French did not accept tuberculosis as a contagious disease until 1889, whereas the Italians and Spanish had classified it so since the beginning of the century (*Illness and Self*, 105).

4. Smith notes that "between 1948 and 1971 streptomycin and its associated drugs reduced the number of deaths by 51 per cent, a saving of about 140,000 lives" (*Retreat*, 247).

5. The white plague has continued in Third World countries and has erupted again in industrial societies everywhere partly as an attendant on the AIDS epidemic, partly as a result of resistant strains of the bacillus, and partly because of the general lowering of hygiene and nutrition among the urban poor.

6. It may not be too fanciful to link her environment with that of the fated Mimi in *La Bohème*, one of the most romantic evocations of urban consumption in the early twentieth century.

7. The connection between tobacco and tuberculosis is suggested by the fact

that tobacco workers showed a marked increase in susceptibility to the disease (Smith, *Retreat,* 214, and Medical Research Committee, *Inquiry,* 36).

8. See Guillaume, *Désespoir au salut,* 81–105, for a French view of the power of the romantic image of tuberculosis. Smith lists the famous victims (*Retreat,* 225–28).

9. On Feb. 3, 1820, after a fit of coughing which led to hemoptysis, Keats said to Charles Brown, "I know the colour of that blood. It's arterial blood. There's no mistaking that colour. That blood is my death warrant. I must die" (quoted in Ward, *John Keats,* 347). Keats' knowledge seems to have come from his own short career as a doctor.

10. Mansfield does mention being the cause of the deaths of guinea pigs later in her treatment, referring to the practice of injecting laboratory animals with the patient's serum to see whether or not the deadly bacillus was still active.

11. Mansfield had her lungs x-rayed in 1920: "It cost me 200 francs & the cocher charged me 15 francs pour aller et retour" (*CL* 3:202), but as Smith notes, at that time x-rays were "very hard to read" (*Retreat,* 146).

12. René and Jean Dubos (*White Plague*) tell the history of these doctors, many of whom were themselves tubercular and died of the disease.

13. A subspecialty in the interdisciplinary study of literature and medicine is the analysis of the work of doctors or close relatives of doctors who were also writers, among them Arthur Conan Doyle. Keats has been given such scrutiny, and other such writers included Smollett, William Carlos Williams, Flaubert, and Gertrude Stein. There have been a number of discussions of the literary form of psychoanalytic case histories, of which Freud was a founding master. But Freud built upon an already formulated procedure for diagnosis, taking its clues further back into childhood as well as into the unconscious. See Abel, *Virginia Woolf,* and Peter Brooks, *Reading for the Plot,* on the "fictions of psychoanalysis."

14. Although this list of diagnostic procedures comes from a 1939 textbook, Margaret C. Heagarty, M.D., informs me that they are still the first ones to be used (letter to the author, Feb. 15, 1993). Obviously contemporary medicine has found many more things to do to a patient in penetrating to lung disease and its causes.

15. Whether the same is true of the lung specialist as a type is an interesting question; there have been some surveys of physician personality types which suggest greater flamboyance for surgeons, for example, and lesser for internists. See Shorter, *Bedside Manners.*

16. It is no wonder that within this intimacy, lung doctors frequently came down with tuberculosis. Katherine Mansfield's own beloved Dr. Sorapure died of consumption.

17. His discrimination of the "SPOT" may have been aided by x-ray, though Mansfield gives no mention of having had such a procedure and 1918 is relatively early for diagnostic radiology. The transition in diagnosis from person-to-person examination to the use of machines to peer into the interior of the body, and to schematize it in the process, constitutes another mode of medical mentality.

18. The only other major experiment with first-person narrativization was "A Married Man's Story," the study of another pathologically self-concerned male figure.

19. I am, of course, indebted to Eve Kosofsky Sedgwick's *Between Men* for aspects of this judgment. I am also indebted to "Katherine Mansfield and the Love That Dare Not Speak Its Name," a paper on Mansfield's homophobia by Bill Scroggie, my student at Indiana University.

20. The uncensored version was first published in 1918 by the Heron Press, a venture that Mansfield and Murry undertook with his younger brother. The uncut version is now available in Alpers' edition of the stories (*DE*), published in England and New Zealand. Because of copyright, this edition is not available in the United States.

21. Like Mansfield herself, most critics see the story as a turning point. See, for example, Alpers, *DE*, 559, and Hankin, *Katherine Mansfield*, 154–63.

22. Mansfield read "The Love Song of J. Alfred Prufrock" aloud at a party at Garsington in 1917 (Alpers, *Life*, 239).

23. Mansfield called "The Love Song of J. Alfred Prufrock" a "short story." Her own Mr. Reginald Peacock seems a similar experiment.

24. Rhoda B. Nathan points out that Mansfield was reading Dostoyevski as she wrote the story and that the opening line of *Notes from the Underground* begins: "I am a sick man" (*Katherine Mansfield*, 110).

25. Preface to *The Ambassadors* (11). Of course, here James is worried, to some extent, about the story getting away from him in length as well as in implication.

Chapter 7: "I prevented you from living at all"

1. For the classic discussion of this complex, see Talcott Parsons, "Definitions of Health and Illness."

2. The episode became an incident in *Women in Love*, where Lawrence managed to admire the individual act of Gudrun Brangwen while eventually denigrating her feminine aggression.

3. This was a designation she suggested in a letter begging L.M. to come to help her when she was seeking to establish a curative household in Hampstead. Claire Tomalin used the term in a play she wrote about Mansfield and Ida Baker; the play was produced in London in 1990.

4. See Marek, for example, who moves from an exposition of the class consciousness in "The Garden-Party" (in which she reads the colonial social disparities as more intensified than resolved at the end) to a review of Mansfield's relationship with L.M. as manifesting itself "in what amounted to class division between the privileged 'artist' and the obedient 'servant'" ("Class Consciousness," 42).

5. This list of the phases of acceptance of dying is taken from Kübler-Ross, *On Death and Dying*, 235. Kübler-Ross's important study of the reactions and needs of terminal patients indicts the dehumanization of treatment in modern hospitals,

but it also points to the isolation and sense of desertion suffered in any setting by a patient who is dying.

6. Interestingly enough, the health history of "Dora's" family shows how pervasive was the late nineteenth century's appropriation of the daughter as nurse for the tubercular patient. Dora's father had tuberculosis, and she nursed him during one of his episodes. He also had venereal disease, which he passed on to his wife; again it was Dora who accompanied her ailing mother to one of the German spas that specialized in treatment of women's gonorrhea. Thus Dora's hysteria seems to have been instigated in part by the pressure of family illness (see Decker, *Freud*, 50–55). Virginia Woolf was also aware of the enslavement of the oldest daughter to ailing fathers.

7. See Herzlich and Pierret (*Illness and Self*)for a discussion of the class struggle in the turn from "consumption to tuberculosis." In this important sociological investigation, the authors pay attention to the social hierarchies in the conception of tuberculosis as the dominating disease of the late industrial culture of the end of the nineteenth century and beginning of the twentieth.

8. It was with Mark Gertler that Mansfield enacted a passionate affair in a Christmas play in 1914, right before she left Murry to rendezvous with Francis Carco in France. Her defiant acting out of a passionate scene with him scandalized Lawrence and put Murry on notice that she was tiring of the close confinement of the Laurentian alternative "family" circle.

9. Smith mentions Mundesley as the "one sanatorium in England for wealthy people who did not want to travel or were advised against going abroad." Its minimum weekly rate was five guineas, a cost that would have been prohibitive for Mansfield (*Retreat*, 129–30).

10. In the early nineteenth century, Hampstead was noted in the guide books to London as having good air—which may have accounted for Keats' choosing to live there. (I am grateful to Royal A. Gettmann for this information.) Smith mentions Mount Vernon as a well-known Hampstead sanatorium (*Retreat*, 96).

11. Dr. Sorapure buoyed her spirits with this advice, but it may have been biased because he too was a fellow sufferer.

12. Saralyn R. Daly sees the story as a satire on the husband (*Katherine Mansfield*, 88–89).

13. I see such a reconciliation in "The Stranger." But "The Fly," a later story, continues to register Mansfield's animus against the patriarchal male.

14. Smith notes that many of the German health spas, with their regimen of heavy meals and "the water cure," had been founded by and for tubercular patients (*Retreat*, 98).

15. Murry was relatively candid in publishing Mansfield's coruscating letters to him, but his acceptance of her accusations always seems to posit him as a bewildered and lost victim and her as distraught by her disease. The letters that he left out of his editions of her letters are the ones that go into specific physical detail and the ones that indicate his meanness with money.

16. L.M. regrets that "nothing was known about collapsing a lung in those days," as if that might have preserved Mansfield from the risk of hemorrhaging (*LM*, 211).

17. Justus's survey of these stories ("Katherine Mansfield: The Triumph of Egoism") seems the most balanced to me, on the whole. "Miss Brill" has been extensively glossed because of the unsteadiness of its focus: on the one hand it makes a dispassionate inventory of the character's favorite notions about herself and the world, and on the other it lodges sympathy for the frailty of her self-esteem in her pathetic vanity about her fur stole. Her last impression of the fox uttering a little cry as she puts it away seems to force the sentiment. Nevertheless, Miriam Mandel's reading in "Reductive Language in 'Miss Brill' " (473–79) misses Mansfield's solidarity with such pathetic women.

18. For an invaluable description of the sources and composition of the story, see Alpers' edition (*DE*, 566–68).

19. See, for example, Mansfield's comment on Dickens' power to be carried away by his own creation (*Journal*, 203). For an appreciation of her stories which emphasizes her "real gaiety and . . . natural sense of comedy" as opposed to her sentimentality, see Katherine Anne Porter, "Art of Katherine Mansfield," 435–36. Don W. Kleine sees "The Daughters of the Late Colonel" as moving from "comic stasis to tragic temporality" (*Patients and Healers*, 426).

Conclusion: *Spes Phthisica* and the Lyric

1. This instance of lyricism in Foucault seems akin to Elaine Scarry's association of pain with the instigation of imagining (*Body in Pain*), and David B. Morris has approached the notion of *spes phthisica* in terms of the romantic experience of affliction (*Culture of Pain*).

2. Sacks' tales are motivated by his interest in their illustration of the resiliency of human adaptation to the most bizarre, and pathetic, of neurological defects. By contrast, Harold L. Klawans, another recent teller of neurological "tales" for popular consumption, focuses on the doctor's role in finding the source of the disease by spotting the telling physical detail. In *Newton's Madness*, Klawans exploits the Sherlock Holmes puzzle of symptoms; ultimately, the hero is the doctor/detective.

3. Studies such as Lewis J. Moorman's do little more than narrate the lives of tubercular artists, while detailing the phenomenon of *spes phthisica*. For an extended critique of the myth of tuberculosis as a disease of "special temperaments," see Sontag, *Illness as Metaphor*, and Guillaume, *Désespoir au salut*.

4. See Smith for a medical assessment of the presumption that the toxemia of tuberculosis was at the origin of this febrile drive to creativity (*Retreat*, 227–28).

5. My formulation is drawn, in part, from Ricoeur's discussion of "expectation, memory, and attention" (*Time and Narrative*, 1:9).

6. See Alpers for details (*Life*, 356–57).

ᑤ Select Bibliography

Abel, Elizabeth. *Virginia Woolf and the Fictions of Psychoanalysis*. Chicago: U of Chicago P, 1989.

Allen, Walter. *The Short Story in Fiction*. Oxford: Clarendon, 1981.

Alpers, Antony. *The Life of Katherine Mansfield*. London: Jonathan Cape, 1980.

Anderson, Walter E. "The Hidden Love Triangle in Mansfield's 'Bliss.'" *Twentieth Century Literature* 28 (Winter 1982): 397–404.

Appiah, Anthony. "Tolerable Falsehoods: Agency and the Interests of Theory." In *Consequences of Theory*, edited by Jonathan Arac and Barbara Johnson, 63–90. Selected Papers from the English Institute, n.s., 14. Baltimore: Johns Hopkins UP, 1991.

Armstrong, Martin. "The Art of Katherine Mansfield." *Fortnightly Review* (Mar. 1923): 464–90.

Bachelard, Gaston. *The Poetics of Space*. Translated by Maria Jolas. Boston: Beacon, 1969.

Bakan, David. *Disease, Pain, and Sacrifice: Toward a Psychology of Suffering*. Chicago: U of Chicago P, 1968.

Bank, Stephen P., and Michael D. Kahn. *The Sibling Bond*. New York: Basic, 1982.

Barker-Benfield, G. J. *The Horrors of the Half-Known Life: Male Attitudes toward Women and Sexuality in Nineteenth-Century America*. New York: Harper, 1976.

Bassuk, Ellen L. "The Rest Cure: Repetition or Resolution of Victorian Women's Conflicts." In Suleiman, 139–51.

Bates, H. E. *The Modern Short Story: A Critical Survey*. London: Thomas Nelson, 1941.

Beauchamp, Sir Harold. *Reminiscences and Recollections*. New Plymouth, New Zealand: Thomas Avery, 1937.

Beeton, Isabella M. *The Book of Household Management*. 1861. New York: Farrar, 1969.

Bell, Barbara Currier. "Non-Identical Twins: Nature in 'The Garden Party' and 'The Grave.'" *Comparatist* 12 (May 1988): 58–66.

Bell, Quentin. *Virginia Woolf: A Biography.* 2 vols. London: Hogarth, 1972.

Bennett, Paula. "Critical Clitordectomy: Female Sexual Imagery and Feminist Psychoanalytic Theory." *Signs* 18 (Winter 1993): 235–59.

———. *Emily Dickinson: Woman Poet.* New York: Harvester, 1990.

Berkman, Sylvia. *Katherine Mansfield: A Critical Study.* New Haven: Yale UP, 1951.

Bernheimer, Charles, and Claire Kahane, eds. *In Dora's Case: Freud—Hysteria—Feminism.* New York: Columbia UP, 1985.

Bigfoot, Carol. "Renaturalizing the Body (with the Help of Merleau-Ponty)." *Hypatia* 6 (1991): 54–73.

Blanchard, Lydia. "The Savage Pilgrimage of D. H. Lawrence and Katherine Mansfield: A Study in Literary Influence, Anxiety, and Subversion." *Modern Language Quarterly* 47 (1986): 48–65.

Blodgett, Harriet. "The Inviolable Self: Reappraising Katherine Mansfield's Women." *New Renaissance* 5 (Fall 1983): 104–12.

Boddy, Gillian. "From Notebook Draft to Published Story: 'Late Spring'/'This Flower.'" In Nathan, *Critical Essays,* 101–12.

———. *Katherine Mansfield: The Woman and the Writer.* Ringwood, Australia: Penguin Books Australia, 1988.

Bowden, George. A Biographical Note on Katherine Mansfield, 1947, ATL.

———. Letter to Andrew Moore. Berkeley, Calif., Feb. 27, 1919, ATL.

Bowen, Elizabeth. Introduction to *Stories by Katherine Mansfield,* by Katherine Mansfield. New York: Vintage, 1956.

Bowlby, John. *Attachment and Loss.* 3 vols. New York: Basic, 1969–80.

Brandt, Allan M. *No Magic Bullet: A Social History of Venereal Disease in the United States since 1880.* New York: Oxford UP, 1985.

Breuer, Josef, and Sigmund Freud. *Studies on Hysteria.* Translated by James Strachey in collaboration with Anna Freud. New York: Basic, 1957.

Brody, Howard. *Stories of Sickness.* New Haven: Yale UP, 1987.

Brooks, Peter. *Reading for the Plot: Design and Intention in Narrative.* New York: Knopf, 1984.

Brooks, Stewart M. *The V.D. Story.* South Brunswick and New York: A. S. Barnes, 1971.

Broyard, Anatole. *Intoxicated by My Illness and Other Writings on Life and Death.* Edited by Alexandra Broyard. New York: Clarkson Potter, 1992.

Bruch, Hilde. *Eating Disorders: Obesity, Anorexia Nervosa, and the Person Within.* New York: Basic, 1973.

Brumberg, Joan Jacobs. *Fasting Girls: The Emergence of Anorexia Nervosa as a Modern Disease.* Cambridge: Harvard UP, 1988.

Bryder, Linda. *Below the Magic Mountain: A Social History of Tuberculosis in Twentieth-Century Britain.* Oxford: Clarendon, 1988.

Burgan, Mary. "Childbirth Trauma in Katherine Mansfield's Early Stories." *Modern Fiction Studies* 24 (1978): 395–412.

Butler, Judith. *Gender Trouble: Feminism and the Subversion of Identity.* New York: Routledge, 1990.

Caplan, Arthur L.; H. Tristram Engelhardt, Jr.; and James J. McCartney, eds. *Concepts of Health and Disease: Interdisciplinary Perspectives.* Reading, Mass.: Addison-Wesley, 1981.

Carco, Francis. *Les innocents.* Paris: Albin Michel, 1927.

Carswell, John. *Lives and Letters: A. R. Orage, Beatrice Hastings, Katherine Mansfield, John Middleton Murry, S. S. Koteliansky, 1906–1957.* London: Faber, 1978.

Caskey, Noelle. "Interpreting Anorexia Nervosa." In Suleiman, 175–89.

Cassavant, Sharron Greer. *John Middleton Murry: The Critic as Moralist.* N.p.: U of Alabama P, 1982.

Cather, Willa. "Katherine Mansfield." In *Not under Forty,* 123–47. New York: Knopf, 1936.

Chauncey, George, Jr. "From Sexual Inversion to Homosexuality: Medicine and the Changing Conceptualization of Female Deviance." *Salmagundi* 58–59 (Fall 1982-Winter 1983): 114–46.

Chodorow, Nancy J. *Feminism and Psychoanalytic Theory.* New Haven: Yale UP, 1989.

———. *The Reproduction of Mothering: Psychoanalysis and the Sociology of Gender.* Berkeley and Los Angeles: U of California P, 1978.

Cixous, Hélène, and Catherine Clément. *The Newly Born Woman.* Translated by Betsy Wing. Minneapolis: U of Minnesota P, 1986.

Clarke, Bruce. "Katherine Mansfield's Illness." *Proceedings of the Royal Society of Medicine* 48 (1955): 1029–32.

Clarke, Bruce, and Wendell Aycock, eds. *The Body and the Text: Comparative Essays in Literature and Medicine.* Lubbock: Texas Tech UP, 1990.

Cox, Sidney. "The Fastidiousness of Katherine Mansfield." *Sewanee Review Quarterly* 39 (1931): 158–69.

Cummings, Katherine. *Telling Tales: The Hysteric's Seduction in Fiction and Theory.* Stanford: Stanford UP, 1991.

Dalsimer, Katherine. *Female Adolescence: Psychoanalytic Reflections on Literature.* New Haven: Yale UP, 1986.

Daly, Saralyn R. *Katherine Mansfield.* New York: Twayne, 1965.

Daniel, Stephen L. "Literature and Medicine: In Quest of Method." In *Literature and Medicine,* edited by D. Heyward Brock, 6:1–12. Baltimore: Johns Hopkins UP, 1987.

Davis, Robert M. "The Unity of 'The Garden Party.'" *Studies in Short Fiction* 2 (Fall 1964): 61–65.

de Beauvoir, Simone. *The Second Sex.* Translated by H. M. Parshley. New York: Knopf, 1952.

Decker, Hannah. *Freud, Dora, and Vienna, 1900.* New York: Free Press, 1991.

Delany, Paul. *D. H. Lawrence's Nightmare: The Writer and His Circle in the Years of the Great War.* New York: Basic, 1978.

de Lauretis, Teresa. "The Female Body and Heterosexual Presumption." *Semiotica* 67 (1987): 259–79.

Deutsch, Helene. *The Psychology of Women: A Psychoanalytic Interpretation.* 2 vols. 1944–45. New York: Bantam, 1973.

Douglas, Mary. *Purity and Danger: An Analysis of the Concepts of Pollution and Taboo.* London: Routledge, 1991.

Drummond, Wilhelmina. "A Psychosocial Study of Katherine Mansfield's Life." In Ricketts, 23–48.

Dubos, René, and Jean Dubos. *The White Plague: Tuberculosis, Man and Society.* 1952. New Brunswick, N.J.: Rutgers UP, 1987.

Dunbar, Pamela. "What Does Bertha Want?: A Re-reading of Katherine Mansfield's 'Bliss.' " In Nathan, *Critical Essays,* 128–39.

DuPlessis, Rachel Blau. *Writing beyond the Ending: Narrative Strategies of Twentieth-Century Women Writers.* Bloomington: Indiana UP, 1985.

Eakin, Paul John. *Fictions in Autobiography: Studies in the Art of Self-Invention.* Princeton: Princeton UP, 1985.

Ehrenreich, Barbara, and Deirdre English. *For Her Own Good: 150 Years of the Experts' Advice to Women.* Garden City, N.Y.: Anchor, 1978.

Eisenbird, Ruth-Jean. "Early and Later Determinates of Lesbian Choice." *Psychoanalytic Review* 69 (1982): 85–109.

Eisholz, Alice. "Psychohistorical Reflections on Changing Body Images for Women." In Offerman-Zuckerberg, 5–15.

Erikson, Erik. *Identity and the Life Cycle.* New York: Norton, 1959.

———. *Identity, Youth, and Crisis.* New York: Norton, 1968.

Feldstein, Richard, and Judith Roof, eds. *Feminism and Psychoanalysis.* Ithaca, N.Y.: Cornell UP, 1989.

Felman, Shoshana, ed. *Literature and Psychoanalysis: The Question of Reading: Otherwise.* Baltimore: Johns Hopkins UP, 1982.

Foucault, Michel. *The Birth of the Clinic: An Archeology of Medical Perception.* Translated by A. M. Sheridan Smith. New York: Random, 1975.

———. *The History of Sexuality.* Translated by Robert Hurley. Vol. 1. New York: Vintage, 1985.

———. *Madness and Civilization.* Translated by Richard Howard. New York: Vintage, 1965.

Franklin, Carol. "Katherine Mansfield and the Charge of Plagiarism." In Ricketts, 75–84.

Freedman, Estelle B.; Barbara C. Gelpi; Susan L. Johnson; and Kathleen M. Weston, eds. *The Lesbian Issue: Essays from SIGNS.* Chicago: U of Chicago P, 1985.

Freud, Sigmund. *Dora: An Analysis of a Case in Hysteria.* Edited by Philip Rieff. New York: Collier, 1963.

———. "Mourning and Melancholia." In *Collected Papers,* 4:152–72. Translated under the supervision of Joan Riviere. New York: Basic, 1959.

————. *The Sexual Enlightenment of Children.* New York: Collier, 1963.

Fromm, Gloria G. "The Remains of Katherine Mansfield." *New Criterion* 6, no. 10 (June 1988): 78–83.

Fullbrook, Kate. *Katherine Mansfield.* Bloomington: Indiana UP, 1986.

Gadd, David. *The Loving Friends: A Portrait of Bloomsbury.* New York: Harcourt, 1974.

Gallop, Jane. *Reading Lacan.* Ithaca, N.Y.: Cornell UP, 1985.

Garner, Shirley Nelson; Claire Kahane; and Madelon Sprengnether, eds. *The (M)other Tongue: Essays in Feminist Psychoanalytic Interpretation.* Ithaca, N.Y.: Cornell UP, 1985.

Garnett, David. *The Flowers of the Forest Being Volume Two of the Golden Echo.* New York: Harcourt, 1956.

Gertler, Mark. MS letters to Sydney Waterlow. Waterlow Papers, ATL.

Gilbert, Sandra, and Susan Gubar. *No Man's Land: The Place of the Woman Writer in the Twentieth Century.* Vol. 1, *The War of the Words,* and Vol. 2, *Sexchanges.* New Haven: Yale UP, 1988, 1989.

Gilligan, Carol. *In a Different Voice: Psychological Theory and Women's Development.* Cambridge: Harvard UP, 1982.

Gogel, Edward L., and James S. Terry. "Medicine as Interpretation: The Uses of Literary Metaphors and Methods." *Journal of Medicine and Philosophy* 12 (1987): 205–17.

Gordon, Ian A. *Katherine Mansfield.* London: Longmans, 1963.

Green, Martin. *The von Richthofen Sisters: The Triumph and the Tragic Modes of Love.* New York: Basic, 1974.

Greenberg, David F. *The Construction of Homosexuality.* Chicago: U of Chicago P, 1988.

Greenberg, Jay R., and Stephen A. Mitchell. *Object Relations in Psychoanalytic Theory.* Cambridge: Harvard UP, 1983.

Gubar, Susan. "The Birth of the Artist as Heroine: Reproduction, the *Kunstlerroman* Tradition, and the Fiction of Katherine Mansfield." In *The Representation of Women in Fiction,* edited by Carolyn G. Heilbrun and Margaret R. Higgonnet, 19–59. Selected Papers from the English Institute. Baltimore: Johns Hopkins UP, 1983.

Guillaume, Pierre. *Du désespoir au salut: Les tuberculeux aux 19e et 20e siècles.* Paris: Aubier, 1986.

Hankin, C. A. *Katherine Mansfield and Her Confessional Stories.* New York: St. Martin's, 1983.

Hanson, Clare. Introduction to "Katherine Mansfield." In Scott, *Gender of Modernism,* 298–305.

————, ed. *The Critical Writings of Katherine Mansfield.* New York: St. Martin's, 1987.

Hanson, Clare, and Andrew Gurr. *Katherine Mansfield.* New York: St. Martin's, 1981.

Hartmann, Heinz. "Psycho-analysis and the Concept of Health." In Caplan, Engelhardt, and McCartney, 361–72.

Hayman, Ronald, ed. *Literature and Living: A Consideration of Katherine Mansfield and Virginia Woolf.* Covent Garden Essays 3. London: Covent Garden, 1972.

Herzlich, Claudine, and Janine Pierret. *Illness and Self in Society.* Translated by Elborg Forster. Baltimore: Johns Hopkins UP, 1987.

Hirsch, Marianne. *The Mother/Daughter Plot: Narrative, Psychoanalysis, Feminism.* Bloomington: Indiana UP, 1989.

Hormasji, Nariman. *Katherine Mansfield: An Appraisal.* Auckland, New Zealand: Collins Bros. & Co., 1967.

Horney, Karen. *New Ways in Psychoanalysis.* New York: Norton, 1939.

Horowitz, Mardi J., ed. *Hysterical Personality.* New York: Aronson, 1977.

Hubbell, George S. "Katherine Mansfield and Kezia." *Sewanee Review Quarterly* 35 (1927): 325–35.

Hughes, Judith M. *Reshaping the Psychoanalytic Domain: The Work of Melanie Klein, W. R. D. Fairbain, and D. W. Winnicott.* Berkeley and Los Angeles: U of California P, 1989.

Hunter, Dianne. "Hysteria, Psychoanalysis, and Feminism: The Case of Anna O." In Garner, Kahane, and Sprengnether, 89–115.

Huxley, Aldous. *Point Counter Point.* London: Chatto & Windus, 1928.

Hynes, Sam. "Katherine Mansfield: The Defeat of the Personal." *South Atlantic Quarterly* 52 (Oct. 1953): 555–60.

Illich, Ivan. *Medical Neurosis: The Expropriation of Health.* New York: Pantheon, 1976.

Irigaray, Luce. *This Sex Which Is Not One.* Translated by Catherine Porter with Carolyn Burke. Ithaca, N.Y.: Cornell UP, 1985.

Isherwood, Christopher. "Katherine Mansfield." In *Exhumations,* 64–72. London: Methuen, 1966.

James, Henry. *The Ambassadors.* New York: Norton, 1964.

James, William. *The Will to Believe, and Other Essays in Popular Philosophy.* New York: Longmans, 1896.

Jameson, Frederic. "Imaginary and Symbolic in Lacan: Marxism, Psychoanalytic Criticism, and the Problem of the Subject." In Felman, 338–95.

Jardine, Alice A. *Gynesis: Configurations of Women and Modernity.* Ithaca, N.Y.: Cornell UP, 1985.

Justus, James H. "Katherine Mansfield: The Triumph of Egoism." *Mosaic* 6 (1973): 13–22.

Kahane, Claire. "Hysteria, Feminism, and the Case of *The Bostonians.*" In Feldstein and Roof, 280–97.

Kaplan, Sydney Janet. *Katherine Mansfield and the Origins of Modernist Fiction.* Ithaca, N.Y.: Cornell UP, 1991.

Katz, Jay. *The Silent World of Doctor and Patient.* New York: Free Press, 1984.

Kegan, Robert. *The Evolving Self: Problem and Process in Human Development.* Cambridge: Harvard UP, 1982.

King, Lester S. *Medical Thinking: A Historical Preface.* Princeton: Princeton UP, 1982.

Klawans, Harold L. *Newton's Madness: Further Tales of Clinical Neurology.* London: Bodley Head, 1990.

Klein, Melanie. *The Psychoanalysis of Children.* London: Hogarth and the Institute of Psycho-analysis, 1932. Revised in collaboration with Alix Strachey by H. A. Thorner. Translated by Alix Strachey. New York: Dell, Delta, 1976.

Kleine, Don W. "Mansfield and the Orphans of Time." *Modern Fiction Studies* 24 (1978): 423–38.

Kleinman, Arthur. *Patients and Healers in the Context of Culture: An Exploration of the Borderland between Anthropology, Medicine, and Psychiatry.* Berkeley and Los Angeles: U of California P, 1980.

Kobler, J. F. *Katherine Mansfield: A Study of the Short Fiction.* Boston: Twayne, 1990.

Kristeva, Julia. "The Pain of Sorrow in the Modern World: The Works of Marguerite Duras." Translated by Katharine A. Jensen. *PMLA* 102 (1987): 138–52.

———. *Powers of Horror: An Essay on Abjection.* Translated by Leon S. Roudiez. New York: Columbia UP, 1982.

———. "Stabat Mater." In Suleiman, 99–118.

Krohn, Alan. *Hysteria: The Elusive Neurosis.* New York: International Universities P, 1978.

Kübler-Ross, Elisabeth. *On Death and Dying.* New York: Macmillan, 1969.

Kundera, Milan. *The Unbearable Lightness of Being.* Translated by Michael H. Heim. New York: Harper, 1984.

Lacan, Jacques. *Écrits: A Selection.* Translated by Alan Sheridan. New York: Norton, 1977.

———. *Feminine Sexuality.* Translated by Jacqueline Rose. New York: Norton, 1982.

Lawrence, D. H. *The Letters of D. H. Lawrence: Volume III, October 1916–June 1921.* Edited by James T. Boulton and Andrew Robertson. Cambridge: Cambridge UP, 1979.

———. *Women in Love.* New York: Viking, 1920.

Lawrence, Frieda. *Frieda Lawrence: The Memoirs and Correspondence.* Edited by E. W. Tedlock. New York: Knopf, 1964.

Lea, F. A. *The Life of John Middleton Murry.* London: Methuen, 1959.

MacLaughlin, Ann L. "An Uneasy Sisterhood: Virginia Woolf and Katherine Mansfield." In *Virginia Woolf: A Feminist Slant,* edited by Jane Marcus, 152–61. Lincoln: U of Nebraska P, 1983.

Magalaner, Marvin. *The Fiction of Katherine Mansfield.* Carbondale: Southern Illinois UP, 1971.

———. "Traces of Her 'Self' in Katherine Mansfield's 'Bliss.'" *Modern Fiction Studies* 24 (Autumn 1978): 413–22.

Mandel, Miriam B. "Reductive Language in 'Miss Brill.'" *Studies in Short Fiction* 26 (Fall 1989): 473–77.

Mansfield, Katherine. *The Aloe with Prelude*. Edited by Vincent O'Sullivan. Wellington, New Zealand: Port Nicholson P, 1983.

———. *The Collected Letters of Katherine Mansfield*. Edited by Vincent O'Sullivan and Margaret Scott. 3 vols. Oxford: Oxford UP, 1984–93.

———. "A Fairy Story." Privately printed.

———. "Fifteen Letters to Virginia Woolf." *Adam* 19 (1972–73): 370–76.

———. *Journal of Katherine Mansfield*. Edited by John Middleton Murry. London: Constable, 1954.

———. "Katherine Mansfield: The Unpublished Manuscripts: Juliet." Edited by Margaret Scott. *Turnbull Library Record* 3 (Mar. 1970): 5–28.

———. "Katherine Mansfield: The Unpublished Manuscripts." Edited by Margaret Scott. *Turnbull Library Record* 3 (Nov. 1970): 129–36.

———. "Katherine Mansfield: The Unpublished Manuscripts." Edited by Margaret Scott. *Turnbull Library Record* 4 (May 1971): 6–20.

———. "Katherine Mansfield: The Unpublished Manuscripts." Edited by Margaret Scott. *Turnbull Library Record* 5 (May 1972): 20–25.

———. "Katherine Mansfield: The Unpublished Manuscripts." Edited by Margaret Scott. *Turnbull Library Record* 6 (Oct. 1972): 5–8.

———. "Katherine Mansfield: The Unpublished Manuscripts." Edited by Margaret Scott. *Turnbull Library Record* 7 (May 1974): 5–14.

———. "Katherine Mansfield: The Unpublished Manuscripts: 'Maata.'" Edited by Margaret Scott. *Turnbull Library Record* 12 (May 1979): 13–28.

———. *Katherine Mansfield's Letters to John Middleton Murry, 1913–1922*. Edited by John Middleton Murry. London: Constable, 1951.

———. *The Letters of Katherine Mansfield*. Edited by John Middleton Murry. New York: Knopf, 1932.

———. "Mary: A Story." *Harper's Monthly Magazine* (1910): 274–76.

———. *Novels and Novelists*. Edited by John Middleton Murry. New York: Knopf, 1930.

———. *Poems of Katherine Mansfield*. Edited by Vincent O'Sullivan. Auckland, New Zealand: Oxford UP, 1988.

———. *The Scrapbook of Katherine Mansfield*. Edited by John Middleton Murry. New York: Knopf, 1940.

———. *The Short Stories of Katherine Mansfield*. New York: Knopf, 1967.

———. *The Stories of Katherine Mansfield: Definitive Edition*. Edited by Antony Alpers. Auckland, New Zealand: Oxford UP, 1988.

———. "Study: The Death of a Rose." *Triad* (July 1, 1908): 35.

Mantz, Ruth Elvish, and John Middleton Murry. *The Life of Katherine Mansfield*. London: Constable, 1933.

Marek, Jayne. "Class Consciousness and Self-Consciousness in Katherine Mansfield's 'The Garden Party.'" *Postscript: Publication of the Philological Association of the Carolinas* 7 (1990): 35–43.

McEldowney, Dennis. "The Multiplex Effect: Recent Biographical Writing on Katherine Mansfield." *Ariel* 16 (Oct. 1985): 111–24.

Mechaire, David. "The Concept of Illness Behavior." In Caplan, Engelhardt, and McCartney, 485–92.

Medical Research Committee [Great Britain National Health Insurance Joint Committee]. *An Inquiry into the Prevalence and Aetiology of Tuberculosis among Industrial Workers, with Special Reference to Female Munition Workers*. London: Government Publication, 1918.

Mendell, Dale. "Early Female Development from Birth through Latency." In Offerman-Zuckerberg, 17–36.

Merlin, Roland. *Le drame secret de Katherine Mansfield*. Paris: Editions du Seuil, 1950.

Meyers, Jeffrey. *Disease and the Novel, 1890–1960*. New York: St. Martin's, 1985.

———. *Katherine Mansfield: A Biography*. London: Hamish Hamilton, 1978.

Michie, Helena. *The Flesh Made Word: Female Figures and Women's Bodies*. New York: Oxford UP, 1987.

Miller, James Alexander, and Arvid Walgreen. *Pulmonary Tuberculosis in Adults and Children*. New York: Nelson, 1939.

Mitchell, Juliet, and Jacqueline Rose, eds. *Feminine Sexuality: Jacques Lacan and the École Freudienne*. Translated by Jacqueline Rose. New York: Norton, 1985.

Monroe, William. "Performing Persons: A Locus of Connection for Medicine and Literature." In Clarke and Aycock, 25–40.

Moore, James. *Gurdjieff and Mansfield*. London: Routledge, 1980.

Moore, Leslie [Ida Constance Baker]. *Katherine Mansfield: The Memories of L.M.* 1971. London: Virago, 1985.

Moormans, Lewis J. *Tuberculosis and Genius*. Chicago: U of Chicago P, 1940.

Moran, Patricia. "Unholy Meanings: Maternity, Creativity, and Orality in Katherine Mansfield." *Feminist Studies* 17 (1991): 105–25.

Morris, David. *The Culture of Pain*. Berkeley and Los Angeles: U of California P, 1991.

Morrow, Patrick. "Katherine Mansfield and World War I." In *Literature and War*, edited by David Bevan, 39–43. Amsterdam: Rodopi, 1990.

Murray, Heather. *Double Lives: Women in the Stories of Katherine Mansfield*. Dunedin, New Zealand: U of Otago P, 1990.

Murry, Colin Middleton. *One Hand Clapping: A Memoir of Childhood*. London: Victor Gollancz, 1975.

———. *Shadows on the Grass*. London: Victor Gollancz, 1977.

Murry, John Middleton. *Between Two Worlds: The Autobiography of John Middleton Murry*. New York: Julian Messner, 1936.

———. *Katherine Mansfield and Other Literary Studies*. London: Constable, 1959.

———. *The Letters of John Middleton Murry to Katherine Mansfield*. Edited by C. A. Hankin. New York: Franklin Watts, 1983.

Murry, Katherine Middleton. *Beloved Quixote: The Unknown Life of John Middleton Murry*. London: Souvenir, 1986.

Nathan, Rhoda B. *Katherine Mansfield*. New York: Ungar, 1988.

———, ed. *Critical Essays on Katherine Mansfield*. New York: G. K. Hall, 1993.

Neaman, Judith S. "Allusion, Image, and Associative Pattern: The Answers in Mansfield's 'Bliss.' " In Nathan, *Critical Essays*, 117–27.

Nebeker, Helen F. "The Pear Tree: Sexual Implications in Katherine Mansfield's 'Bliss.' " *Modern Fiction Studies* 24 (1978): 545–51.

Nehls, Edward. *D. H. Lawrence: A Composite Biography*. 3 vols. Madison: U of Wisconsin P, 1957.

"The 'New' Doll's House Is Pleasing Visitors." *Mansfield News* (Katherine Mansfield Birthplace Society) 5 (May 1992): 1.

Newton, Esther. "The Mythic Mannish Lesbian: Radclyffe Hall and the New Woman." In Freedman, Gelpi, Johnson, and Weston, 7–25.

Nicolson, Nigel. *Portrait of a Marriage*. New York: Bantam, 1974.

Nightingale, Florence. *Notes on Nursing: What It Is and What It Is Not*. London, 1859. Facsimile ed., Philadelphia: Lippincott, 1946.

Ober, William B. *Boswell's Clap and Other Essays: Medical Analysis of Literary Men's Afflictions*. Carbondale: Southern Illinois UP, 1979.

———. *Bottom's Up! A Pathologist's Essays on Medicine and the Humanities*. Carbondale: Southern Illinois UP, 1987.

O'Connor, Frank. *The Lonely Voice*. Cleveland: World Publishing, 1963.

O'Faolain, Sean. *The Short Story*. London: Collins, 1948.

Offerman-Zuckerberg, Joan, ed. *Critical Psychophysical Passages in the Life of a Woman: A Psychodynamic Approach*. New York: Plenum, 1988.

Orage, A. R. *Selected Essays and Critical Writings*. Edited by Herbert Read and Denis Saurat. Freeport, N.Y.: Books for Libraries P, 1967.

Orton, William. *The Last Romantic*. London: Cassell, 1937.

O'Sullivan, Vincent. *Katherine Mansfield's New Zealand*. London: Muller, 1975.

Parkin-Gounelas, Ruth. *Fictions of the Female Self: Charlotte Brontë, Olive Schreiner, Katherine Mansfield*. New York: St. Martin's, 1991.

———. "Katherine Mansfield's Piece of Pink Wool: Feminine Signification in 'The Luftbad.' " *Studies in Short Fiction* 27 (Fall 1990): 495–507.

Parsons, Talcott. "Definitions of Health and Illness in the Light of American Values and Social Structure." In Caplan, Engelhardt, and McCartney, 57–81.

The Pearl: A Journal of Facetiae and Voluptuous Reading. Selections from Volumes 1–18/July 1879–December 1880, with items from *The Oyster*. Sevenoaks, Kent: New English Library, 1984.

Poovey, Mary. " 'Scenes of an Indelicate Character': The Medical 'Treatment' of Victorian Women." In *The Making of the Modern Body*, edited by Catherine Gallagher and Thomas Laqueur, 137–68. Berkeley and Los Angeles: U of California P, 1987.

Porter, Katherine Anne. "The Art of Katherine Mansfield." *Nation* 145 (1937): 435–36.

Pritchett, V. S. "Books in General." Review of *The Collected Stories of Katherine Mansfield* by Katherine Mansfield. *New Statesman and Nation* (Feb. 2, 1946): 87.

———. "Katherine Mansfield." *New Yorker* 26 (Oct. 1981): 196–200.

Proust, Marcel. *Cities of the Plain.* Translated by C. K. Scott-Moncrieff. New York: Modern Library, 1955.

Rich, Adrienne. *Of Woman Born: Motherhood as Experience and Institution.* New York: Bantam, 1977.

Ricketts, Harry, ed. *Worlds of Katherine Mansfield.* Palmerston North, New Zealand: Nagare P, 1991.

Ricoeur, Paul. *Time and Narrative.* 3 vols. Translated by Kathleen McLaughlin and David Pellauer. Chicago: U of Chicago P, 1984–88.

Rifflet-Lemaire, Anika. *Jacques Lacan.* London: Routledge, 1977.

Riley, Denise. *"Am I That Name?": Feminism and the Category of "Women" in History.* Minneapolis: U of Minnesota P, 1988.

Roof, Judith. *A Lure of Knowledge: Lesbian Sexuality and Theory.* New York: Columbia UP, 1991.

Rorty, Amelie Oksenberg, ed. *The Identities of Persons.* Berkeley and Los Angeles: U of California P, 1976.

Rosen, David H. *Lesbianism: A Study of Female Homosexuality.* Springfield, Ill.: Charles C. Thomas, 1974.

Roudinesco, Elisabeth. *Jacques Lacan and Co.: A History of Psychoanalysis in France, 1925–1985.* Translated by Jeffrey Mehlman. Chicago: U of Chicago P, 1990.

Ruddick, Lisa. *Reading Gertrude Stein: Body, Text, Gnosis.* Ithaca, N.Y.: Cornell UP, 1990.

Sacks, Oliver. *The Man Who Mistook His Wife for a Hat and Other Clinical Tales.* New York: Summit, 1985.

Sagan, Eli. *Freud, Women, and Society: The Psychology of Good and Evil.* New York: Basic, 1988.

Scarry, Elaine. *The Body in Pain: The Making and Unmaking of the World.* New York: Oxford UP, 1985.

Schleifer, Ronald. *Rhetoric and Death: The Language of Modernism and Postmodern Discourse Theory.* Urbana: U of Illinois P, 1990.

Schneider, Elizabeth. "Katherine Mansfield and Chekhov." *Modern Language Notes* 50 (1935): 394–97.

Scott, Bonnie Kime, ed. *The Gender of Modernism: A Critical Anthology.* Bloomington: Indiana UP, 1990.

Scroggie, Bill. "Katherine Mansfield and the Love That Dare Not Speak Its Name." Paper presented at the Twentieth Century Literature Conference, University of Louisville, Louisville, Ky., 1993.

Sears, Pauline Snedden. *Doll Play Aggression in Normal Young Children: Influence of Sex, Age, Sibling Status, Father's Absence.* Psychological Monographs: General and Applied, edited by Herbert S. Conrad, vol. 65. Washington, D.C.: American Psychological Association, 1951.

Sedgwick, Eve Kosofsky. *Between Men: English Literature and Male Homosocial Desire.* New York: Columbia UP, 1985.

———. *The Epistemology of the Closet.* Berkeley and Los Angeles: U of California P, 1990.

Selver, Paul. *Orage and the New Age Circle: Reminiscences and Reflections.* London: Allen, 1959.

Shanks, Edward. "Katherine Mansfield." *London Mercury* 18 (1928): 286–93.

Sharland, James Cragg. *The Settler's Guide and Household Companion: A Compendium of Useful Information and Hints for the Preservation of Health and the Prevention of Disease, etc.* Auckland, New Zealand: Wilsons & Horton, 1878.

Shaw, Helen, ed. *Dear Lady Ginger: An Exchange of Letters between Lady Ottoline Morrell and D'Arcy Creswell together with Ottoline Morrell's Essay on Katherine Mansfield.* London: Century, 1983.

Shorter, Edward. *Bedside Manners: The Troubled History of Doctors and Patients.* New York: Simon, 1985.

———. *A History of Women's Bodies.* New York: Basic, 1982.

Siegel, Carol. "Virginia Woolf's and Katherine Mansfield's Responses to D. H. Lawrence's Fiction." *D. H. Lawrence Review* 21, no. 3 (Fall 1989): 291–311.

Slavney, Phillip R. *Perspectives on "Hysteria."* Baltimore: Johns Hopkins UP, 1990.

Smith, F. B. *The Retreat of Tuberculosis, 1850–1950.* London: Croom Helm, 1988.

Smith-Rosenberg, Carol. "The Female World of Love and Ritual: Relations between Women in Nineteenth-Century America." *Signs* 1 (Autumn 1975): 1–30.

Sontag, Susan. *Against Interpretation.* New York: Farrar, 1966.

———. *Illness as Metaphor.* New York: Vintage, 1979.

Steiner, George. *Language and Silence: Essays on Language, Literature, and the Inhuman.* New York: Atheneum, 1967.

Stimpson, Catharine R. "Zero Degree Deviancy: The Lesbian Novel in English." *Critical Inquiry* 8 (Winter 1981): 363–79.

Suleiman, Susan Rubin, ed. *The Female Body in Western Culture: Contemporary Perspectives.* Cambridge: Harvard UP, 1986.

Taylor, Donald S., and David A. Weiss. "Cracking the Garden Party." *Modern Fiction Studies* 4 (1958–59): 361–64.

Taylor, Robert W., A.M., M.D. *A Practical Treatise on Genito-Urinary and Venereal Diseases and Syphilis.* 3d ed. New York: Lea Bros. & Co., 1904.

Temoshok, Lydia, and C. Clifford Attkisson. "Epidemiology of Hysterical Phenomena: Evidence for a Psychosocial Theory." In Horowitz, 143–222.

Tomalin, Claire. *Katherine Mansfield: A Secret Life.* New York: Knopf, 1988.

Twaddle, Andrew C. *Sickness Behavior and the Sick Role.* Boston: G. K. Hall, 1979.

Vicinus, Martha. "Distance and Desire: English Boarding-School Friendships." In Freedman, Gelpi, Johnson, and Weston, 43–65.

Wagenknecht, Edward. "Katherine Mansfield." *English Journal* 17 (1928): 272–84.

Waldron, Phillip. "Katherine Mansfield's *Journal.*" *Twentieth Century Literature* 20 (Jan. 1974): 11–18.

Walker, Barbara G. *The Woman's Dictionary of Symbols and Sacred Objects.* San Francisco: Harper, 1988.

Ward, Aileen. *John Keats: The Making of a Poet.* New York: Viking, 1963.

Weeks, Jeffrey. *Coming Out: Homosexual Politics in Britain from the Nineteenth Century to the Present.* London: Quartet, 1977.

———. *Sex, Politics, and Society: The Regulation of Sexuality since 1800.* London: Longman, 1981.

Wevers, Lydia. "How Kathleen Beauchamp Was Kidnapped." In Nathan, *Critical Essays,* 37–47.

Wilcox, Helen; Keith McWaters; Ann Thompson; and Linda R. Williams, eds. *The Body and the Text: Hélène Cixous, Reading and Teaching.* London: Harvester, 1990.

Williams, Linsly R. *Tuberculosis: Nature, Treatment, and Prevention.* New York: Funk, 1924.

Willy, Margaret. *Women Diarists: Celia Fiennes, Dorothy Wordsworth, Katherine Mansfield.* London: Longmans, 1964.

Wilt, Judith. *Abortion, Choice, and Contemporary Fiction: The Armageddon of the Maternal Instinct.* Chicago: U of Chicago P, 1990.

Winnicott, D. W. *Home is Where We Start From: Essays by a Psychoanalyst.* Edited by Clare Winnicott, Ray Shepherd, and Madeleine Davis. New York: Norton, 1986.

———. *Human Nature.* New York: Schocken, 1988.

———. *The Maturational Process and the Facilitative Environment.* New York: International Universities P, 1965.

———. *Playing and Reality.* New York: Routledge, 1989.

———. *Through Paediatrics to Psychoanalysis.* London: Hogarth, 1975.

Wood, Alice L. "The History of Artificial Feeding in Infants." In *Lydia J. Roberts Award Essays,* 21–29. Chicago: American Dietetic Association, 1966.

Woolf, Leonard. *Beginning Again: An Autobiography of the Years 1911 to 1918.* New York: Harcourt, Brace, and World, 1963–64.

Woolf, Virginia. *The Diary of Virginia Woolf.* 5 vols. Edited by Anne Olivier Bell. New York: Harcourt, 1977–84.

———. *Night and Day.* San Diego: Harcourt, 1920.

Wright, Celeste T. "Katherine Mansfield and the 'Secret Smile.'" *Literature and Psychology* 5 (1955): 44–48.

———. "Katherine Mansfield's Dog Image." *Literature and Psychology* 10 (1960): 80–81.

———. "Katherine Mansfield's Father Image." *English Studies* 11 (1955): 137–55.

∽ *Acknowledgments*

I AM GRATEFUL for permission to quote from the following sources: The Society of Authors as the literary representative of the estate of Katherine Mansfield, for letters, poems, and journal passages; Alexander Turnbull Library in Wellington, New Zealand, for passages from Mansfield's manuscripts published in the *Turnbull Library Record* and for quotations from the letters of Mark Gertler (in the Waterlow Papers) as well as unpublished letters of Mansfield and her family; and Alfred A. Knopf, Inc., for portions of *The Short Stories of Katherine Mansfield*. Photographs are published here with the permission of the Alexander Turnbull Library and the Library of Congress. James Moore and Claire Tomalin have helped me in my pursuit of rare photographs for this book.

In the long course of completing this study, I have been helped by the friendly and knowledgeable professional librarians at the Alexander Turnbull Library in Wellington, New Zealand; the Lilly Library and the research library at Indiana University–Bloomington; the Berg Collection at the New York Public Library; and the Newberry Library, in Chicago. I wish to acknowledge, especially, the help of Margaret Scott and Janet Hornsey in New Zealand and Ann Bristow in Bloomington. Antony Alpers has given me insights not only from the text of his biography of Mansfield but from private conversation.

I have been aided by research and travel grants from Indiana University–Bloomington, and at the critical beginning of my turning from literary criticism to medicine, I had the good fortune of participating in an interdisciplinary faculty seminar on illness sponsored by the Dean of Faculties Office. My colleagues during this year of study have a part in this book: Mary Ann Baker, Bonnie Brownlee, Ann Carmichael, Ellen Dwyer, Jeanne Peterson, Steve Stowe, and Peggy Thoits. I have been helped by generous research support in connection with my holding the Marquette University Women's Visiting Chair in Humanistic Studies from 1992–93. The sisterly enthusiasm of the alumnae at Marquette was decisive in my seeing this study to completion. And I have been generously encouraged by the following friends and colleagues: Don Gray,

Kathryn Flannery, Gayle Margerhita, Alice Falk, Carolyn Mitchell, Susan Gubar, and Linda David—all at Indiana University—and Claudia Johnson, John Watkins, and Christine Kreuger at Marquette. My research assistants, Beth Steffen and Michelle Kuchta at Marquette and Mary Carlson at Indiana, have been among my most valued colleagues, as were the members of the graduate seminars on Mansfield and Woolf which I taught at Indiana in 1990 and Marquette in 1992. Grace Buonocore has given me the security of a sharp and sympathetic editorial eye.

At the beginning of this book, I acknowledged "the Margarets"; I acknowledge my debts to the men in my family here. My father, John Patrick Heagarty, M.D., gave me my sense of medical practice as a possibly humane and invariably engrossing area of study. My son, Harry, has been the unfailing and cheerful supporter of my work. My husband, Bill, has always been my most astute and sympathetic critic; he must have this final word of gratitude.

Index

Library of Congress Cataloging-in-Publication Data

Burgan, Mary.

  Illness, gender, and writing : the case of Katherine Mansfield /
Mary Burgan.

    p. cm.

  Includes bibliographical references and index.

  ISBN 0-8018-4873-3 (hc : acid-free paper)

   1. Mansfield, Katherine, 1888–1923—Criticism and interpretation.
2. Feminism and literature—New Zealand—History—20th century.
3. Women and literature—New Zealand—History—20th century.
4. Authors, New Zealand—20th century—Health and hygiene.
5. Mansfield, Katherine, 1888–1923—Health. 6. Women authors—
Health and hygiene. 7. Psychoanalysis and literature. 8. Authorship—
Sex differences. 9. Body, Human, in literature. 10. Sex role in
literature. I. Title.

PR9639.3.M258Z587 1994

823'.912—dc20

                                          94-4107

                                            CIP